THE INNER WORLD

A PSYCHO-ANALYTIC STUDY OF
CHILDHOOD AND SOCIETY IN INDIA

THE INNER WORLD

A Psycho-analytic Study of Childhood and Society in India

SUDHIR KAKAR

SECOND EDITION

DELHI
OXFORD UNIVERSITY PRESS
OXFORD NEW YORK

Oxford University Press, Walton Street, Oxford OX2 6DP

London Glasgow New York Toronto
Delhi Bombay Calcutta Madras Karachi
Kuala Lumpur Singapore Hong Kong Tokyo
Nairobi Dar es Salaam Cape Town
Melbourne Auckland

and associates in
Beirut Berlin Ibadan Mexico City Nicosia

First published 1978

Revised and enlarged edition 1981
Second impression 1982
Paperback edition published 1982

Typeset by Eastend Printers, Calcutta 700014
printed by Mohan Makhijani at Rekha Printers Pvt. Ltd.,
A102/1 Okhla Industrial Estate, Phase II, New Delhi 110020
and published by R. Dayal, Oxford University Press
2/11 Ansari Road, Daryaganj, New Delhi 110002

for Apeksha, Rahul and Shveta

Contents

Contents

Preface to the First Edition

I like to think of this book as a contribution to social psychology in general and the social psychology of Hindu society in particular. Readers will quickly discover that I view social psychology as a study of the psychic representation in individuals of their society's culture and social institutions. This conception diverges somewhat from the dominant academic tradition in the subject which is relatively a-cultural and a-historical and is more concerned with studying the reactions of individuals in the 'here-and-now' situations of social stimulus.

This book first began to take shape in a seminar 'Childhood and Society in India', which I gave at the Sigmund-Freud Institute of Psycho-analytic Training and Research in Frankfurt in the summer of 1972. I am grateful to Professor Clemens De Boor and the Institute's Training Committee for their encouragement. The work on this study was continued and completed with the help of a Senior Fellowship of the Indian Council of Social Science Research during 1975–76. I am extremely grateful to the Council and especially to its member-secretary Mr. J. P. Naik for the support which freed me from academic commitments and allowed me to work undisturbed on the manuscript for almost eighteen months. My colleagues at the Centre for the Study of Social Systems, Jawaharlal Nehru University, provided a hospitable environment during the period of this fellowship.

Discussions with psycho-analytic colleagues, both in Germany and India, have considerably helped in giving final shape to this work. The detailed comments of Erik Erikson, respected teacher and dear friend, have been invaluable. Above all, I owe a special debt of gratitude to Pamela Daniels. She helped to shape many of the ideas in this book. Without her personal involvement, critical acumen and sympathetic support this book could not have been written in its present form.

CHAPTER I

Introduction

Aims and Approach

This book is concerned with the psychological themes which pervade Indian childhood, and relates these themes to the traditions and institutions of culture and society in India. Broadly speaking, I have attempted to describe the emergence of these psychological themes out of the interplay between universal processes of human development and the Indian cultural milieu. This milieu includes the religious ideals and historical traditions as well as the social institutions which are specific, if not exclusive, to Indian society.

My approach in this study has been configurational. And yet, as I am acutely aware, to do full justice to each element of the configuration requires a multiple expertise to which I cannot lay claim. In spite of watchful efforts to keep each dimension—individual, social, cultural and historical—constantly in mind when thinking about the Indian 'psyche', the configuration is apt to become lopsided, as the observer finds himself accenting the dimension which reflects his dominant professional experience and personal interest. And although this inevitable emphasis on one dimension, on individual psychological development in my case, may be initially useful and even necessary as an organizing device, it tends to develop an independent importance, an existence all its own. Perhaps this is just as well, a shortcoming with a 'secondary gain'. For, although a configurational approach is essential to understand the 'Indianness' of Indians, the claim to have given equal attention to all aspects of the configuration can easily become an expression of ignorance or arrogance, or both.

The primary dimension of this study, its organizing principle, is individual development. And yet, even this dimension must be further circumscribed. For, as we know, and as Anna Freud has systematically shown, there exist 'developmental lines' for almost every aspect of personality.[1] Thus, in the development of psycho-sexuality, Sigmund Freud charted for us a sequence of libidinal stages. In the area of intellectual function and the development of complex thought processes, Piaget observed and described a sequence of stages of cognitive development. There are developmental lines for numerous other aspects of personality—the growth of the capacity for moral choice; the chronology of the defence activity in the integration of personality; the evolution of an individual sense of industry from the first play on one's own and one's mother's body, and through toys, games and hobbies, to adult work.

My discussion of human development in India is organized around yet another basic developmental line or sequence, one which describes the arc of growth in terms of the individual's reciprocity with his social environment, where, for a long time, the members of his immediate family are the critical counterplayers. Erik Erikson has given us the model in his conceptualization of an epigenetic sequence of stages of 'psycho-social growth', a sequence which leads from the infant's utter dependence on the nurturing care of a mothering person to the young adult's emotional self-reliance and sense of identity. Identity, as used here, is meant to convey the process of synthesis between inner life and outer social reality as well as the feeling of personal continuity and consistency within oneself. It refers to the sense of having a stake in oneself, and at the same time in some kind of confirming community. Identity has other connotations, perspectives which extend beyond the individual and the social to include the historical and the cultural. It is, as Erikson's many writings on the subject reveal,[2] a subtle concept, the essential meaning of which is more accessible to intuitive grasp than amenable to systematic elaboration: it is forever on the tip of the mind, so to speak. The concept is ideally suited to integrate the kinds of data—cultural, historical and psychological—which must be included in a description of the 'Indianness' of Indians: the network of social roles, traditional values, caste customs and kinship regulations with which the threads of individual psychological development are interwoven. In this special sense, this book is also an exploration in Indian identity.

I have drawn the data for this study from diverse fields. Anthropological accounts, sociological studies, mythology and folk tales, clinical impressions and historical reflections have all provided grist for a common mill. As this 'common mill' is the shared inner world—its unfolding in individual life cycles as well as its manifestation in Indian society—clinical impressions and analysis of such symbolic products as myths and rituals, fables and art are prominent through-

out. The high reliance I have placed on these two modes of understanding—analysis of clinical evidence and interpretation of myths—
reflects, in part, the nature of my subject, in part, the nature of my
training in psycho-analytic psychology. I want to clarify here what
I believe to be the scope and the limitations of this essentially psycho-
analytic method.

Feelings, impulses, wishes and fantasies—the dynamic content of
the inner world—occupy the deepest recesses of the psyche. Ephemeral to consciousness, rarely observable directly, they are none the
less real enough. And it is through introspection and empathy (vicari-
ous introspection) that the inner world of an individual becomes
accessible to consciousness and its myriad meanings can be grasped
by an outside observer.[3] Consistent and systematically practised introspection and empathy, essential to most forms of psychotherapy, are
fundamental to the kind of psychological understanding I have aimed
at in this study. This capacity for empathic understanding and interpretation is more likely between people who share the same cultural
background. When the words, dreams and behaviour, the inhibitions,
desires and sensitivities, of the observed are intimately resonant with
the observer's own, he can spot 'clues' that might appear insigni-
ficant or incomprehensible to a neutral or alien observer. This does
not mean that a trained observer has no access to the interior psychological process of individuals outside his own culture, for much of
this is indeed universal. In spite of culturally distinct manifestations
of the unconscious, communication and empathy between individuals
belonging to different cultures is certainly possible. However, other
things being equal, such as unconscious resistances in the observer,
or the possibility of empathizing wrongly (that is, of courting one's
own projections), the quest for psychological truth is less encumbered
when both the observer and his subjects belong to the same culture.

Attempts to derive this kind of psychological understanding from
strictly anthropological material, such as accounts of child-rearing
practices, have produced problematic results. For, although certain
kinds of behaviour shared by many individuals in a group may be
related to common practices of child rearing and socialization, these
early experiences are only the initial links in a much longer chain of
developmental influences; they are not to be viewed as causative. As
many writers have pointed out, similar adult patterns of behaviour
and feeling may be manifested by individuals whose early experiences
were quite different, if later common experiences followed; and vice

versa.[4]

The importance of anthropological studies is that they ground generalizations based on psycho-analytic deductions in the everyday realities of a given culture. They pinpoint and describe just what the critical, common early childhood experiences *are* in that culture. Moreover, formulations of character type, based solely on psycho-analytic observations, require the tempering perspective of anthropology to identify and verify which social classes or cultural communities include a given type more or less frequently. This is a paramount consideration in India, and elsewhere, for observations gleaned directly from clinical psychotherapy reflect but a small, élite sample of a large, heterogeneous population.

The insight gained through psychological observations of individuals, through extrapolating from clinical evidence, can be immensely enriched and deepened by an analysis of the symbolic products of their society. Popular plays and songs condense and dramatize shared fantasies; the psychological constellations they represent offer clues to the sensitivities and defences of the audiences they attract and hold. Among the various symbolic manifestations of any culture, myths in their classical form, or popularized and bowdlerized in legends and folk tales, occupy a special niche of honour. They are a rich and ready mine of psychological information for the psychoanalytic prospector. Myths, in one sense, are individual psychology projected onto the outside world; they let what is actually going on 'inside' happen 'outside'. Myths not only convey communal versions of the repressed wishes and fantasies of early childhood, functioning as a kind of deep freeze for socially unacceptable impulses; they also reflect the nature of an individual's interpersonal bonds within his culture. They can be read as a kind of collective historical conscience, instructions from venerable ancestors on 'right' and 'wrong', which serves to bind the members of a group to each other and thus to forge a collective identity, separate and distinct from the collective identities of other groups.[5]

I do not mean to imply that myths serve only a psychological purpose. Throughout history, they have preserved the memory of historical events, codified religious rituals, dramatized social conflicts, and given aesthetic form to the creative spirit of culture. There are as many different methods of interpreting a myth as there are nuggets of meaning within it. One could extract universal themes by a comparative analysis of myths, as in the work of James Frazer, or take a traditional or a Marxist historical approach, looking for evidence of historical events symbolic of new political alliances or of economic transformations. One could employ the structural method of Propp and Lévi-Strauss, or the theological and ritualistic interpretations of Hindu pundits, or even adopt the moralistic literalism of the nineteenth century German nature school in which one god is Thunder or Death while another goddess is Harvest or Life. In this study, however, I have chosen to interpret Indian mythology within a psycho-social framework (with the accent on the first part of the term). My 'reading' of the myths and legends of the Hindu tradition, many of which I first heard with fascination as a child, reflects the influence on my thinking over the last decade of psychoanalytic theory, particularly its emphasis on the unconscious and on the infantile dimensions of the inner life. Infantile is not meant here in any derogatory sense, but refers to the basic preoccupations of all children: birth, death, bodily functions and the pleasure or guilt associated with them, sexual organs and sexual feelings, and relationships within the family. We play and replay these infantile themes, consciously or unconsciously, throughout our individual life cycles; elaborated and legitimated through the decorum of symbolism and artistry, they are the basic stuff of human mythology.

Every major Hindu myth has many (some say, infinite) variations; thus the interpretation of Hindu mythology can be a rewarding experience for just about every school of myth analysis. Anyone with the inclination, time and patience to go through the dense, defiant overgrowth of myths contained in the Indian epics and the *Puranas* is almost certain to come upon a variation which illustrates his or her particular theoretical standpoint. Although I may not always have successfully resisted the temptation to choose versions which support my theses most aptly, my conscious effort has been to concentrate on the common elements of a myth in all its variations and to use the best-known popular versions. By 'popular' I mean the familiar versions of the classical myths, the versions most likely to be known to an 'average' Indian: those narrated by family elders or by professional *religiosi* at festive and sacral occasions, enacted in folk plays and dance dramas, or portrayed in the easily available paperback accounts of the Hindu gods.

The role of myths, especially those of religious derivation, in defining and integrating the traditional elements and the common features of identity and society in Hindu India—certainly in the past, and in most parts of the community till today—cannot be over-estimated. Yet, at the same time, we become sharply aware of the 'Indianness' of Indians when we compare, intuitively or systematically, the dominant psychological modalities of India with those of other societies. As the distinct individuality of a person unfolds and becomes visible in a network (or 'field' in the Lewinian sense) of relationships, so this 'Indianness', the separation of the culturally generated from the universal aspects of behaviour, becomes vivid when viewed against a backdrop of other cultural consolidations.

Because I have lived, worked and been trained in Europe and the United States as well as in India, these 'other' cultures with which I compare India are mainly those of the West. I have, however, been necessarily mindful of the autonomy of each society. It has not been my purpose to evaluate one society, whether Indian or Western, in terms of the other. I have not interpreted a particular psychological trait in members of one society as a neurotic symptom or as an unfortunate deviation from some universal norm incorporated only by the other. I have proceeded, rather, on the assumption that both societies offer distinctive solutions to universal human dilemmas, that both (in secular psychological terminology) have specific normative conceptions of what constitutes the 'healthy' personality and of how social relations should be organized to achieve this elusive ideal.

The tenets of ego psychology and psychotherapy in the West, for instance, postulate a highly complex personality which constantly works to create a common solution for the strivings of all its psychic sub-structures, a process which demands a maximum of synthesizing and integrating activity on the part of the ego.[6] In India, on the other hand, the ideal of psychological wholeness or 'maturity', as we shall see later, is quite compatible with an ego which is relatively passive and less differentiated. Any ideal of psychological maturity which presumes to translate experiences and practices in one society into universal norms for others should give us pause. I am reminded of the Indian fable of six blind men and an elephant in which one man, after touching the animal's tail, sought to impose on the others his absolute conviction that the elephant was a snake.

Questions about the 'essential nature' of the Indian personality are not new. With different emphases and with different aims in mind, these questions have been asked and answered often enough. Thus, as early as *c.* 300 B.C., Megasthenes, the Greek ambassador to the court of Chandragupta, remarked of Indians:

Death is with them a very frequent subject of discourse. They regard this life as, so to speak, the time when the child within the womb becomes mature, and death as a birth into a real and happy life for the votaries of philosophy. On this account they undergo much discipline as a preparation for death. They consider nothing that befalls men to be either good or bad, to suppose otherwise being a dream-like illusion, else how could some be affected with sorrow and others with pleasure, by the very same things, and how could the same things affect the same individuals at different times with these opposite emotions?[7]

Among other things, Megasthenes's observations on the Indian 'national character' serve to direct our attention to the problem of generalization, for, with intuitive good sense, Megasthenes did not speak of all Indians but confined himself to one social group, the 'Brachmanes' or Brahmins.

When talking of 'others', whether these others be Indians, Americans or Chinese, the temptation to generalize and to give our conclusions' an aesthetically satisfying order, however artificial and superficial, is all too often irresistible. Distinctions among social, religious, or economic groups within a culture are as inconvenient as they are intractable. The tendency to see other groups in monolithic, even stereotypical terms, the better to accommodate our projections and idealizations, is all too common: a tendency which usually defies common sense and scientific evidence at one and the same time. Whether we designate the shared characteristics of a people as 'basic character structure' (Kardiner, Linton), or 'national character' (Benedict, Gorer, Mead), or 'social character' (Fromm), the qualifications need to be carefully spelled out in order to prevent a misuse of these concepts and the riding of private hobby horses of prejudice. David Hume, writing in 1741, was outspoken in his criticism of the tendency to oversimplify in interpreting the 'national character' of others. 'The vulgar are apt to carry all national characters to extremes,' he wrote, 'and having once established it as a principle that any people are knavish, or cowardly, or ignorant, they will admit of no exception, but comprehend every individual under the same censure. Men of sense condemn these undistinguishing judgements; though at the same time they allow that each nation has a particular set of manners, and that some particular qualities are more frequently to be met with among one people than among their neighbours.'[8]

At first glance, one might despair of making any legitimate, fruitful generalizations at all about a society as complex and heterogeneous as India. It would appear to be a foolish or desperate task to try to distil some common psychological themes from the welter of distinct regional, linguistic, caste, class and religious sub-identities which go to make up India.

Many social scientists might argue that in such a situation generalizations should not be attempted at all without national surveys of beliefs, attitudes and acts factually shown to be characteristic of a random sample. Others, both Indians and foreigners, impressed by what seems to be a hard-core unity in the diversity of Indian culture, argue that national statistics may be helpful in such an effort but are not essential.

Let me then describe the limits of this work. First, this book deals primarily with Hindu India, and with the cultural traditions and psycho-social identity of so-called 'caste' Hindus at that. Moreover, my observations do not purport to be a definitive statement about Hindus throughout India; rather, they are meant to illustrate a dominant mode in the wide and variable range of Hindu behaviour. The use of 'Hindu' and 'Indian' interchangeably in the text reflect not a misperception of synonyms, but simply the demands of readability, although, in fact, other religious groups in India have been profoundly influenced by the dominant Hindu culture. Even so, the effort to uncover unifying themes and to concentrate on the integrating aspects rather than on the (admittedly) large number of variations and deviations within the Hindu culture may still be considered by some a task of doubtful feasibility. Yet I have ventured to do this for at least two reasons: first, hypotheses have to be advanced if they are ever to be tested;[9] and second, I believe that the generalizations that have evolved out of this study possess an underlying truth resonant with the psychological and cultural actualities of upper caste Hindu childhood and society.

Culture and Personality

However we choose to define it,[10] the overwhelming importance of cultures in personality formation is now recognized by most dynamic psychologies. The old nature vs nurture, heredity vs environment, controversy boils down (as such controversies often do) to an acknowledgement of every individual's dual heritage: our biological-physical endowment indelibly embellished by the culture of the particular society which surrounds us from the beginning of life, enveloping us like the very air we breathe and without which we do not grow into viable human beings.[11]

Culture is so pervasive that even when an individual seems to break away from it, as in states of insanity, the 'madness' is still influenced by its norms and rituals. As George Devereaux has suggested, in the predictable and pre-patterned symptoms of such ethnic psychoses as *amok*, *latah*, *koro*, the respective culture seems to be giving the directive, 'Don't become insane, but if you do, you must behave as follows. . . .'[12] Thus, even in a condition of extreme stress, the individual takes from his culture its conventions or traditions in implementing and giving form to an idiosyncratic disorder, the culture providing, as it were, the patterns of misconduct. The basic intra-psychic processes, defence mechanisms and conflicts in human development have been recognized as universal; there are, however, cultural differences in the *Ablauf* of these processes, in the relative importance of the mechanisms of defence, as well as in the intensity and the form of the conflicts. Moreover, different cultures shape the development of their members in different ways, 'choosing' whether childhood, youth or adulthood is to be a period of maximum or minimum stress. In India, for instance, in contrast with Germany or France, it is early childhood rather than adulthood which is the 'golden age' of individual life history. Such preferential imagery influences a culture's perspective on the different stages of the human life cycle as well as the intensity of individual nostalgia for the 'lost paradise' of childhood.

Let us turn here to several controversial issues within the sphere of personality and culture: What is the nature of a culture's influence on the individual? How and when does this influence seem to become critical over the course of individual development?

In psycho-analytic thought, Freud, as early as 1897, suggested an intrinsic antagonism between man's instinctual demands and the social restrictions of his culture.[13] He returned to this subject in his later years and elaborated on it in considerable detail: *Civilization and Its Discontents* and *The Future of an Illusion* are masterpieces, with that particular ring of liberating truth which transforms sceptical reservations into partisan enthusiasm. Freud's main theme, the 'burden of culture', has been taken up by later writers who have, however, not substantially amended his insights or added to his lucid expositions.[14] In the post-Freudian era of psycho-analytic thought, there has been a gradual shift in focus away from the allegedly inherent opposition between the wishes, drives and impulses of individual personality on the one hand and the repressive constraints of culture on the other, to an exploration and exegesis of the complementarity of what was formerly opposed. It is now generally accepted that the newborn infant brings with him an innate capacity or readiness to adapt to any culture into which he may be received. His innate potential for growth, for learning, for relationships, can normally be expected to unfold in culturally appropriate ways in the course of interaction with the world around him.[15] Erikson has expressed this shift succinctly: 'Instead of emphasizing what the pressures of social organization are apt to deny the child, we wish to clarify what the social order may first grant to the infant as it keeps him alive and as, in administering to his needs in specific ways, it introduces him to a particular cultural style.'[16] In spite of the liability to charges of 'functionalism', that is, charges of taking the mere existence of specific cultural patterns and social institutions as sufficient proof of their 'inevitability', I have focused on adaptation rather than on conflict. I have chosen to elaborate on the 'fit' between psychological themes, cultural style and social institutions rather than pointing out the oppressive inconsistencies which certainly exist, and have existed, not only in Indian society but in all other complex societies as well.

The adaptive viewpoint outlined above is, to my mind, not only fruitful generally in clarifying the evolutionary aspects of individual and cultural development; it also has a specific relevance for this study. Ever since Max Weber's analysis of Indian society, many Western (and Indian) social scientists have interpreted social institutions such as caste and the extended family as oppressive, in the sense of hindering the growth of such personality traits as 'independence', 'initiative', 'persistence' and 'achievement motivation' in the individual. Such interpretations, however, are intimately related to a historically determined, culturally specific *Weltanschauung* of the ideal 'healthy' personality cast in the Faustian mould, a world-view which is being increasingly questioned, if not openly repudiated, by certain classes and sub-cultures of youth in the West itself. In their preoccupation with what they thought Indian society denied the growing child, many social scientists overlooked or paid only perfunctory attention to those qualities which the Indian cultural and social order granted the individual. In a twist of historical fate, whereas the emphasis among certain 'modern' Indians is on change, on breaking with tradition and acquiring the life styles, goals and skills consonant

with European and American middle-class values, the values of continuity and cooperation in Indian culture, the psychological and
social dimensions of which are at the heart of this study, are, in turn,
perceived as fundamental to the process of radical change by many
young men and women in the Western world.

Cultural traditions, as Freud recognized long ago, are internalized
during childhood in the individual's superego, the categorical conscience which represents the rights and wrongs, the prohibitions and
mores, of a given social milieu: 'The superego of the child is not
really built up on the model of the parents, but on that of the parents'
superego; it takes over the same contents, it becomes the vehicle of
tradition and of all the age-long values which have been handed down
in this way from generation to generation. . . . The ideologies of the
superego perpetuate the past, the traditions of the race and the
people, which yield but slowly to the influences of the present and to
new developments, and, as long as they work through the superego,
play an important part in man's life.'[17] But the roots of culture in the
psyche penetrate below the crusty layer of the superego. Mediated
through persons responsible for the infant's earliest care, cultural
values are, from the beginning, an intimate and inextricable part of
the *ego*. As the organizing principle of the personality, the ego is, of
course, that which differentiates and mediates between 'I' and 'you',
between what is 'inside' and what is 'outside'. The development of
the ego, as many psycho-analytic writers have systematically pointed
out, cannot be comprehended except in its interdependence with the
society into which an individual child is born, a society represented
in the beginning by the mother and other culturally-sanctioned
caretakers.[18]

It is the mother's responses and 'cues' which at first help give
shape to the infant's brand new individuality and nurture his capacity, in culturally approved ways, to turn passive, receptive experience
into active volition and mastery. The way in which the mother, and
later, other caretakers responsible for the growing child's welfare,
responds to her child is inseparable from the traditions of child-
rearing in her culture. That is, a mother's responses to her infant
depend not only upon her emotional stance towards motherhood
deeply rooted in her own life history, or upon the inborn constitution of her child (whether he is cuddly or rigid, active or placid) but
also upon her culture's image of the role of motherhood and of the
nature of a child.

In India, for example, mothers and the families that surround them share the traditional idea of the 'twice-born'--namely, the belief that a child is not born as a member of society until between the ages of five and ten. This belief reflects the rather sharp distinction between the *individual* human being and the *social* human being, a distinction which is expressed in the ancient codes of conduct, the *Dharmasastras*, as follows: 'Till a boy is eight years old he is like one newly born and only indicates the caste in which he is born. As long as his *upanayana* ceremony is not performed the boy incurs no blame as to what is allowed or forbidden.'[19] I do not mean to suggest that all, or even most people in India live by a conscious philosophical understanding of the twice-born state, or have heard of Daksha, the ancient god-sage from whom this quotation is said to derive. I merely want to emphasize that this view of the nature of a child—a completely innocent being who is a gift of the gods, to be welcomed and appreciated and even indulged for the first few years of life—is so deeply rooted in the Hindu world-image that it influences every aspect of adults' relationships with children. In turn, the myriad 'messages' emanating from these transactions, shape and form the child's developing ego in rather specific ways which are characteristic of the culture. One may indeed talk of a cultural part of the ego and emphasize its role as the earliest and the 'more primary' carrier of a culture's traditions.

Personal Word

I would like to close this introduction with a personal word. As with many scientific and creative endeavours, this book has not only grown out of a professional interest but is also related to personal needs. The journey into Indian childhood to discover the sources of Indian identity is also a return into a personal past, a reconnaisance of my own origins. Almost certainly, one of the motives for becoming a traveller in my own psycho-social country has been my experience, shared by many other Indians, of studying, working and living for long stretches of time in Europe and in the United States. At some time during this self-chosen exile, a more or less protracted cultural confrontation, with the self as the battleground, becomes almost inevitable. I have learned to recognize in myself and in other 'modern' Indians the phases of violent rejection and passionate extolling of all things Indian. For this is one of the ways in which this confrontation manifests itself, as the ego attempts to integrate experiences at different points of the life cycle, to try somehow to bring the Indian 'background' and the Western 'foreground' onto a single canvas. I have been thus aware, in myself and in many other Indian expatriates, of a deep and persistent undercurrent of nostalgia, almost sensual in character, for the sights, smells, tastes, sounds of the country of our childhood. The expression of affects without restraint, the *being* in emotions, the infectious liveliness amidst squalor—in short, the intensity of life—is a deep, diffusely seductive siren song for Indian intellectuals. At the same time, this nostalgia is not 'modern', but something to be vaguely ashamed of, if not violently banished from consciousness.

Insights into Indian identity have, in addition to any claims to the advancement of knowledge, a therapeutic effect in so far as they have clarified and engaged the deeply Indian parts of myself, thereby strengthening a sense of personal and historical continuity. This is an important consideration, since rapid historical change or 'modernization' and the attendant psychological confrontation with other, seemingly more assertive and 'successful' world-images, have provoked in many Indians anxious feelings of having come unmoored, of being adrift. The problem is especially acute in the case of modern Indian intellectuals who have chosen to locate themselves in the vanguard of this change. I would like to think of this study as a part of an intellectual tradition more than a hundred years old, starting with Ram Mohan Roy (1774–1833), a tradition devoted to the vicissitudes of Indian identity in modern times. Thus this book also incorporates a personal avowal, a *Bekenntnis*, which in an earlier generation was eloquently articulated by Nehru:

As I grew up and became engaged in activities which promised to lead to India's freedom, I became obsessed with the thought of India. What was this India that possessed me and beckoned to me continually, urging me to action so that we might realize some vague but deeply felt desire of our hearts? The initial urge came to me, I suppose, through pride, both individual and national, and the desire, common to all men, to resist another's domination and have freedom to live the life of our choice. . . . But it was not enough to satisfy the questioning that arose within me. What is this India, apart from the physical and geographical aspects? What did she represent in the past; what gave strength to her then? How did she lose that old strength? And has she lost it completely? Does she represent anything vital now, apart from being the home of a vast number of human beings? How does she fit into the modern world?[20]

The confrontation with the past in order to enlarge the margins of freedom in the present, the assessment of weaknesses and strengths and the search for their roots, is a therapeutic approach to history and I feel a strong sense of emotional kinship and common purpose as I go on to read:

India with all her infinite charm and variety began to grow upon me more and more, and yet the more I saw of her the more I realized how very difficult it was for me or for anyone else to grasp the ideas she had embodied. . . . Though outwardly there was diversity and infinite variety among our people, everywhere there was that tremendous impress of oneness, which had held all of us together for ages past, whatever political fate or misfortune had befallen us. The unity of India was no longer merely an intellectual conception for me: it was an emotional experience which overpowered me. That essential unity had been so powerful that no political division, no disaster or catastrophe, had been able to overcome it. It was absurd, of course, to think of India or any country as a kind of anthropomorphic entity. I did not do so. I was also fully aware of the diversities and divisions of Indian life, of classes, castes, religions, races, different degrees of cultural development. Yet I think that a country with a long cultural background and a common outlook on life develops a spirit that is peculiar to it and that is impressed on all its children, however much they may differ among themselves. . . .[21]

This search for the 'peculiar spirit' of India—identity, in modern parlance—is an increasing preoccupation among most Indian intellectuals today. What Nehru sought for himself and his countrymen in Indian history, I have tried to recapture in Indian life history. On a personal plane, *The Inner World* is a psycho-social discovery of India.

CHAPTER II

The Hindu World Image

An exploration of the psychological terrain of the Indian inner world must begin with the cluster of ideas, historically derived, selected and refined, through which Hindu culture has traditionally structured the beliefs and behaviour of its members. At the heart of this cluster of governing ideas is a coherent, consistent world image in which the goal of human existence, the ways to reach this goal, the errors to be avoided, and the obstacles to be expected along the way are all dramatically conveyed. I am not talking here of Hindu philosophy in the sense of abstract intellectualized concepts accessible only to an élite priesthood of interpreters, but of the prescriptive configuration of ideal purposes, values and beliefs which percolate down into the everyday life of the ordinary people and give it form and meaning.

The world image of traditional Hindu culture, like those of other societies, provides its members with a sanctioned pattern, a template which can be superimposed on the outer world with all its uncertainties and on the flow of inner experience in all its turbulence, thus helping individuals to make sense of their own lives. Shared by most Hindus and enduring with remarkable continuity through the ages, the Hindu world image, whether consciously acknowledged and codified in elaborate rituals, or silently pervading the 'community unconscious',[1] has decisively influenced Indian languages as well as ways of thinking, perceiving and categorizing experience. This image is so much in a Hindu's bones he may not be aware of it. The self-conscious efforts of westernized Hindus to repudiate it are by and large futile based as they are on substantial denial. 'For such images', Erikson writes, 'are absorbed early in life as a kind of space-time which gives coherent reassurance against the abysmal estrangements emerging in each successive stage and plaguing man throughout life. . . . And even where such explicit world images are dispensed with in the expectation—or under actual conditions—of "happiness" or "success", they reappear implicitly in the way man reassures himself when feeling adrift.'[2]

The Theme of Fusion—Moksha

As posited by Hindu culture, the ultimate aim of existence, the chief *purushartha* ('man's meaning'), is *móksha* or *mukti*. The term *moksha* has been variously taken to mean self-realization, transcendence, salvation, a release from worldly involvement, from 'coming' and 'going'. Yet in Hindu philosophy it is also described as the state in which all distinctions between subject and object have been transcended, a direct experience of the fundamental unity of a human being with the infinite. The Upanishads, which dwell upon this theme of perfect union, describe the state in metaphorical, even passionate language: 'just as the person, who in the embrace of his beloved has no consciousness of what is outside or inside, so in this experience nothing remains as a pointer to inside or outside. It is the entry into *brahman*, a merging with *brahman*, eating of *brahman*, breathing of *brahman's* spirit. It is the unity of self and the world.'[3]

The difficulty with such descriptions is that they have meaning only for the initiated and they communicate different things to different people. Western readers will perhaps find a resonant evocation of a *moksha*-like state in the shimmering meta-language of Blake:

All are Human, & when you enter into their Bosoms you walk
In Heavens & Earths, as in your own Bosom you bear your Heaven
And Earth & all you behold; tho' it appears Without, it is Within,
In your Imagination, of which this World of Mortality is but a
  Shadow.[4]

For many, the essence of *moksha* can be grasped, however fleetingly, through vivid visual symbols such as the Hindu image of Shakti and Shakta—the energy and the inert, the Doer and the World —with their thighs clasped around each other in an eternal embrace; or the Taoist inverted black and white fishes of Yin and Yang. For the limitations of language become all too clear when one seeks to convey an experience which is, almost by definition, beyond words. Yet I am not an artist, but a psychologist. I cannot be content with approaching *moksha* merely through visual images but must also attempt an understanding through the psychological means at my disposal. This is an important task, although a mystic himself might advise letting well enough alone, since it is the ideal of *moksha*, in principle generalizable to all Hindus, which conveys (if only preconsciously) the possibility of a 'mystical' experience to every Indian. In

the West, this singular realm of experience is conceivable only to an
élite of artists, poets and 'God's fools'. The point is that in India the
idea of *moksha* is not deviant, but central to the imagery of the culture.
Any psycho-social study of Hindu India must necessarily grapple
with this phenomenon, however difficult or professionally disconcert-
ing the attempt may be.

Freud was ill at ease trying to describe such feeling-states as
moksha. 'Oceanic feeling' was his collective term for mystical, ecstatic, *zazen* or *samadhi* experiences.[5] Among a good many later psychologists his caution and diffidence have degenerated into suspicion and
disbelief of the so-called 'mystic' states. But 'oceanic feeling', contrary to Freud's expectations, can now be physiologically differentiated; and *samadhi* ('attainment of oneness') which, at least in the
school of Raja Yoga, is held to be the precondition of *moksha*, has
been postulated by Roland Fischer to be a heightened state of 'trophotropic' arousal, qualitatively different from other states of heightened self-awareness included in the category 'ergotropic' arousal. It
will help to clarify the relationship of *samadhi* to other states of
consciousness if we reproduce Fischer's chart.[6] (Fig. 1)

It is not clear whether by the generic term '*samadhi*' Fischer means
any one of the four 'imperfect' *samadhis*, or the perfect *asamprajnata*
samadhi itself. Yet even the perfect *samadhi* of yoga is described in
Hindu texts as a blissful trance of a transitory nature. *Moksha*, on the
other hand, is not a temporary surge of oceanic feeling, but a
constant and fully aware living-in-the-ocean. Ramana Maharshi,
one of the greatest of the Indian sages credited with having achieved
this state, compared the pre-requisite *samadhi* to a bucket of water
which is submerged in the water of a well: the 'self' immersed in
the 'greater self', with the rope and the bucket ('ego') remaining
there to draw the individual self out again.[7] But he likened *moksha*
to the waters of a river merged in those of the ocean. Or, groping for
another simile, he wrote that in *moksha* 'this ego is harmless; it is
like the skeleton of a burnt rope—though it has a form it is of no
use to tie anything with'.[8]

One of the main difficulties in trying to arrive at a psychological
understanding of such states as *moksha* is terminological. The descriptions in Hindu texts and the subjective accounts of sages
commonly held to have achieved this ideal of 'non-duality', as it is
sometimes called, contain a variety of synonymously used nouns. The
semantic confusion among 'I', 'self', and 'ego', and among their

counterparts 'other', 'world', 'macro-cosmos', etc. is exaggerated in translation from Sanskrit or from any Indian vernacular to English.

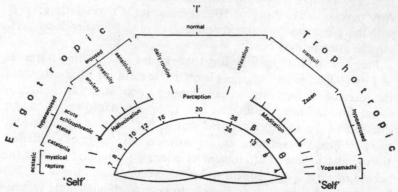

Fig. 1. Varieties of conscious states mapped on a perception-hallucination continuum of increasing ergotropic arousal (left) and a perception-meditation continuum of increasing trophotropic arousal (right). These levels of hyper- and hypoarousal are interpreted by man as normal, creative, psychotic, and ecstatic states (left) and Zazen and samadhi (right). The loop connecting ecstasy and samadhi represents the rebound from ecstasy to samadhi, which is observed in response to intense ergotropic excitation. The numbers 35 to 7 on the perception-hallucination continuum are Goldstein's coefficient of variation specifying the decrease in variability of the EEG amplitude with increasing ergotropic arousal. The numbers 26 to 4 on the perception-meditation continuum, on the other hand, refer to those beta, alpha, and theta EEG waves (measured in hertz) that predominate during, but are not specific to, these states.

A perfect correspondence between terms which are, even in their original usage, difficult to pin down in a precise definition, simply does not exist. But such semantic difficulties, we should remember, are not uncommon in other systematic psychologies that seek to understand the processes of mental life through disciplined introspection. I refer here primarily to psycho-analytic psychology and its extensive literature, in which, as Heinz Hartmann has pointed out, clear distinctions between the terms ego, self and personality are by no means always drawn.[9]

Since the perfect *samadhi* of yoga is the closest approximation we have, experientially and psychologically, to what *moksha* may conceivably mean, I want to attend to the self and the functioning of the psychic system, particularly the ego, in the *samadhi* state. Ego here is to be understood in the psycho-analytic sense. It is not a synonym for individual personality; it does not refer to the subject as opposed to the object of experience; nor does it stand for that narcissism or self-pride often conveyed in everyday usage by words like 'egotistical'. By ego I mean the inner agency of the psyche which screens and synthesizes the impulses, needs, emotions and memories from within and the impressions, ideas, expectations and opportunities from outside, both of which become part of our consciousness and call for some kind of action. The ego, following Freud's model, is one of the three principal psychic substructures, its counterparts being the primitive id and the constraining superego. The individual ego is in a state of constant flux, mediation and exchange between inner and outer, past and present, unconscious and self-conscious, self and society, between the instinctual and the institutional in human life. The ego is unconscious in that one can become aware of its work but not of *it*. The self, on the other hand, following Erikson, is preconscious in the sense that it becomes conscious when 'I' reflects upon it, or rather upon the various selves—body, personality, social roles—which make up the composite, or whole self.[10] The counterplayers of the self are 'others', or more precisely, the selves of others. This, of course, leaves one with the problem, more metapsychological than psychological, of the 'I'. For 'I' is neither self, which is the object of 'I', nor ego, a psychic agency. 'I', as Hindus would say, is pure consciousness, the *atman* of Vedantic thought whose only counterplayer is *brahman*.

As described in the texts, and in the accounts of religious teachers, *moksha* can be understood to mean that a person living in this state has an all-pervasive current of 'I'. 'I' is the centre of awareness and existence in all experienced situations and in all possible selves. 'I' is a constant and continuous presence in all the transient selves— the bodily self in the throes of sexual excitement or in the pain of sickness; the personal self at play, dreaming and reflecting or at work, planning and constructing; the social self in the generational role of parent and householder or of son or subordinate. *Moksha*, however, is not limited to gaining this awareness of 'I' in a composite self. Rather, it is held that this ultimate 'man's meaning' is not realized until a person also has a similar feeling of 'I' in the selves of others, an empathy amplified to the point of complete identification. Until this awareness of 'I' in the composite self and in the generalized 'other' is established and maintained, man, Hindus would say, is living in *avidya*: ignorance or false consciousness. And his perception of himself, of the outside world and others around him, remains *maya*: a fragment, an apparent reality which, even if it is socially shared and sanctioned as *matam* ('opinion about reality'), is not *tatvam*, the ultimate, true reality known only to the liberated man.

In the Hindu ideal, reality is not primarily mediated through the conscious and pre-conscious perceptions, unconscious defences and rational thought processes that make up the ego; it emanates from the deeper and phylogenetically much older structural layer of personality—the id, the mental representative of the organism's instinctual drives. Reality, according to Hindu belief, can be apprehended or known only through those archaic, unconscious, pre-verbal processes of sensing and feeling (like intuition, or what is known as extra-sensory perception) which are thought to be in touch with the fundamental rhythms and harmonies of the universe. The Hindu conception of ego-oriented reality as *maya* helps to explain the average Hindu's fascination and respect for the occult and its practitioners. Astrologers, soothsayers, clairvoyants, sadhus, fakirs and other shamanic individuals who abound in Indian society are profoundly esteemed, for they are thought to have begun to transcend the bonds of *maya*.

The distinctions between reality and *maya*, between *vidya* and *avidya*—true and false consciousness—illustrate a fundamental difference between Hindu and Western world images, as well as a discrepancy in the modes of thought and apperception, which even the best-intentioned movements of cultural ecumenism cannot hope to bridge satisfactorily. The maintenance of ego boundaries—between 'inside' and 'outside', and between 'I' and 'others'—and the sensory experiences and social relations based on these separations, is the stuff of reality in Western thought and yet *maya* to the Hindus. The optimal discrimination of this reality of separateness, expressed in terms of heightened ego functions such as reality sense, reality testing and adaptation to reality, is the stated goal of most Western psychotherapies, but of paltry importance in the Hindu ways of liberation. A good reality sense, according to psycho-analysis, shows itself in the absence of a conscious feeling of the self or the various selves. This, however, is precisely the situation which the Hindu ways of liberation would seek to reverse. And if in the course of development, the child learns to differentiate between himself and

what is not a part of him, between 'me' and 'not-me'—a process in
which the individual's sense of space, time, causality and individuality
is formed, and ego boundaries are constituted—then in a certain
sense the Hindu ways of liberation, as we shall see later, seek to undo
this process of ego development. Nor in the Hindu scheme of things
is this 'undoing' what Ernst Kris meant by 'regression in the service
of the ego', in which a return to beginnings serves to realign the
defensive ego functions so that the adult ego is strengthened and
augmented from the experience. Rather, the intention is to effect a
complete revolution in man's psychic organization by providing new
goals and different modes of perception which radically alter the
subjective experiencing of 'reality'. Perhaps the contrasts (and the
similarities) between the psycho-analytic and the Hindu approaches
to the task of 'liberating' or engaging individual consciousness can be
best illuminated through a specific elaboration of one of the best
known Hindu techniques, Raja Yoga.

Yoga and psycho-analysis

The eight steps of Raja Yoga, the last of which results in *samadhi*,
are divided into three phases in the classical blueprint:

	RAJA YOGA		EIGHT STEPS
	Three phases		
Phase I	PREPARATION:	(ETHICAL)	1. yama
			2. niyama
		(PHYSIOLOGICAL)	3. asana
			4. pranayama
Phase II	INTEGRATION:	First step in trans-formation of *chitta*	5. pratyahara
Phase III	MEDITATION:	Samyama	6. dharana
			7. dhyana
			8. samadhi

Fig. 2

The phases are said to require a number of years of practice before
samadhi is even conceivable. The first phase is *preparation*, both
ethical and physiological. The ethical preparation consists of the first
two yoga steps *yama* and *niyama*, rules for everyday living without
which one cannot become a yogi: nonviolence, truthfulness, non-
stealing, continence, cleanliness, austerity, study and so forth. The
physiological preparation through the next two steps *asana* and

pranayama—bodily postures and breathing exercises—has as its objective a healthy body. As Vivekananda put it, 'Each man must begin where he stands, must learn how to control the things that are nearest to him. This body is very near to us, nearer than anything in the external world.'[11]

The practice of yoga proper actually begins in the fifth step, *pratyahara*, which constitutes the second phase which I would call integration. The yoga texts and the commentaries of various teachers who have tried to explain and elaborate on *pratyahara* make up a fascinating literature in many respects, especially in its delineation of the relationship between conscious and unconscious mental processes. For our purposes here, it suggests some provocative parallels between the Hindu and the psycho-analytic view of mental life.

The object of this phase is the *chitta*, 'even nearer than the body', the fundamental concept in the Hindu model of the human psyche. *Chitta* is very similar to the id of the psycho-analytic model, the part of the psychic organization which represents the elemental, instinctual drives of the organism. Hindu texts sometimes also use *chitta* in a dynamic sense to characterize *all* unconscious mental processes. Thus, if Freud described the id as 'a chaos, a cauldron full of seething excitations',[12] the concept of *chitta* can be evoked through similar imagery. Some Hindu texts draw the metaphor of a monkey, restless by nature, who drinks wine and becomes even more restless. As if this were not enough, he is stung by a scorpion, and (to complete the image of uncontrolled restlessness) a demon enters him. *Chitta*, in its normal state, is compared to this monkey, drunk with wine, smarting under the scorpion bite and possessed by a demon.[13] In the course of everyday life, *chitta* is bound up with the bodily organs; it exists in the 'scattered' form of outwardly directed activity and manifests itself in the individual's experiences of pleasure and pain, as well as in the 'darkening' form manifested in human aggression.

But the 'scattered' and 'darkening' forms, together with their manifestations of pleasure, pain and aggression, are not the natural state of *chitta*. These forms, the Hindu texts maintain, come into existence with birth and become ever more solidified in the course of human growth and development. *Chitta's* 'natural state', its real nature, is the 'one-pointed' form in which its fundamental aim of 'I' awareness and the non-duality of 'I' and 'other' can be realized. *Chitta's* aim is the aim of human life, the essential meaning underlying the various yoga practices.

At first glance the Hindu view of *chitta* appears to contrast sharply with the predominant psycho-analytic concept of the id as essentially blind and maladaptive instinctuality, ever moving towards indiscriminate discharge. This view, as Bernard Apfelbaum has shown in an exhaustive critique, sets up an opposition between the ego and the id, in which the ego must be ever watchful and strengthened to control the eruptions out of the 'ever seething cauldron'.[14] Hindu thinkers have not postulated this kind of permanent opposition between the two psychic systems. Although recognizing the restlessness and the driven character of the *chitta*, they have attributed to it a specific aim identical with the purpose of human life, not at odds with it. The Hindu view finds some parallel in later statements of Freud's such as, 'The power of the id expresses the true purpose of the individual organism's life',[15] and, 'The development of the individual seems to us to be a product of the interaction between two urges, the urge towards happiness which we usually call "egoistic", and the urge towards union with others in the community, which we call "altruistic".'[16]

Chitta, the Hindus maintain, strives towards its own transformation. The scattered and the darkened drives are capable of maturation towards their final 'one-pointed' form in which their unique aim is 'altruistic', the union of 'I' and the 'not–I'. If one lends credence to philosophical speculations arising out of developments in modern biology, the Hindu emphasis on interdependence, symbiosis and fusion in the human organism is in the mainstream of the life-sciences. Responses such as aggression are viewed not as primary but as secondary developments in evolution: necessary for the regulation of symbiosis, rather than designed to break or disturb the fundamental 'altruism' of living organisms.[17]

What are the scattered and darkening drives which Hindu religious teachers through the centuries have exhorted their followers to 'gather', 'concentrate' and transform? The principal texts consistently attest to the primary importance of sexuality. In Hindu mythology, sexuality is a rampant flood of polymorphous pleasure and connection, disdaining the distinctions between the heterosexual, genital imperatives of conventional sex and sweeping away incestual taboos. Shiva, the god of ascetics and yogis, does not always find respite from sexual desire, for 'when Siva failed to be satisfied by making love to Gauri, his wife, he then went naked into the Pine Forest in the guise of a madman, his *linga* (phallus) erect, his mind full of desire, wishing to obtain sexual pleasure with the wives of the

3

sages'.[18] As a medieval Bengali text somewhat woefully remarks, 'if such illustrious personages as Brahma (the Creator), Maharudra (Shiva), and Parasara, the father of the sage Vyasa, were lustful, in fact so lustful that they pursued their own daughters, what can you expect of unreconstructed man?'[19] The recognition of human sexuality and of its necessary transformation is then the main task of liberating yoga. This transformation, however, is envisioned as sublimation rather than repressive self-control, for Hindu yogis have always shown a healthy respect for the power of the libido: 'Sex energy has got tremendous potency. But mere abstention without converting it into higher mental power (*ojas shakti*) is dangerous. Mere abstention . . . may lead to various kinds of mental and physical disease.'[20] The alleged location of *chitta* at *muladhara* (according to mystical physiology, a point equidistant from the anus and the urethral canal which can be the focus of intense sexual excitement and which probably corresponds to the embryologically important seminal colliculus) leaves no doubt about the primacy of sexuality in the *chitta*.

Another one of those metaphors in which Hindu thinkers seemed to revel compares *chitta* to a lake with muddy and agitated water which sends up waves, the *vrittis*, and thus hides the bottom, the 'I', which is visible only if the water is calm and the ripples have subsided. These ripples or waves are the mental functions—perception, inference, delusion, dream, sleep and memory—all of which have their ultimate source in the *chitta*. Vivekananda, commenting upon one of Patanjali's aphorisms on memory, sleep and dreams, says, 'For instance you hear a word. That word is like a stone thrown into the lake of *chitta*: it causes a ripple and that ripple rouses a series of ripples. This is memory. So it is in sleep. When the peculiar kind of ripple called sleep throws the *chitta* into a ripple of memory, it is called a dream. Dreaming is another form of the ripple which in the waking state is called the memory.'[21]

To summarize the Hindu concept of *chitta* and its importance in the process of attaining *moksha*: All mental processes are grounded in *chitta* which has as its specific aim 'I' awareness and fusion with the 'Other'. Usually this aim is not fulfilled since *chitta* is attached to the organs of the body and exists restlessly in scattered and darkening forms. But *chitta* (and its underlying drive constellation) is capable of transformation, through 'gathered' and 'concentrated' forms, into the final 'one-pointed' form which is its true aim. Only in radical acknowledgement of *chitta*, by diving deep through its calm waters, can man realize *moksha* and thus comprehend true 'reality'.

Pratyahara (literally, a 'gathering towards') is thus the first step in *chitta's* transformation. The yogic technique used in this stage bears a striking resemblance to that of free association in psycho-analytic therapy. To quote Vivekananda again:

The first lesson, then, is to sit for some time and let the mind (*chitta*) run on. The mind is bubbling up all the time. It is like that monkey jumping about. Let the monkey jump as much as he can; you simply wait and watch. . . . Give it rein. Many hideous thoughts may come into it; you will be astonished that it was possible for you to harbour such thoughts; but you will find each day *chitta's* vagaries are becoming less and less violent, that each day it becomes calmer. . . . It is tremendous work; it cannot be done in a day. Only after a patient, continuous struggle for years can we succeed.[22]

The yogis saw the regression that takes place in this phase as a necessary one in the service of the *chitta*, not the restless, dark and demonic *chitta*, but the calmable, effulgent and benign one containing altruistic drive representations through which the Upanishadic injunction of *atmanam viddhi*—'Know the I'—can be fulfilled. The presence of a guru to guide and monitor this process is essential. But the guru's function is not to help strengthen the ego's autonomy or to enlarge its domain through insights into the hidden reaches of the mind. Rather, given the goal of calming *chitta* and the gradual merging of the ego and the (transformed) id, the guru's role in *pratyahara* is to sanction and facilitate this process of integration while all the while keeping a watchful eye on the 'patient's' ego lest it be prematurely engulfed. The presence of the guru provides the necessary support against the danger of psychotic breakdown. Unlike the alert, sanctioning support conveyed in words in most Western psychotherapies, the guru's support is given through 'look, touch and silence'—the language of the *chitta*.

The third and last phase in Raja Yoga is concentrated meditation. Here the final transformation of the *chitta* from the 'gathered' to the 'one-pointed' form takes place. The three steps of this phase are *dharana*, *dhyana* and *samadhi*. With *samyama*, as the three steps are sometimes collectively called, the yogi moves into a phase in which a comparison with psycho-analysis is no longer possible. The tasks are different from those entertained by classical psycho-analysis; more than that, the language of our psychological concepts, with its diagnostic bent, was not designed to reflect the flavour and the meaning of a subjective experience which throughout the centuries has eluded theoretical pursuit and been communicated through symbolic language and allegory. The instructions to the yogi in this phase read like exercises in primal creation: Concentrate the *chitta* on sun, water, ice, stones, the texts say, till the image becomes clear and fixed, 'inside', unchanging, whether the eyes are closed or open, the objects present or absent. Create the outer world and the physical nature inside. Meditate on the stone's reality till the stone becomes transparent. Form the perception of a lotus flower which has eighty-four thousand petals, each petal eighty-four thousand nerves, each nerve eighty-four thousand rays where every ray can be seen clearly. Form and meditate on the image of *brahman* sitting in the middle of the lotus flower and discover that 'I' am *brahman* and 'I' am the world.[23]

Tentatively and carefully, we can yet attempt to raise some psychological questions which may contribute to our understanding of the total experience. Does cognition in the state of *samadhi* change from an autonomous function of the adult ego to a process which rests in a primary, undifferentiated 'ego–id matrix'? Are some of the reported experiences in *samadhi* similar to the phenomenon known in Western psychology as 'depersonalization', in which the individual feels unreal as he loses connection with his body, his subjective time sense becomes disturbed, and the external world takes on an improbable aspect? Is the strong feeling of being in love with the whole of creation reported by Indian sages similar to the diffused eroticism of an infant's primary narcissism? Is there any relation between the liberated man's *samadhi* and the symbiotic form of infantile psychosis described by Mahler?[24]

From all accounts, biographies, reports of professional psychologists and psychiatrists, it would appear that the experience of *samadhi* cannot be easily pigeonholed in psychopathological categories. To live in this state, it seems, does *not* mean to experience the external world as an utterly subjective phenomenon, as in hallucinations or delusions of the schizoid or schizophrenic kind. Rather, *samadhi* seems to be an intensely creative approach to external reality and the world of facts, an apperception in which everything happening outside is felt to be a creative experience of the original artist within each one of us and recognized as such with (what Blake would call) *delight*. Most persons harbour tantalizing 'forgotten' traces of this kind of curiosity, originality and delight universal in the early years of childhood. For at a certain stage of life, in late infancy, we do not see the world as something outside ourselves, to be recognized in detail, adapted, complied with and fitted into our idiosyncratic inner world, but as an infinite succession of creative acts. The ideal of *moksha*, then, incorporates a recovery of this creative feeling—not as an ephemeral transition of childhood, nor as a schizophrenic episode, but in the fully aware activity of a mature adult. Using clinical syndromes such as depersonalization to comprehend the *samadhi* experience may falsely convey a conviction of understanding, the kind of understanding that may come when one confidently uses tested and tried instruments even though they are inappropriate to the matter at hand. Medard Boss has put this in much stronger, almost polemical, language: ' . . . How foolish is the oft repeated Western assertion that the exercises of the Indian holy men in becoming one with "Brahman" had as a result a weakening or dissolution of their consciousness, and their personality! . . . If one can talk of man in general in such terms, then neither in the East nor in the West have I ever met more fully aware personalities, people who were more "conscious", mature, sober, and strong, than the best of the Indian holy men. . . .'[25]

Some psychologists have interpreted the striving for *moksha* as a response to psychic stress—that is, a regression to the undifferentiated phase of infancy in which child and mother are united in symbiotic intimacy, and withdrawal to a (potentially controllable) inner world of personal experience. As a partial explanation of the psychological basis of such a cultural ideal, and in the case of some individual Hindus, this explanation may be true. Yet to see *moksha only* as an expression of the nostalgic wish for infantile omnipotence may be to fall from the frying pan of teleological thinking in which the planned goals of life explain present actions, into the fire of 'originological' fallacy in which the beginnings are *completely sufficient* to account for present longings. At the same time, Hindu thinkers and yogis have not denied the element of nostalgic reverence for childhood in their ideal of the liberated man. This is amply borne out by statements such as those of Radhakrishnan: 'The child is much nearer the vision of the self. We must become as little children before we can enter into the realm of truth. . . . The need for being born again is insisted upon. It is said that the wisdom of babes is greater than that of scholars.'[26] Or, in the words of Vivekananda: 'I am fully persuaded that a baby, whose language consists of unintelligible sounds, is attempting to express the highest philosophy.'[27] The question arises whether this high valuation of infancy and the longing to return to the origins of life in search of an eternal future must be called 'infantile' and 'regressive', with their pejorative connotations and negative developmental implications. For if, as Freud himself came to believe, the power of the unconscious id expresses the true purpose of individual psychic life, then the aim of *samadhi* transcends the merely infantile, and the concurrence of the ego in this and similar aims involves something other than ego dissolution or ego slavery.

I believe that much of the mutual misunderstanding between psycho-analysis and the yogas can be attributed to their different 'visions of reality', their different images of the nature of man and the world he lives in. Visions of reality are composites of certain verifiable facts, acts of speculation and articles of faith that unite groups of human beings in specific cultural consolidations. They necessarily involve looking at inner and outer reality from certain angles while ignoring others, and appeals to the 'evidence' by adherents of one or the other vision rarely lead to the development of a more inclusive, 'universal' vision but only succeed in emphasizing their essential relativity.

The psycho-analytic vision of reality, for example, is primarily influenced by a mixture of the tragic and the ironic.[28] It is tragic in so far as it sees human experience pervaded by ambiguities, uncertainties and absurdities where man has little choice but to bear the burden of unanswerable questions, inescapable conflicts and incomprehensible afflictions of fate. Life in this vision is a linear movement in which the past cannot be undone, many wishes are fated to be unfulfilled and desires ungratified. Fittingly enough, Oedipus, Hamlet and Lear are its heroes. The psycho-analytic vision is however also ironic in so far as it brings a self-deprecating and detached perspective to bear on the tragic: the momentous aspects of tragedy are negated and so many gods are discovered to have clay feet. It tends to foster a reflective adaptation and deliberative acceptance. The tragic vision and its ironic amelioration are aptly condensed in Freud's offer to the sufferer to exchange his unbearable neurotic misery for ordinary human unhappiness. On the other hand, the yogic (or more broadly, the Hindu) vision of reality is a combination of the tragic and the romantic. Man is still buffeted by fate's vagaries and tragedy is still the warp and woof of life. But instead of ironic acceptance, the yogic vision offers a romantic quest. The new journey is a search and the seeker, if he withstands all the perils of the road, will be rewarded by an exaltation beyond normal human experience. The heroes of this vision are not the Oedipuses and the Hamlets but the Nachiketas and the Meeras.

These different visions of reality, as I have stressed above, combine both the objective and the subjective. Their aim is to impose a meaning on human experience and not the discovery of an absolute truth. Inevitably they set up ideals and goals of life which may converge in some respects yet diverge in others. To call such deviations 'pathological' or 'ignorant' is to confuse a vision of reality with *the* reality and thus to remain unaware of its relativity.

The esoteric practices of Raja Yoga described above are the province of a small religious élite—the 'talented' few who devote their entire lives to the realization of *moksha* through systematic unswerving introspection. For the vast majority of Hindus, men and women, however, there are other traditionally sanctioned 'ways' that also lead towards the ideal state. An individual may choose from among these according to the dictates of his or her temperament and life circumstances. There are, for instance, the way of *Bhakti* or intense devotional activity; the way of Karma Yoga or selfless work, the chosen path of Gandhi; and the way of Jnana or the cultivation of the capacity to distinguish between the real and the apparent. Whatever path he follows, every Hindu is aware of the difficulty, even the improbability, of reaching the ideal state in a single lifetime. This is illustrated in the story of a yogi who, when told by Narada, the god-sage, that he would attain *moksha* after he had been born as many times as there were leaves on the tamarind tree, began to dance for joy, exclaiming, 'Ah, I shall attain *moksha* after such a short time!'

From the point of view of this study—the Hindu inner world—it is not the precise details and the actual possibilities of the 'fusion' experience that interest us so much as the contribution of the *moksha* ideal to a basic and specific form of Hindu religiosity. In the West, there have been individuals, such as St John of the Cross and Martin Buber, who have emphasized something very similar as an ideal of human life, but these and other advocates of the inner truth of mystical experience are a small minority, deviant strangers to the conventional ways of Western culture. But the 'primary processes' and 'pre-rational' goals of man's inner world have traditionally been a paramount concern of the Hindu culture as a whole—whether manifested in obsessive preoccupation, in systematic exploration and exercise, or simply in a universally shared respectful fascination. The ideal gives an abiding sense of purpose to the individual Hindu's life, a goal to be actively striven for, or patiently awaited through the cycle of many lives. For to a Hindu, *moksha*—and by implication, the possible transformation of *chitta*—is a cherished fact. Even when forgotten in the mundane cares of daily living, or banished from awareness at certain stages of life, *moksha* persists as the main element in the 'ideology of the superego', providing an unconscious ethical direction to the course of life. This 'altruistic' longing, even when conscious, may be rarely discussed, and admitted to strangers only in moments of unmasked intimacy; yet it remains the universal beacon of 'higher feeling' in the lives of most Hindus, cutting across class distinctions and caste boundaries, bridging the distance between rural and urban folk, between the illiterate and the educated. Without this all-important perspective of *moksha*, Gandhi's apparently contradictory convictions are as incomprehensible to the political scientist as the daily meditations of an Indian physicist in the prayer room of his house are to his Western colleagues.

In ancient India, the emphasis on *moksha* as the goal of life was exquisitely conscious and freely articulated. Every cultural endeavour, whether in the sciences or in the arts, explicitly acknowledged as its goal the bringing of human beings ever closer to this state. Works on politics, economics, fine arts, law, social organization or erotic life were slanted and interpreted according to this ideal, for *moksha* was considered *sarva-vidya-pratistha*—the basis of all knowledge. This intimate connection between the goal of life and spheres of cultural expression is perhaps best illustrated in the Hindu view of art.

From cave paintings to temple sculpture, from Sanskrit drama to classical dance and music, Indian art was traditionally dominated by the goal of creating (by the artist), evoking (in the audience), and absorption (by both) of *rasa*. *Rasa*, literally, means 'taste', or 'essence', or 'flavour'; it is the aesthetic counterpart of *moksha*. *Rasa* consists first in the creation of one of the eight emotional states—love, laughter, sorrow, anger, high spirits, fear, disgust and astonishment —in the theme or subject of a work of art. Second, it implies the evocation of the same emotional state in the spectator, listener or reader. And finally, it summons the complete mutual absorption of the artist and the audience in the emotional state that has been so created. *Rasa* is not an objective quality of beauty or form by which the artist is judged 'good' or 'bad'. In music, for example, the texture of sound or purity of tone is not the point of *rasa*, as anyone who has heard the Dhrupad singing of the elder Dagar brothers can testify. Nor does *rasa* imply the kind of artistic curiosity that poses new problems or discovers fresh solutions. *Rasa* in art, as *pratyahara* in yoga, is a sojourn in the inner world, an exploration of the unconscious; it is the aesthetic mode of transcendence—of quieting the turmoil of *chitta* and bringing it nearer to its perfect state of pure calm.

Artistic creation is traditionally viewed as a product of the artist's *sadhana*, similar to the yogi's meditation. Thus the ancient treatises on sculpture and painting enjoined the artist not to be distracted by the world around him, by the transience of external 'reality', but first to journey inward, to know and make vivid the inner landscape before turning his observing eye to the outside. The subjects of the outside world are then to be transformed into artistic creation through creative apperception rather than through literal reproduction of 'clinical' reality. It is said that when Valmiki composed the *Ramayana*, although he was quite familiar with the ancient story, he prepared himself through many years of *sadhana* until he could see the protagonists acting and moving 'inside' him as though in real life. Art, in the Hindu view, succeeds in its goal when the artist's unconscious, expressed in the finished work of art or in the unfolding grace of musical performance, 'reverberates' or 'swings together' with the unconscious of the listener. The effect and the subjective experience of a fully realized *rasa* in a work of art is very similar, I believe, to those rare moments of communion in Western psychotherapy when silence is neither an expression of the patient's resistance nor the reliving of a past event in which silence played an important role, but expresses a deep resonance between the therapist's and the patient's unconscious.

Psychologically, Indian art requires and inspires in the artist and in the audience a kind of ego awareness which does not involve intense concentration or extreme alertness. The essence of an Indian *raga* in music, for example, is grasped only when the ego is in a state of partial concentration, diffuse attention or reverie, a state which is encouraged and gently guided by the unfolding of the *raga* itself. The psychic states of both the artist and the listener are ideally symbolized in the image of Maheshamurti in the Elephanta caves: his large open eyes without any pupils convey exactly the mood of simultaneous wakefulness and somnolence necessary for art to fulfil its purpose, the creation and evocation of *rasa*.

Formally, ancient Indian art relied upon a variety of technical devices and a skilful combination of sensory experiences to induce in the viewer or the listener the kind of ego consciousness described above. As Richard Lannoy has pointed out, cave paintings and Sanskrit drama (as well as classical music) characteristically slow down our sense of time, use words and images (and tones) to draw us into a whirlpool of multiple perspectives, and emphasize a cyclical rather than a linear narrative structure.[29] These are 'psychedelic' techniques —sufficient to explain the aesthetic vertigo, and the complaints of monotony and repugnance on the part of many older Europeans, as well as the enthusiastic receptivity of many young Westerners when confronted with Indian art for the first time. Ajanta frescos, Vaisnava paintings and classical *ragas*, with no central emphasis, no dramatic crisis and apparently no structure, are not designed for those who require of experience something to 'hold on to', 'to get their teeth into', and for whom the relaxation of ego attention, the art of letting go, means (unconsciously) to open the flood gates of the personality to the primal forces of instinctuality and to expose oneself to the unknown within.

Man, not as a discrete presence but absorbed in his surroundings; ego, not in opposition to the id but merged with it; individual, not separate but existing in all his myriad connections: these versions of human experience provided the main thematic content of Indian art. In Sanskrit drama and verse, this is expressed in a marked preference for the theme of union (and separation). In Kalidas's *Meghduta* ('The Cloud Messenger') the drama is in the forlorn state of the lover exiled from his home and separated from his wife; in Bhavabhuti's *Uttara-rama-charita* ('Rama's Later History') it is in the desertion of Sita; while in the best known play of them all, Kalidas's *Shakuntalam*, replete with the reunion symbolism of water—tranquil pools and turbulent streams, rushing rivers and deep lakes—this central theme of union attains its highest poetic expression. In the graphic and plastic arts it is the same: the figures of the Ajanta frescos appear to retreat and then 'emerge from a mysterious, undifferentiated continuum', the temple sculptures are an 'all-encompassing labyrinth flux of the animal, human and divine . . . visions of life in the flesh, all jumbled together, . . . suffering and enjoying in a thousand shapes, teeming, devouring, turning into one another'.[30]

This unitary vision of *soma* and psyche, individual and community, self and world, me and not-me is present in most forms of popular culture in India even today. Many religious rites and folk festivals, from the pious devotions of communal *kirtans* in the temples to the orgiastic excesses of *holi*, are partially attempts at breaking out of the shell of individual existence. Nor does this vision of communion rule out its opposite, the expression of loss and separation and a nostalgic longing for reunion with a beloved 'Other', the divine or the mortal lover. This theme characterizes renowned Hindu poetry like Tagore's as well as the widely popular devotional *bhajans*. When it comes to Indian light classical music, the *ghazals*, *thumris* and *dadras* of northern India, pathos is everything; and the sentimental delight of the audience leaves little doubt about the main criterion of aesthetic merit. The presence or absence of these sentiments of pathos and longing differentiates even the much-maligned and ubiquitous filmsongs into the spiritually elevating or the merely pleasing.

Moving away from the realm of the classical and popular arts, we see that the belief in an underlying unity among categories which are kept rigorously separate in Western thought, such as body and mind, is an integral part of Indian language, thought and phenomenology. For example, in the practice of psychosomatic medicine, as Erna Hoch reports, 'it is very natural for Indian patients to associate certain physical symptoms with a corresponding mental or emotional phenomenon. If one tries to differentiate whether a person who says "my heart does not feel like it" or "my liver is not doing its work" actually means the physical organ or some emotional disturbance, one often evokes puzzlement, as a separation of the two has never been made in the patient's way of thinking. It is only the more emancipated, Westernized Indian who makes his body a scapegoat and insists that a certain symptom is plainly physical and cannot possibly have anything to do with his emotions.'[31] Hoch recounts the case history of an Indian farmer who comes to the doctor with complaints a Westerner would explain in terms of bodily symptoms, but who in response to the doctor's initial inquiry about his trouble, can answer simply, 'my mind is bad'. The very word for health in Hindi—*svastha*, from the root '*swa*' (I) and '*astha*' (stable)—implies something which is resident, present or stable in the 'I': not in the body, not in the mind, not in the various organs or selves, but in the underlying *atman*.

In this discussion so far, I have explored some of the byways of the main concept of traditional Hindu culture, emphasized its pervasive influence in all fields of cultural endeavour, touched upon its continuing relevance in the world image of contemporary Hindus and, from this perspective, I have ventured to compare Hindu and Western (psycho-analytic) views of mental life. Often enough, I found myself writing as a Hindu with a 'vested' share of his community's preconscious world image; and the quotations from Hindu sources carry, of course, an implicit seal of personal approval. I could not quite hide a partisan enthusiasm for a conception of human experience which resembles, yet spiritually and intellectually surpasses, the timeless simplifications of magical or animistic thinking that often prove irresistible to the child within each one of us. For there is something majestic—and yes, also quixotic and anarchic in the context of Indian politics and economy—in a cultural ideal which has as its goal the liberated, rather than the successful or the 'achieving' man; which emphasizes the possibility of man's realization rather than his salvation; which considers the exploration and enrichment of the inner world of experience a vital life task; and which relies on the practice of a cultivated subjectivity and introspection to gain knowledge of the self and the world. Yet a study such as this also calls for 'objectivity', taking the distance necessary to examine the ideal —this 'nostalgia of the Indian soul'—critically from the standpoint of depth psychology.

The essential psychological theme of Hindu culture is the polarity of fusion and separation. To be sure, this is a universal theme, a dynamic counterpoint between two opposite needs, to merge into and to be differentiated from the 'Other', where the 'Other' is all which is not the self. The language used by Ramana Maharshi in describing *sahaja samadhi*, with its profuse symbolism of fusion and connection —water, river, ocean, well and rope—expresses the tension inherent in the theme of fusion. For example, rope has universal symbolic significance as an extension of all forms and techniques of communication; it is a means of joining or holding things together. Yet, as we know from clinical experience, the 'meaning' of rope can shift from a representation of union to the denial of separation; the rope now becomes something dangerous and must be destroyed or 'burnt'.[32]

The relationship between fusion and separation in the individual is asymmetrical; each of us seeks to right the balance by constantly moving back and forth in the psychic space between the two poles.

A permanent balance between the poles is, of course, impossible to achieve, given the constant flux of psychological experience—the 'business of living'.

The psychological importance of the theme of fusion and separation lies in its intimate relation to the human fear of death. This fear has little to do with the knowledge of one's mortality, with the fact of dying. For death can be perceived, as it has been by many who have sought it voluntarily, as the bearer of varied gifts: peace, quiet, and perhaps revenge on those who are left behind and must now mourn. Rather, the 'fear' of death is related to the terrible, inadmissible fact of life, namely, that one once was, and will be again, non-existent. We mask our denial of death in our anxious fear of it. For in the individual unconscious death simply does not exist. As Yudhishthira in the Indian epic *Mahabharata* expressed it: 'The strangest thing in the world is that each man, seeing others die around him, is still convinced that he himself is immortal.' Psychologically speaking, a pervasive fear of death betrays either the fear of loss of a love object or the fear of loss of individuality in fusion with the object.

The quality of this fear, psycho-analysis would maintain, is determined by two inescapable facts of life: human imagination and dependence. Our imagination and capacity for fantasy enable us to envision chasms of blackness and emptiness just outside the comforting confines of reality as we have learned to know it. And our lifelong dependence on other human beings forces us to live as if on an edge: on one side, should we stumble and fall, is a state of complete dependence and defencelessness which snuffs out individuality; on the other, is a state of utter independence and the loneliness that comes with it. The fear of death, then, contains these two elements: the fear of dependence and obliteration as an individual in the state of fusion, and the fear of unimaginable loneliness, emptiness and desolation in the state of separation. Both fears are rooted in early infancy, when they are first and most directly experienced. It is in this period of complete dependence upon others that a child's extravagant imagination and unchecked fantasies may transform these fears into horrors unimaginable to an adult. Only gradually, as a child's ego develops, do these fears become attached to specific persons and specific situations and thus lose their earlier archaic quality where they were related to a vague but omnipresent 'Other'.

Hinduism has attempted to confront *and* resolve the fear of death (as well as the 'constituent fears' it embraces) in its elaboration of *moksha* as the goal of human life. The Greek ambassador Megasthenes, a perceptive witness in his host country two thousand years ago, was quite right in his observation that death was the main preoccupation of the learned men of Hindu society. For Hindus, the 'right', 'healthy' or 'true' fulcrum on the continuum between fusion and separation is much closer to the fusion pole than in Western cultures. Hindu culture is governed in these matters not by the golden mean but by a staunch belief in the golden extreme. In its most consequential refinement, Raja Yoga, Hindu culture has gone even further in rejecting the 'norm' of a dynamic balance between fusion and separation as an essential condition of mental health. Disintegration of individuality in the state of fusion, Raja Yoga maintains, leads to a higher form of integration; the striving to extinguish individual independence leads to a much higher form of *interdependence*. Yet for most Hindus Raja Yoga remains an ideal approachable only by especially gifted souls who can endure and transcend the archaic anxiety, the 'walk through the valley of the shadow of death', vividly described in the accounts of Ramakrishna and Ramana Maharshi.[33]

If the concept of *moksha* incorporates the ideal of fusion, implicitly it also defines the Hindu's personal and cultural sense of hell, separation from others and from the 'Other'. Any inner shift towards, or desire for, autonomy arouses the most severe of the culturally supported anxieties: the fear of isolation and estrangement that are visited upon the completely autonomous human being. For most Hindus who (unconsciously or preconsciously) have rejected any version of the ideal of autonomy as well as the actual everyday processes of 'individuation', and yet at the same time share the universal human anxiety that is the dark side of the fusion ideal, the movement towards the goal of *moksha* has necessarily to be a slow one through a full life lived in *dharma*, the second important concept of the Hindu world image.

Life Task and Life Cycle—Dharma

In the Hindu philosophical tradition, *dharma* is the central concept of *Mimamsa*, the intensely activist philosophy of the first two parts of the Vedas. First mentioned in the *Rigveda*, the concept of *dharma* has evolved gradually as each historical era has spawned its own interpretation in terms of its own needs and actuality. The list of formal treatises on *dharma*, from Gautama's *Dharmasastra* (*c.* 600

B.C.) to the present day, covers 172 pages in Kane's *History of Dharmasastra*. Today *dharma* is variously translated as 'law', 'moral duty', 'right action', or 'conformity with the truth of things'. But in each of its various patterns, *dharma* as the image of the human life cycle, (*asramadharma*) or *dharma* as the principle underlying social relations, there runs a common thread: *Dharma* is the *means* through which man approaches the desired goal of human life. As the *Vaisesikasutra* has it, *dharma* is 'that from which results happiness and final beatitude'.[34] It is what Lao Tse called the Tao, 'The Way'.

Hindu culture has consistently emphasized that as long as a person stays true to the ground-plan of his life and fulfils his own particular life task, his *svadharma*, he is travelling on the path towards *moksha*. But how does the individual acquire the knowledge of his *svadharma*, and thus of 'right actions'? This is a complicated matter, and, as it happens, a relative one. Hindu philosophy and ethics teach that 'right action' for an individual depends on *desa*, the culture in which he is born; on *kala*, the period of historical time in which he lives; on *srama*, the efforts required of him at different stages of life; and on *gunas*, the innate psychobiological traits which are the heritage of an individual's previous lives. 'Right' and 'wrong' are relative; they emerge as clear distinctions only out of the total configuration of the four 'co-ordinates' of action. The individual can never *know* in any absolute sense, nor even significantly influence this configuration. It is given.

In lessening the burden of individual responsibility for action, Hindu culture at the same time alleviates the pain of guilt suffered in other societies by those whose (real or fantasied) actions transgress rigid thou-shalt and thou-shalt-not axioms. Instead, a Hindu's actions are governed by a more permissive and gentle, but much more ambiguous, thou-canst-but-try precept. One of the psychosocial consequences of this ethical relativism, or uncertainty, is the generation in the individual Hindu, from the earliest childhood, of a pervasive doubt as to the wisdom or efficacy of individual initiative. To size up a situation for oneself and proceed to act upon one's momentary judgement is to take an enormous cultural as well as a personal risk. For most Hindus such independent voluntary action is unthinkable.

But if the search for certainty is futile, one can at least increase one's sense of psychological security by acting as one's ancestors did in the past and as one's social group does at present. Right action and individual *svadharma* thus increasingly come to mean traditional action and *jati* (caste) *dharma*, in the sense that an individual's occupational activity and social acts are right or 'good' if they conform to the traditional pattern prevalent in his kinship and caste groups. Suspicion of innovation and unconscious avoidance of activities not charted in traditional maps are the consequences. The Hindu view of action is necessarily a conservative one; it harks back to a 'golden age', and harbours the sceptical conviction that social change is superfluous, an importunate deviation from traditional ways.

Activity or occupation itself—whether that of a shoemaker or a priest, a housewife or a farmer, a social worker directly serving others or a yogi apparently indifferent to the suffering around him—is equally good and equally right if it is a part of the individual's life task and accepted by him or her as such. The culture assures that any activity, if fulfilled in the spirit of *svadharma*, leads equally towards the universal goal of life: 'Better one's own *dharma*, bereft of merit, than another's well performed; the death in one's own *dharma* is praiseworthy, the living in another's is fearsome.'[35]

Much of the teaching and transmission of Hindu cultural values to the next generation takes place through the narration of stories and parables by mothers, grandmothers and others in the circle of the extended family. The concept of *svadharma* is no exception. A favourite story tells of a king who was strolling along the banks of the Ganges river with an entourage of his ministers. It was the monsoon season and the river was in spate, swirling, flowing towards the sea. The broad sweep of the swollen river and its strong current filled the king with awe. Suddenly mindful of his own insignificance, he addressed his ministers: 'Is there no one on this earth who can reverse the flow of this river so that it flows from the sea to the mountains?' The ministers smiled at the king's naïveté, but a courtesan who overheard his question stepped forward and addressed the river thus: 'O, Mother Ganges, if I have striven to fulfil my *dharma* as a courtesan by giving my body to all comers, without distinguishing rich from poor, handsome from ugly, old from young, then reverse your flow!' The waters were still for a moment, as if in deliberation, and then the river started to flow backwards.

An individual's work, or more generally any activity through which he 'acts on the world', has two aspects or aims for the Hindu. The first is to earn a living and to satisfy the worldly purposes of accomplishment, power and status, the householder's desire to create and care for a family, and perhaps also the broader social goal of community service. Hindus can be as absorbed as anyone in obtaining the means of sensuous enjoyment and recognition from others and, as we shall see later, these goals and pursuits are positively prescribed by the culture for the 'householder' at a certain stage of life. Yet, accompanying this outward, worldly activity is a preconscious, culturally generated belief that the real purpose of activity is within the individual. The measure of a man's work lies not only in what it enables him to achieve and maintain in the outside world, but also in how far it helps him towards the realization of his *svadharma*: how far it prepares him 'inside' and brings him nearer to that feeling of inner calm which is the dawning of wisdom and the prerequisite for *moksha*. Like the child's absorption and pleasure in his play which, without his conscious awareness, prepares him for adult work, in the Hindu scheme of things this very 'adult work' is valued not so much for the external rewards it brings, the intrinsic fascination it holds, or the social respect it insures in the present, as for the developmental apprenticeship it provides. It is a necessary refinement of the self in the unfolding of the Hindu life cycle.

This sense of *dharma* as the spirit rather than the content of activity is, I believe, related to the individual Hindu's notable tolerance of life styles other than his own. Hindus tend to accept casually deviance or eccentricity which in the West might be anxiously labelled antisocial or psychopathological, requiring 'correction' or 'cure'. Usually, of course, in its extreme manifestations, this kind of acceptable deviance is a group phenomenon, sanctified by tradition and formalized in recognized rituals; only then is it fully legitimized as the working out of a particular *svadharma*. Consider the flamboyant example of the groups of transvestites, dressed in women's clothes, who are often seen in the streets of large cities and towns. Earning their living as male prostitutes and through donations on certain festival occasions such as the birth of a child (when they appear before the house of the newborn ritually mouthing and mimicking obscenities), the transvestites can point with pride to their ancient traditions, their own holy places and their origin in one of the mythical Pandava brothers, Arjuna the famed warrior, who was transformed into a woman for one year. The transvestites, like other 'bizarre' groups of professional beggars, faith-healers or those sadhus who go about clothed only 'in the infinite', are as integral to the Hindu social order as the members of the Calcutta stock exchange, Hindi film-stars or the more familiar peasant-householders.

4

The idea that every individual's *svadharma* is unique enhances a deeply held belief in a pervasive equality, at a personal level, among all human beings. This conviction of personal equality is independent of prescriptive criteria for *social conduct* which contribute to a society of rampant inequalities. It is more a belief that each individual has a dignified, rightful place and function in the society, a belief which transcends the formal patterns of deference to caste, class and family hierarchies, but does not hold the promise of an egalitarian soçiety. This quality of mutual respect, the recognition that others share a common humanity and a common life goal while fulfilling various distinct *svadharmas*, is often manifest in even the most feudal of master-servant relationships, and it can humanize personal encounters in the most bureaucratic of settings. Yet this very tolerance may also lapse into an indifference to the fate of those not bound to an individual by traditional ties of caste and kinship.

Dharma as a social force

The social aspect of *dharma* is suggested in the etymology of the word itself which derives from the root *dhr* (to uphold, to sustain, to nourish). *Dharma* is social cement; it holds the individual and society together. As the *Mahabharata* expresses it, 'Neither the state nor the king, neither the mace nor the mace-bearer, governs the people; it is only by *dharma* that people secure mutual protection.'[36] *Dharma* is both the principle and the vision of an organic society in which all the participating members are interdependent, their roles complementary. The duties, privileges and restrictions of each role are prescribed by an immutable law, the *sanatan* or 'eternal' *dharma*, and apply equally to the king as to the meanest of subjects.

Hindus share the belief that the legitimacy of social institutions lies in the *dharma* they incorporate rather than in utilitarian contractual agreements and obligations. Traditional social structures, incorporating the social elements of *dharma*, are accepted and respected by most Hindus as fundamentally viable and just. Criticism and suggestions for reform in certain historical periods are not meant to question the institutions as such, but are designed to bring them closer to the ideal blueprint laid down by the 'eternal law'. Moreover, it is generally believed that social conflict, oppression and unrest do not stem from the organization of social relations, but originate in the *adharma* (not *dharma*) of those in positions of power. Institutions in India are thus personalized to an extent inconceivable in the West;

individuals who head them are believed to be the sole repository of the virtues and vices of the institutions; as human beings, such individuals in authority are thought to be accessible to appeal, open to the impulse of mercy and capable of actions unconstrained by the rule of the 'system'. Many are the poignant stories of simple farmers in the early days of British rule who responded to an act of injustice by government officials by spending their all 'in the vain hope of reaching the Queen, and gaining her ear, at Windsor. Heartbroken pilgrims for the most part, who died of want and disillusionment far from the home, and villages that they would never see again.'[37]

Any tendency towards social reform in India moves not to abolish hierarchical institutions or to reject the values on which they are based, but to remove or 'change' the individuals in positions of authority in them. When an institution is not working, it is taken for granted that the power-wielders have veered from the path of *dharma*. Gandhi's concept of 'trusteeship', his unsuccessful attempts to convince the mill and factory owners to consider the wealth they accumulate as held in trust for the welfare of society rather than for their personal expenditure, is just such an effort to 'reconstruct' a group of power-holders, to bring them home to an appreciation of *dharma* as social responsibility.

Indian mythology is replete with instances in which *dharma* deteriorates to such an extent that the Preserver Vishnu must assume human form to re-establish it by annihilating those responsible. The culprits are almost always to be found in positions of temporal or spiritual authority. Thus, King Hiranyakashipu who, through years of ascetic practices, secured Shiva's promise that he would never be killed by a man or an animal and that he would not die either on earth or in the air, unleashed such a reign of terror that *dharma* was endangered. Vishnu had to take the form of Narsingha—half man, half lion—and kill the king by putting him across his thighs and ripping open his chest with his nails to keep to the letter of Shiva's boon.

Perhaps it should be re-emphasized that *dharma* in its social aspect, which influences the individual's experience of institutions in familial, social, economic and political spheres as well as his connection with these institutions, exists largely at a preconscious level and is rarely the subject of conscious scrutiny. Thus, for most Hindus, social change implicitly means a change of authority figures rather than a restructuring of institutions or of the prevalent networks of authority and dependency; but if India seems a paradise for politicians and politicking, it is the despair of forces committed to structural change. This does not mean that revolutionary change in Indian society is impossible. Social and environmental stresses can reach such proportions that preconscious beliefs are called consciousness, recognized as the vestiges of a personal–cultural past, reinterpreted negatively, and superseded by deliberate and conscious attempts to reject them unconditionally in planning the direction of institutional change.[38] At this time, however, this kind of psychological revolutionary situation (as distinct from political or economic circumstances), in which a *totalistic rejection of the personal–cultural past* is the prerequisite for radical action, does not exist either among India's various political élites or among the masses of the people. Depending upon political persuasion, the beliefs associated with *dharma* can be hailed as a bulwark of Indian social stability or disparaged as a hindrance in the path of revolutionary change. In what conceivable circumstances a psychologically revolutionary situation may indeed develop in India is a subject to which I will return in a later chapter.

Dharma as image of the life cycle (asramadharma)

Dharma is not only the principle of individual action and social relations but also the ground-plan of an ideal life cycle in the sense that it defines the tasks of different stages of life and the way each stage should be lived. Like modern theories of personality, the Hindu model of *asramadharma* conceptualizes human development in a succession of stages. It holds that development proceeds not at a steady pace in a smooth continuum, but in discontinuous steps, with marked changes as the individual moves into each new phase of life: proper developmental progress requires the meeting and surmounting of the critical task of each phase in the proper sequence and at the proper time.

Essentially, *asramadharma* is the Hindu counterpart of the epigenetic principle applied to man's development in relation to his society and, as I have shown in detail elswhere, it is very similar to Erikson's well-known theory of psychosocial stages of growth.[39] Contrasting with Erikson's model, which is clinical and developmental, the Hindu view proposes 'ideal' images in the Platonic sense. In outlining the stages of life and the specific tasks of each stage, the Hindu model does not chart the implications for mental health if the tasks remain unfulfilled, but emphasizes the importance of the scrupulous progression from task to task and from stage to stage in the ultimate realization of *moksha*. Or, in the popular saying: 'It is only he who has built a house, planted a tree and brought up a son, who is ready for the final effort.' A schematic comparison of the two models showing the specific tasks for each stage and the strength or 'virtue' accruing from a successful resolution of each task is illuminating, not least of all for the clinical validation it provides of many ancient Hindu propositions on the conduct and course of the 'ideal' life cycle. This convergence should not seem remarkable since both the religious endeavour to give meaning to the stages of life and the clinician's attempt to connect and correlate the attributes of these stages must be based on what evolution has created: human growth and development.

Erikson's Scheme		Hindu Scheme	
Stage	Specific Task and 'Virtue'	Stage	Specific Task and 'Virtue'
1. Infancy	Basic Trust vs. Mistrust: Hope	Individual's 'pre-history' not explicitly considered	Preparation of the capacity to comprehend *dharma*
2. Early Childhood	Autonomy vs. Shame, Doubt: Willpower		
3. Play Age	Initiative vs. Guilt: Purpose		
4. School Age	Industry vs. Inferiority: Competence	1. Apprenticeship (*brahmacharya*)	Knowledge of *dharma*: Competence and Fidelity
5. Adolescence	Identity vs. Identity Diffusion: Fidelity		
6. Young Adulthood	Intimacy vs. Isolation: Love	2. Householder (*garhasthya*)	Practice of *dharma*: Love and Care
7. Adulthood	Generativity vs. Stagnation: Care	3. Withdrawal (*vanaprastha*)	Teaching of *dharma*: Extended Care
8. Old Age	Integrity vs. Despair: Wisdom	4. Renunciation (*sannyasa*)	Realization of *dharma*: Wisdom

Fig. 3

The image of the course of an ideal life cycle, as described in the stages of *asramadharma*, is deeply etched on the Hindu psyche. The strength and persistence of this tradition was brought home vividly to me in a series of interviews with four brothers running a large modern business in Calcutta. The eldest brother, in his early sixties, was increasingly turning away from family and business affairs to concentrate on matters of spiritual development. He did not talk of *retiring* from his work and his role as head of the extended family, which had involved him profoundly during the major part of his adulthood, but of an *active* renunciation of his previous concerns. The transition certainly contained elements of grief and discontent; yet the eldest brother's subjective experience of the step he was taking had an overall quality of hopeful renewal rather than a regretted end. The second eldest brother, in his fifties, who had taken over the responsibilities of chief executive of the family firm a couple of years before, was beginning to see his major task more and more as encouraging and 'nurturing' the growth and development of his younger brothers and others of the next generation coming into the business rather than gathering personal laurels through a spectacular increase in the company's profits, or other financial feats. The two younger brothers, in their late thirties, were immersed in their work and their families, while fully enjoying a hectic social life and all the sensual pleasures that wealth can provide in India. These four modern, highly Westernized brothers were living out their respective *svadharmas* as businessmen, thereby realizing, with feelings of inner well-being, the ancient tradition of *asramadharma*. Nor is this an isolated example. At a preconscious level of awareness, a vast majority of traditional Hindus are convinced that failure to renounce the life-concerns of an outlived life stage, as well as a premature commitment to tasks that are appropriate only for a later stage of life, are 'bad' for the individual. Thus, consistency in interests, attitudes and activities over time, from youth to old age, is not an estimable virtue but a sign of insufficiency.

Ideas of Time and Destiny

I come now to perhaps one of the most difficult and misunderstood concepts of Hindu culture, *karma*, the third essential idea in the Hindu world image. In the following discussion I do not aim to give a philosophical account of the origin and rationale for this concept, but rather, I am interested in ascertaining and describing the place and influence of the idea of *karma* in Hindu psychology.

The popular Indian understanding of *karma*, which says little about its preconscious meaning for individual Hindus, comes through in the following interview in a north Indian village: 'Even at the time of death a man should wish to do good deeds and wish to be reborn in a place where he can do good deeds again. Then he will get enlightenment and come to know of his past lives. After many lives, a man attains *mukti* (*moksha*). . . . If one does evil deeds, his form changes and he falls lower, till he becomes a *jar* (an inanimate thing).'[40] Other Hindus, when pressed for their sense of *karma*, are likely to express the same twin ideas: namely, the endless cycle of birth, growth and death, in which an individual soul (*jiva*) progresses or regresses through levels of existence, above and below the human one, touching the highest possibilities of pleasure and serenity, or plumbing the lowest depth of pain; and, second, the control of this movement by the *karma* of the individual soul, by the balance of 'right' and 'wrong' actions, the proportions of *dharma* and *adharma*.

Karma influences the Hindu world image in two fundamental ways: in the Hindu's experience of time, and in the formation of his cosmology. The way in which a culture estimates and elaborates ideas of time and destiny provides insight into the psychological organization of its individual members. This connection has been stressed by others, notably Spengler: 'The historical environment of another is a part of his essence, and no such other can be understood without the knowledge of his time-sense, his destiny-idea and the style and degree of acuity of his inner life. In so far therefore as these things are not directly confessed, we have to extract them from the symbolism of the alien Culture. And as it is thus and only thus that we can approach the incomprehensible, the style of an alien Culture and the great time-symbols belonging thereto acquire an immeasurable importance.'[41]

Time, in the Hindu culture, is symbolized by the image of *Kala*, worshipped as the god of death and inexorable fate who gives birth to beings, causes them to ripen and mature, and then (like the Greek *Chronos*) devours them. Thus human time is seen as a cycle, characterized by origination, duration and disappearance *ad infinitum*. In Hindu art, *Kala* is often portrayed as a fearful god with bulging eyes and a wide open mouth. In front of the mouth are tiny, tumbling human figures reaching to the earth in an arc, with no evident clue as to whether these figures are emerging from, or disappearing into, the god's mouth. Yet this divisibility, periodicity and flux of time, according to Hindu belief, is only an apparent phenomenon, the worldly manifestations of permanent, absolute or real time in all its empirical plurality. The distinction between 'real' and 'human' time is reminiscent of the distinction between reality and *maya*. Real time, contained within Brahman and not spilled out as seed, is homogeneous, indivisible and motionless. It is experienced as such in *moksha*. Just as space, the classical Hindu thinkers maintained, is divided into appearances by the objects present in it, so is time differentiated into temporal zones of greater or smaller proportions, varying from a moment to an astronomical age, by the arising, enduring and disappearing of empirical beings. This sense of the motionless density of time is of course similar to the way in which an individual experienced time in his 'prehistory'. For before the self takes shape, before the perceptual system becomes differentiated, we live without memories of what has gone before or expectations of what lies ahead; and time is thus motionless.

The awareness of the movement and direction of time in the West, the heightened consciousness of its units—years, days, hours—the sensitivity and sometimes obsessive attention to its passage, is not shared by Hindus in the same degree. This fact is reflected in linguistic usage. Although a highly developed language like Hindi has a number of synonyms (not found in Western languages) for a natural object such as the moon, terms descriptive of its appearance in different phases and seasons, the words denoting time itself are given much more cavalier treatment. Thus, not only is the meaning of the word *Kal* (from *Kala*) derived from the syntax and context of the sentence, it also depends upon the inflection of the voice which conveys the speaker's mood. *Kal* can mean tomorrow or yesterday, a moment or an age; it may refer to an event which just happened, or to a future likelihood (as in the Spanish *mañana*).

Relatively speaking, time for a Hindu does not have the impersonal and objective (nor the sometimes driving, coercive) quality it has for the average Westerner. In India, historical events have little immediacy in the lives of individuals; they seem to recede almost instantly into a distant past, to become immemorial legend. Gandhi's murder, only a little more than twenty-five years ago, has already assumed the mythical form of the 'death of a hero'. In the individual's subjective chronology, it is merged with other similar historical events which took place hundreds of years ago—as 'the past'. On the other hand, mythical figures like Rama or Hanuman are as actual and as psychologically real (if not more so) as recent historical characters such as Ramakrishna or Shivaji.

This telescoping of different periods of time may catch the modern social scientist off-guard in his pursuit of the data of oral history by means of the reminiscences of Hindu peasantry. Ostensibly chronological, factual personal accounts, for instance, are apt to be a mixture of memories of the informant's childhood as well as the childhoods of his contemporaries, and may also include the biographical details of a long-deceased but memorable relative who was revered aloud by the family during the individual's youth. The Hindu time sense is more psychological than historical; it has the dream-like quality of timeless time as it exists in the human unconscious.

Unconscious as destiny

What prevents the individual from living in *dharma*, separates him from an intuitive understanding of right action, and thus hinders his progress towards the destined goal of *moksha*? This is the question the concept of *karma* addresses, thereby completing Hinduism's philosophical response to the fundamental issues of human existence. This question also takes us on a short excursion into the conceptual psychology of ancient Hindus, formalized in various philosophical texts and at the same time constituting a shared pool of intuitive 'common knowledge', a psychology which can legitimately be described as originating in a specific metaphysical need.

According to Hindu psychological theory, the newborn infant is not a *tabula rasa* but comes equipped, as it were, with a highly personal and individual unconscious characterized by a particular mixture of three fundamental qualities or *gunas*: *sattva* (clarity, light), *rajas* (passion, desire) and *tamas* (dullness, darkness). In the Hindu idea of destiny the unconscious has an innate tendency to strive towards clarity and light, just as *chitta's* aim is to mature from its scattered and darkening forms. Yet the other two qualities of the unconscious, passion and darkness, are concurrent and omnipresent, their relative strength differing from one infant to another. And if the cause of 'wrong' actions—of *adharma*—is 'begotten by the quality of *rajas*, all consuming and all polluting, . . . our enemy here on earth', then it follows that an individual may, by reason of his innate *guna* constellation, need to expend much more conscious and unremitting effort to live in *dharma* than another whose unconscious is characterized by a more 'propitious' mix. In any case, a constant intimacy with the unconscious together with a recognition and 'control' of impulses and fantasies, in short, the exploration and conquest of inner space, are essential aspects of living in *dharma*. For, 'A person consists of his desires. And as his desire so is his will; and as his will so is his deed; and whatever deed he does that will he reap.'[42] And, 'Let the wise man guard thoughts, for they are difficult to perceive, very artful, and they rush wherever they list. . . .'[43]

The balance of the *gunas* is a dynamic one, perpetually changing as each impulse, each desire, each thought and each action leaves its trace on the unconscious *chitta*. For many, in spite of their best efforts during a lifetime to tilt this balance in the direction of *sattva*, the initial handicap of innate dispositions (*samskaras*) which shape the unconscious at the beginning of life may prove insurmountable. The *karma* theory, as it unfolds, assures the individual that none of his efforts has been wasted, for he will start the next life with the balance of *gunas* attained at the close of his previous existence. The unconscious, then, occupies a central place in the Hindu world image and theory of the meaning of human life; the origin and constitution of the unconscious are not biological but metaphysical, its nature depending upon the 'actions' (in the widest sense of the word) of a previous life.

Karma is not just a doctrine of 'reincarnation', 'fatalism' or 'predestination'; it is a promise of hope. Given the innate tendency of the unconscious towards light (*sattva*), combined with an individual's personal efforts in this direction (*dharma*), *karma* assures that attainment of the goal of existence (*moksha*) is certain even though there are apt to be many setbacks in the process—a process which may require a number of rebirths and many life cycles for its completion. For the average Hindu, questions of whether this doctrine is a necessary myth or whether it is reasonable and compatible with 'scientific' knowledge do not arise. Such ideas are not based on a logic of extension or linear reasoning, but are absorbed as a kind of dream-like, intuitive inner orientation early in life. In Spengler's terms, these are 'destiny-ideas' as opposed to 'causality-principles', calling for 'life experience and not scientific experience, the power of seeing and not that of calculating, depth and not intellect'.[44]

Urban, industrialized life in India, as elsewhere in the world, breeds all manner of anxiety and dislocation, and is providing clinicians with a fair share of case-history material. Thus, in our modern patients we find confirmation of traditional Hindu psychological concepts and 'interpretations'. The doctrine of *karma*, and especially the psychological notions associated with it, exercise a considerable influence on Hindu mental life. A woman patient in her early thirties, becoming aware of her aggressive impulses towards her husband as revealed in a dream, spontaneously exclaimed, 'Ah, these are due to my *samskaras*. However hard I try to be a good wife, my bad *samskaras* prevent me.' This tendency to stress the *samskaras*, the innate, constitutional dispositions, rather than acknowledging and 'working through' conflicting emotions, thoughts and actions in the context of one's life history is a culturally specific form of resistance in psychotherapy with Indian patients. Moreover, this resistance is evident in adult attitudes towards a child's growth and development. Because Hindus do not view infant nature as universal, or infinitely malleable, there is little pressure and no urgency to try to 'mould' a child in one or another parentally desired, culturally approved image. Even the newborn is considered partially autonomous, in the sense of having been born with a unique and specific constellation of *gunas*. The very specificity of the *gunas* constellation imposes certain limits on the socialization of any child.

With the cultural acceptance of the notion of *samskara*, there is little social pressure to foster the belief that if only the caretakers were good enough, and constantly on their toes, the child's potentialities would be boundlessly fulfilled. With the Hindu emphasis on man's inner limits, there is not that sense of urgency and struggle against the outside world, with prospects of sudden metamorphoses and great achievements just around the corner, that often seems to propel Western lives. In any case, given the *totality* of the Hindu world image, such a struggle would be viewed as taking place on the wrong battlefield and fought with the wrong weapons.

The power of the *samskaras* is dramatically illustrated by the popular fable of the mouse-girl and the holy man. If I repeat the fable here it is not only because I like to tell stories (which is true) but also because these fables exquisitely capture the essence of the Hindu world image.

On the left bank of the Ganges, there once lived a holy man called Yajnavalkya together with his wife. One day, as he was meditating, he felt something small and soft fall into the nest of his hands. He opened his eyes and saw that it was a small female mouse which must have fallen down from the claws of an eagle circling above. The holy man had pity on the mouse, and using his occult powers, transformed it into a small girl and took her home. The girl grew up as the daughter of the house, and when she reached marriageable age

Yajnavalkya's wife reproached him one day, saying, 'Don't you see your daughter is mature now and needs a husband?' Yajnavalkya answered, 'You are right. I have decided that she should have the best possible husband in all the worlds.' He then called the sun-god, and when he appeared Yainavalkya said, 'I have chosen you as my son-in-law.' He then turned to the girl and asked her, 'Would you like the light of three worlds as your husband?' But she answered, 'Ah, father, he is much too plump and redfaced. Find me another husband.' The holy man smiled and asked the sun whether he knew of anyone who was better than he. The sun answered, 'Oh, holy man! The cloud is even stronger than I am, at least when it covers me.' Yajnavalkya called the god of clouds, but once again when he asked his daughter's consent she replied, 'Oh, father, he looks much too morose. Find me a better husband.' Yajnavalkya asked the cloud whether there was someone in the world better than he. The cloud answered, 'The mountain is better, for it can stop me.' The holy man called the mountain god, but the moment he appeared the girl cried out, 'Oh, father, he is too massive and clumsy, find me a better husband.' Yajnavalkya's patience was nearly exhausted, but since he loved his daughter, he asked the mountain whether he knew of some-one who was even better. The mountain answered, 'The mouse can bore as many holes in me as it wants to. Considering that, it must be stronger than I am.' Yajnavalkya called the mouse, and as soon as the girl saw him, she exclaimed, 'Father! This is the only husband I can be happy with. Ah, can't you change me into a mouse?' The holy man fulfilled her wish. And as the two mice disappeared into the bushes, he walked back home, smiling to himself and saying, 'Al-though the sun, the cloud and the mountain stood before her as suitors, the mouse-girl needed to become a mouse again. Her nature could not be denied.'

In conclusion, it remains to be noted that the preconscious system of beliefs and values associated with the concepts of *moksha*, *dharma* and *karma* forms a meta-reality for Hindus. Above and beyond the objective world of phenomena capable of validation which we term 'real', and the individual distortions and denials of these phenomena which we are accustomed to calling 'unreal', such world images (in any culture) constitute a third distinct category, both 'real' and 'unreal', a meta-reality which is neither deterministically univer-sal nor utterly idiosyncratic but which fills the space between the two. It is culturally specific and harboured or accepted, often un-

consciously, as the heart of a community identity. Like the evidence
of the senses which more often than not goes unquestioned, the
meta-reality of a culture is also rarely summoned for conscious
examination; yet it exercises an influence on individual thought and
behaviour that is somewhat comparable to the working of the reality
and pleasure principles. Instinctual and reality demands, it seems,
have their counterpart in cultural imperatives. Denial of these imperatives can create tension and dis-ease in the individual. For such a
meta-reality is not a system of abstractions, to be more or less hazily
comprehended during the adult years; it is a part of the actuality of
psychology and culture, absorbed by the child in his relationship with
his adult caretakers from the very beginning of life as the underlying
truth of the world in which he will spend his life—a world first
conveyed to him by his mother.

CHAPTER III

Mothers and Infants

The first months of human life are a period of wordless oblivion which is of root significance for individual development. At once timeless and fleeting, infancy is the foundation for all later psychological experience. Moreover, the nature of an individual's first relationship—with his mother—profoundly influences the quality and 'dynamics' of social relations throughout his life.

Recognition of the crucial role of this original relationship, the mother–infant 'dyad' as the genetic psychologist Edward Simmel has called it,[1] for the development of all subsequent social relations has been relatively late in coming in the social sciences. Thus, although Freud mentioned its importance in 1895 in one of his earliest papers and often elaborated on the psychological reciprocity between mothers and infants, he came to appreciate its full significance in emotional development only towards the end of his life. By 1938, he described the mother's importance to the infant as 'unique, without parallel, established unalterably for a whole lifetime as the first and strongest love-object and as the prototype of all later love-relations —for both sexes'.[2] It is within this dyad that a person first learns to relate to the 'Other' and begins to develop his capacity to love (in its widest sense); it is here that an individual originates as a social being. As adults, all of our affiliations and intimacies bear the stamp of our particular kind of infancy. Indeed, as anthropologists such as Kardiner, Benedict and Mead have shown, the specific emotional colouring of many of a society's cultural institutions can be directly attributed to the dominant quality or mode of the first relationship, not in the sense of simple causal connection, but in the complementarity and reciprocal influence between the mother–infant dyad and other institutionalized forms of social relations.

In spite of the general consensus on its significance, the mother–infant dyad remains intellectually elusive and relatively unexplored. In part, because of its archaic, wordless nature, it is but dimly reflected in the free associations of psycho-analytic patients and hence in clinical reconstructions. Hypotheses and speculations on the emotional development of the infant and on what actually transpires between him and his mother in the course of their repeated early encounters are thus derived from a variety of sources: direct observation of infants, experimental data in neo-natal cognition, treatment of psychotic patients, and deductions from the conceptual framework of psycho-analysis. The following short summary of existing knowledge of the emotional state of infancy is highly condensed.[3] Such a description, however minimal, is a necessary background for the elaboration of the dominant mode of the mother–infant relationship in Hindu society and for an interpretation of its consequences for adult personality, its influence on the organization of social relations and its relevance to the elaboration of cultural ideals.

During the first few months of life, the infant lives in a psychological state which has variously been termed 'undifferentiated', 'non-differentiated', or 'unintegrated'. These terms are basically similar; all imply that at the beginning of life there is no clear and absolute distinction between conscious and unconscious, ego and id, psyche and *soma*, inside and outside, 'I' and what is 'not-I', nor even between the different parts of the body. Only gradually, through constant exchanges with the mothering person, does the infant begin to discriminate and differentiate these opposites which are initially merged, and thus to take his first steps on the road to selfhood. The emotional or affective quality of this process of differentiation and inner integration is determined by the vicissitudes of the infant's tie to his mother. Whether all that is 'not-I' will forever remain vaguely threatening, replete with forebodings of an undefined nature, a danger to be avoided, or whether the infant will emerge from this phase feeling that the outside world is benevolently disposed and basically trustworthy; whether a reassuring sense of inner continuity and wholeness will predominate over a sense of falling to pieces and life forever lived in disparate segments: these are some of the developmental questions which originate in infancy. Furthermore, there is no comparable period of life in so far as the adaptive learning that takes place, learning which is mediated almost solely through the mother's instrumentality, when the mother is the principal caretaker of infants as she is in most cultures.

It is the mother's face—which the baby's eyes begin to 'grasp' and follow from about the age of four weeks, even when nursing—which becomes crystallized as the first visual precept from a jumble of light blurs, the first meaningful image out of a chaos of 'things' without meaning. It is on the mother's body, on her breast and through her hands that tactile perception and orientation are learned and practised. It is her rhythms of movement and quiet, her body warmth and smell, which differentiate the baby's other sensitivities, his sense of equilibrium and movement and his sensuality, while her voice is the sound stimulus which is the prerequisite for his own development of speech. Thus, the mother's *sensory presence* is of vital importance for the infant's earliest developmental experiences and awakenings.[4]

This emphasis on the mother's significance and power does not mean that the infant is completely helpless or passive in his relationship with her. From the beginning, he too is actively involved—looking, listening and, with the development of manual co-ordination, touching, handling, grasping—in maintaining connection and communication with his mother. Ethologists have designated this innate predisposition to activity–the five basic instinctive responses of sucking, clinging, following, crying and smiling–as a 'species-specific behaviour pattern' designed to further the human infant's survival by keeping him near the mother. Whether the ethological hypothesis is appropriate remains a controversial issue;[5] and even given the infant's predisposition to this kind of activity and the innate equipment which makes it possible, 'the vital spark has to be conferred on the equipment through exchanges with another human being, with a partner, with the mother'.[6] She is the 'facilitating environment' for these earliest processes of development. Without her contact and facilitation, the infant's first experiences take place in a psycho-social void, and his development is likely to be severely disturbed.

The infant's development and the relationship with the mother which nurtures it are optimal only when that relationship becomes a kind of psychological counterpart to the biological connection of pregnancy. Psychologists have variously described this optimal condition as 'mutuality', 'dual unit', 'reciprocity' or 'dialogue'. All these terms seek to convey that what is good and right for one partner in the relationship is also good and right for the other. The reciprocity between the mother and infant is a circular process of action–reaction–action in which, ideally, the mother welcomes her infant's unfolding activities and expressions of love with her own delighted and loving responses, which in turn stimulate the baby to increase his efforts and to offer his mother further expressions of gratification and attachment. This mutuality is by far the most important factor in enabling an infant to create a coherent inner image of a basically reassuring world and to lay the foundation for a 'true self'; without it, he is likely to become a bundle of reactions which resignedly complies with, or is in constant struggle against, the outer world's infringements. It is the mother who helps her infant learn to deal with anxiety without feeling devastated, and to temper and manage the inevitable feelings of frustration and anger.

For many years, psycho-analytic psychologists were preoccupied with the infant's need for succour in its most literal form: the need to be fed. The manifest nature of this need, together perhaps with the symbolic nostalgia and charm evoked by the image of a nursing baby and his mother, led to an almost exclusive focus on the variability of feeding practices in the mother–infant relationship as the central dynamic factor in personality formation. Anthropological observations of feeding and weaning activities were relied upon in an almost ritualized manner, as a primary source for the explanation of dominant personality characteristics within a given culture. Without underestimating the effect of the nursing situation and the feeding moment on personality—the vicissitudes of orality, as psycho-analysts would call it—it is fair to note that the nutritional need and its satisfaction is only one element, albeit an important one, in the total configuration of the mother–infant dyad. For the crucial social interaction, through which an individual begins to separate himself out and become a person, the infant needs his mother as a whole human being, not merely as a satisfier of hunger and thirst; or, to state it plainly, what the infant requires is not a breast but a mother. Feeding must be viewed as a part of a total communication process in which not only the mother's breast but also the quality of her movement, voice and touch affects the quality of the infant's sensory and emotional lease on life. The breast can be viewed, then, as a symbol for the mother, while feeding and weaning are but symbols for the inevitable processes of attachment and separation in human development. That is, whether or not they are representative of the quality of mothering in any culture, they are the most tangible (and symbolically loaded) aspects of nurturing. What psychologists and anthropologists alike must observe more carefully is not the false controversy between breast and bottle feeding, or how conscientiously the

5

mother carries out her nursing duties, or how and when she weans her child, but the total emotional climate, the gestalt, of mothering.

Psycho-social Matrix of Infancy: Feminine Identity in India

Whether her family is poor or wealthy, whatever her caste, class or region, whether she is a fresh young bride or exhausted by many pregnancies and infancies already, an Indian woman knows that motherhood confers upon her a purpose and identity that nothing else in her culture can. Each infant borne and nurtured by her safely into childhood, especially if the child is a son, is both a certification and a redemption.

At the same time, each individual woman approaches motherhood at her particular crossroads of *desa, kala, srama* and *gunas*,[7] and with her unique constellation of values, expectations, fears and beliefs about the role and the experience of mothering. She meets her newborn infant with the emotional resources and limitations of her particular personality; these are the 'matrix' of her child's infancy.[8] Her identity as a Hindu woman has evolved out of the *particulars* of her life cycle and childhood, out of the dailiness of her relationships as daughter in her parents' family and as wife and daughter-in-law in her husband's family, and out of the universals of the traditional ideals of womanhood absorbed by her from childhood onwards. Whether a particular mother is reserved or responsive to a particular infant, and in what circumstances, depends on a wide range of variables, not the least of which is her ordinal position in her original family (whether she was a firstborn female or the fourth daughter in a row, or the first little girl after a line of sons . . .) as well as the sex and ordinal position of the infant who now needs and claims her love and care. It is not the purpose of this study to explore the range of individual maternal receptivity. Rather, we will focus on the vivid ideals of womanhood and motherhood in India, the common themes which in a traditional society such as India pervade and circumscribe the identities of individual women.

First of all, where and when tradition governs, an Indian woman does not stand alone; her identity is wholly defined by her relationships to others. For although in most societies, a woman (more than a man) defines herself in relation and connection to other intimate people, this is singularly true of Indian women. The dominant psycho-social realities of her life can be condensed into three stages:

First, she is a daughter to her parents.

Second, she is a wife to her husband (and daughter-in-law to his parents).

Third, she is a mother to her sons (and daughters).

How, then, do daughters fare in 'mother India'? The frank answer is that it is difficult to know, at least as exhaustively and 'in depth' as I would like to. The reason for this lies in the fact that data, of all kinds, are uneven or unavailable. Anthropological accounts refer, implicitly or explicitly, to the development of boys, and skim the subject of female childhood or skip it altogether. Myths, too, are sparing of their bounty towards daughters, for in a patriarchal culture myths are inevitably man-made and man-oriented. Addressing as they do the unconscious wishes and fears of men, it is the parent–son rather than the parent–daughter relationship which becomes charged with symbolic significance.[9]

These limitations are real enough, but they need not be forbidding. On the contrary, they challenge the psycho-analytic researcher to mine the existing material thoroughly and to construct an interpretive bridge for future work. There are, for example, in anthropological accounts, both a consistent indication of the marked preference for sons all over India, and at the same time, somewhat paradoxically, abundant allusion to the warmth, intimacy and relaxed affection of the mother–daughter bond.[10] Statistics document the higher rate of female infant mortality, and call attention to the fact that whatever health care and schooling are available in India, daughters are the last to receive it.[11] In the realm of literature, although the mainstream mythology and classical texts of Hinduism have been the preserves of men, there are parts of the oral tradition—ballads, folksongs and couplets sung by women in different parts of the country, a few folk-tales—which give us clues to the psychological constellation of daughterhood in India. Leavened with clinical impressions, these various sources can be judiciously drawn together to sketch a portrait of Indian girlhood.

The preference for a son when a child is born is as old as Indian society itself. Vedic verses pray that sons will be followed by still more male offspring, never by females. A prayer in the *Atharvaveda* adds a touch of malice: 'The birth of a girl, grant it elsewhere, here grant a son.'[12] As MacDonell observes, 'Indeed daughters are conspicuous in the *Rigveda* by their absence. We meet in hymns with prayers for sons and grandsons, male offspring, male descendants and male issue and occasionally for wives but never daughters. Even forgiveness is asked for ourselves and grandsons, but no blessing is ever prayed for a daughter. When *Agni* is born it is as if it were a male infant. They clap their hands and make sounds of rejoicing like the parents of a new-born son. There is no such rejoicing over the birth of a daughter.'[13] The ancient *Pumsavana* rite, still performed over pregnant women in traditional Hindu households, is designed to elicit the birth of a male infant and to magically change the sex of the unborn child if it be a female.

Contemporary anthropological studies from different parts of India and the available clinical evidence assure us that the traditional preference for sons is very much intact.[14] At the birth of a son drums are beaten in some parts of the country, conch-shells blown in others and the midwife paid lavishly, while no such spontaneous rejoicing accompanies the birth of a daughter. Women's folk-songs reveal the painful awareness of inferiority—of this discrepancy, at birth, between the celebration of sons and the mere tolerance of daughters. Thus, in a north Indian song the women complain:

> Vidya said, 'Listen, O Sukhma, what a tradition has started!
> Drums are played upon the birth of a boy,
> But at my birth only a brass plate was beaten.'[15]

And in Maharashtra the girl, comparing herself to a white sweet-scented jasmine (*Jai*) and the boy to a big, strong-smelling thorny leaf (*kevada*), plaintively asks: 'Did anyone notice the sweet fragrance of a *jai*? The hefty *kevada* however has filled the whole street with its strong scent.'[16]

Of course there are 'valid' ritual and economic reasons—we will come to the psychological ones later—for 'sexism' in Indian society. The presence of a son is absolutely necessary for the proper performance of many sacraments, especially those carried out upon the death of parents and imperative to the well-being of their souls. In addition to her negligible ritual significance, a daughter normally is an unmitigated expense, someone who will never contribute to the family income and who, upon marriage, will take away a considerable part of her family's fortune as her dowry. In the case of a poor family, the parents may even have to go deep in debt in order to provide for a daughter's marriage. The *Aitareya Brahmana* (like other older texts) probably refers as much as anything else to the economic facts of life when it states flatly that a daughter is a source of misery while a son is the saviour of the family.[17]

As in other patriarchal societies, one would expect the preference for sons, the cultural devaluation of girls, to be somehow reflected in the psychology of Indian women. Theoretically, one possible consequence of this kind of inequity would be a heightened female hostility and envy towards males, together with a generally pronounced antagonism between the sexes. I do not have sufficient evidence to be categorical; yet my impression is that these phenomena do not, in general, characterize the inner world of Indian women. The dominant myths, for example—unlike, say, *A Thousand and One Nights*—show little evidence of strain in relationships between the sexes. And, as I have shown elsewhere, aggression occurring between members of the same sex is significantly greater than between members of opposite sexes in India.[18]

It can be argued that male dominance and strong taboos against feminine aggression may inhibit the expression of female resentment against men and serve to redirect this hostility against male children. For if a woman perceives that the fundamental premise of the absolute status hierarchy between the sexes is merely gender, and if she is prevented from expressing her rage and resentment at this state of affairs, either because of cultural taboos, social inferiority or her dependence upon men, then her unconscious destructive impulses towards male children are liable to be particularly strong, this being her only possible revenge against a pervasive oppressive masculinity. Again, excepting certain communities, this does not appear to be characteristic of Indian women, given the evidence of songs, tales and other kinds of folklore.[19]

The third possibility is that girls and women in a dramatically patriarchal society will turn the aggression against themselves and transform the cultural devaluation into feelings of worthlessness and inferiority. There is scattered evidence that such a propensity indeed exists among many communities of Indian women, that hostility towards men and potential aggression against male infants are often turned inward, subsumed in a diffuse hostility against oneself, in a conversion of outrage into self-deprecation. At least among the upper middle class women who today seek psychotherapy, the buried feeling, 'I am a girl and thus worthless and "bad" ', is often encountered below the surface of an active, emancipated femininity. One patient, for example, staunchly maintained that her parents' separation took place because of her father's disappointment that she was born a girl and not a boy, although in fact, as she herself was aware, the parents had separated shortly before her birth. Some of the traits connected with low self-esteem—depressive moodiness, extreme touchiness and morbid sensitivity in interpersonal relations —come through in the testimony of modern, educated Indian girls in the non-clinical interviews reported by Margaret Cormack in *The Hindu Woman*.[20] And their less educated, rural sisters give vent to similar feelings through the medium of folk-songs: 'God Rama, I fall at your feet and fold my hands and pray to you, never again give me the birth of a woman.'[21]

I have deliberately used the words 'possibility' and 'propensity' in the above discussion rather than ascribe to Indian women a widespread depressive pattern. In the first place, for the cultural devaluation of women to be translated into a pervasive psychological sense of worthlessness in individual women, parents' and other adults' behaviour and attitudes towards the infant girls in their midst—the actualities of family life—must be fully consistent with this female depreciation. Secondly, the internalization of low self-esteem also presupposes that girls and women have no sphere of their own, no independent livelihood and activity, no area of family and community responsibility and dominance, no living space apart from that of the men, within which to create and manifest those aspects of feminine identity that derive from intimacy and collaboration with other women. And, in fact, these two circumstances exist in India, to mitigate the discriminations and inequities of patriarchal institutions.

From anthropological accounts and other sources, we know of the lenient affection and often compassionate attention bestowed by mothers on their daughters throughout their lives.[22] 'I turn the stone flour mill with the swiftness of a running deer; that is because my arms are strong with the mother's milk I drank.'[23] This, and other couplets like it, sung by women all over India, bear witness to the daughter's memory of her mother's affection for her and to the self-esteem and strength of will this has generated in turn. Thus, in the earliest period of emotional development, Indian girls are assured of their worth by whom it really matters: by their mothers.

The special maternal affection reserved for daughters, contrary to expectations derived from social and cultural prescriptions, is partly to be explained by the fact that a mother's unconscious identification with her daughter is normally stronger than with her son.[24] In her daughter, the mother can re-experience herself as a cared-for girl. And, in Indian society, as we shall see later, a daughter is considered a 'guest' in her natal family, treated with the solicitous concern often accorded to a welcomé outsider, who, all too soon, will marry and leave her mother for good. Mindful of her daughter's developmental fate, the mother re-experiences the emotional conflicts her own separation once aroused, and this in turn tends to increase her indulgence and solicitude towards her daughter.

In addition to her mother's empathic connection with her, as an Indian girl grows up her relationships with others within the extended family further tend to dilute any resentment she may harbour for her brothers. Among the many adults who comprise a Hindu family there is almost always someone in particular who gives a little girl the kind of admiration and sense of being singled out as special that a male child more often receives from many. In such a family system, every child, irrespective of sex, stands a good chance of being some adult's favourite, a circumstance which softens the curse of rivalry, envy and possessiveness which often afflicts 'modern' nuclear families. And of course when a girl is the only daughter, such chances are increased immeasurably. Thus in folk-tales, however many sons a couple may have, there is often one daughter in their midst who is the parents' favourite.

Finally, in traditional India, every female is born into a well-defined community of women within her particular family. Although by no means does it always resound with solidarity and goodwill, the existence of this exclusive sphere of femininity and domesticity gives women a tangible opportunity to be productive and lively, to experience autonomy and to exercise power. It also allows a special kind of inviolate feminine privacy and familiar intimacy. Getting along with other women in this sphere, learning the mandatory skills of householding, cooking and childcare, establishing her place in this primary world: these relationships and these tasks constitute the dailiness of girlhood in India. Moreover, this experience of 'apprenticeship' and the activities that transpire in this feminine sphere are independent of the patriarchal values of the outside world. And when necessary, other women in the family—her mother, grandmother, aunts, sisters and sisters-in-law—are not only an Indian girl's teachers and models but her allies against the discriminations and inequities of that world and its values. Often enough, in the 'underground' of female culture, as reflected in ballads, wedding songs and jokes, women do indeed react against the discriminations of their culture by portraying men as vain, faithless and infantile.[25] All these factors help to mitigate (if not to prevent) the damage to a girl's self-esteem when she discovers that in the eyes of the culture she is considered inferior to a boy, a discovery which usually coincides with the awareness of gender identity in late childhood.

Late childhood marks the beginning of an Indian girl's deliberate training in how to be a *good woman*, and hence the conscious inculcation of culturally designated feminine roles. She learns that the 'virtues' of womanhood which will take her through life are submission and docility as well as skill and grace in the various household tasks. M. N. Srinivas, for example, reports on the training of young girls in Mysore:

It is the mother's duty to train her daughter up to be an absolute docile daughter-in-law. The *summum bonum* of a girl's life is to please her parents-in-law and her husband. If she does not 'get on' with her mother-in-law, she will be a disgrace to her family, and cast a blot on the fair name of her mother. The Kannada mother dins into her daughter's ears certain ideals which make for harmony (at the expense of her sacrificing her will) in her later life.[26]

In the *bratas*, the periodical days of fasting and prayer which unmarried girls keep all over India, the girl's wishes for herself are almost always in relation to others; she asks the boons of being a good daughter, good wife, good daughter-in-law, good mother, and so forth.[27] Thus, in addition to the 'virtues' of self-effacement and self-sacrifice, the feminine role in India also crystallizes a woman's connections to others, her embeddedness in a multitude of familial relationships.

If the self-esteem of Indian girls falters during the years of early puberty, this is intimately related to the fact that at precisely this developmental moment, a time of instinctual turbulence and emotional volatility, her training in service and self-denial in preparation for her imminent roles of daughter-in-law and wife is stepped up. In order to maintain her family's love and approval—the 'narcissistic supplies' necessary for firm self-esteem—the girl tends to conform, and even over-conform, to the prescriptions and expectations of those around her.

The adult personality of Indian women is not only moulded through this (unconscious) manipulation of her precarious feelings of worthiness as an adolescent, it is also distinctly influenced by the culturally sanctioned maternal indulgence of daughters. As we have noted above, daughterhood in India is not without its rewards, precisely because the conditions of womanhood are normally so forbidding. In contrast to the son's, a daughter's training at her mother's hands is normally leavened with a good deal of compassion, for which, as ever, there are traditional as well as psychological explanations. Manu expressly enjoins that kindness be shown to the daughter as she is 'physically more tender and her emotions are more delicate', and other ancient commentators forbid any harshness towards her, even in words.[28] The learned Medhatithi puts the whole matter into its 'proper', that is, its ritual, perspective: 'By reason of the marriage having taken the place of *Upanayana** it follows that just as in the case of men all the ordinances of the *Srutis*, *Smritis* and custom become binding upon them after the *Upanayana*, before which they are free to do what they like and are unfit for any religious duties, so for women also there is freedom of action before marriage, after which they also become subject to the ordinances of the *Srutis* and *Smritis*.'[29] Little wonder that for an Indian girl rebellion against the constraints of impinging womanhood, with its circumscription of identity, becomes impossible. She internalizes the specific ideals of womanhood and monitors her behaviour carefully in order to guarantee her mother's love and approval, upon which she is more than ever dependent as she makes ready to leave home. For all the reasons described above, the irony of an Indian girl's coming-of-age is that to be a good woman and a felicitous bride she must be more than ever the perfect daughter.

Sita: the ego ideal

For both men and women in Hindu society, the ideal woman is personified by Sita, the quintessence of wifely devotion, the heroine of the epic *Ramayana*. Her unique standing in the minds of most Hindus, regardless of region, caste, social class, age, sex, education or modernization, testifies to the power and pervasiveness of the traditional ideal of womanhood. Sita, of course, is not just another legendary figure, and the *Ramayana* is not just another epic poem. It is through the recitation, reading, listening to, or attending a dramatic performance of this revered text (above all others) that a Hindu

*The sacrament for boys, usually occurring between the ages of five and eight, which initiates them as full-fledged members of the society.

reasserts his or her cultural identity as a Hindu, and obtains religious merit. The popular epic contains ideal models of familial bonds and social relations to which even a modernized Hindu pays lip service, however much he may privately question or reject them as irrelevant to the tasks of modern life.

Sita, like the other principal figures in the epic—Rama, Lakshman, Hanuman—is an incomparably more intimate and familiar heroine in the Hindu imagination than similar figures from Greek or Christian mythology are in the fantasies and deliberations of an average westerner. This intimate familiarity does not mean historical knowledge, but rather a sense of the mythical figure as a benevolent presence, located in the individual's highly personal and always actual space-time. From earliest childhood, a Hindu has heard Sita's legend recounted on any number of sacral and secular occasions; seen the central episodes enacted in folk plays like the *Ram Lila;* heard her qualities extolled in devotional songs; and absorbed the ideal feminine identity she incorporates through the many everyday metaphors and similes that are associated with her name. Thus, 'She is as pure as Sita' denotes chastity in a woman, and 'She is a second Sita', the appreciation of a woman's uncomplaining self-sacrifice. If, as Jerome Bruner remarks, 'In the mythologically instructed community there is a corpus of images and models that provide the pattern to which the individual may aspire, a range of metaphoric identity',[30] then this range, in the case of a Hindu woman, is condensed in one model. And she is Sita.

For western readers unacquainted with the myth, the legend of Sita, in bare outline, goes like this: One day as King Janaka was ploughing, an infant sprang up from the ground whom he named Sita.* The child grows up to be a beautiful girl whom the king promises to give in marriage to any man who can bend the wonderful bow in his possession. Many suitors—gods, princes, kings, demons —vie for Sita's hand but none is even able to lift the bow, until Rama, the reincarnation of Vishnu and the hero of the epic, comes to Janaka's country and gracefully snaps the bow in two. After their wedding, Sita and Rama return to Ayodhya, which is ruled by Rama's father, Dasharatha.

After some time Dasharatha wants to abdicate in favour of Rama who is his eldest son. But because of a promise given to the mother of one of his younger sons, he is forced to banish Rama to the forest

*The name Sita means a furrow, a universal symbol for the feminine genitalia.

for fourteen years. Rama tries to persuade Sita to let him proceed in his exile alone, pointing out the dangers, discomforts and deprivations of a homeless life in the forest. In a long, moving passage Sita emphasizes her determination to share her husband's fate, declaring that death would be preferable to separation. Her speech is an eloquent statement of the *dharma* of a Hindu wife:

For a woman, it is not her father, her son, nor her mother, friends nor her own self, but the husband, who in this world and the next is ever her sole means of salvation. If thou dost enter the impenetrable forest today, O Descendant of Raghu, I shall precede thee on foot, treading down the spiky *Kusha* grass. In truth, whether it be in palaces, in chariots or in heaven, wherever the shadow of the feet of her consort falls, it must be followed.[31]

Both Rama and Sita, mourned by the citizens of Ayodhya who adore their prince and future king, proceed to the forest in the company of Rama's brother Lakshman. The *Ramayana* then recounts their adventures in the forest, most prominent and terrible among them being Sita's kidnapping by the powerful king of the demons, Ravana, and her abduction to Lanka. In Lanka, Ravana's kingdom, Sita is kept imprisoned in one of the demon-king's palaces where he tries to win her love. Neither his seductive kindnesses nor his grisly threats are of any avail as Sita remains steadfast in her love and devotion to Rama.

Meanwhile, Rama raises an army from the *Vanar* (monkey) tribes in order to attack Lanka and bring back Sita. After a long and furious battle, he is victorious and Ravana is killed. Doubting Sita's fidelity through the long term of her captivity, Rama refuses, however, to accept her again as his wife until she proves her innocence and purity by the fire ordeal in which the fire-god Agni himself appears to testify to her virtue. The couple then return to Ayodhya where amidst the citizens' happy celebrations Rama is crowned king.

But Sita's ordeal is not yet over. Hearing of rumours in the city which cast suspicion on the purity of his queen, Rama banishes her to the forest where she gives birth to twins, Lava and Kusha. She and her children live an ascetic life in a rustic hermitage, Sita's love for Rama unfaltering. When the twins grow up, she sends them back to their father. On seeing his sons, Rama repents and Sita is brought back to Ayodhya to be reinstated as queen. On her arrival, however, Rama again commands her to assert her purity before the assembled court. His abiding mistrust, and this further demand prove too much for the gentle queen who calls on her mother, the earth, to open up and receive her back. The earth obliges and Sita disappears where she was born.

How are we to interpret the legend of Sita? Philip Slater has pointed out that a myth is an elaborately condensed product, that there is no one 'correct' version or interpretation, for no matter how many layers one peels off, there will remain much to be explained.[32] In the interpretation that follows, I will set aside such elements as social history, religious ritual and artistic embellishment, although I am well aware of their importance to myth-making. Rather, my aim is to attend to the themes in the Sita legend from a psycho-analytic and psycho-social perspective. In this kind of interpretation we must ask questions such as: How does the myth influence the crystallization of a Hindu woman's identity and character? What role does it play in helping to ward off or assuage feelings of guilt and anxiety? How does it influence her attitude towards and images of men? How does it contribute to the individual woman's task of 'adapting to reality' and to the society's task of maintaining community solidarity? And finally do the different mythological versions of a single underlying theme correspond to different 'defensive editions' of unconscious fantasy at different life stages of those to whom the myths speak?[33]

The ideal of womanhood incorporated by Sita is one of chastity, purity, gentle tenderness and a singular faithfulness which cannot be destroyed or even disturbed by her husband's rejections, slights or thoughtlessness. We should note in passing that the Sita legend also gives us a glimpse into the Hindu imagery of manliness. Rama may have all the traits of a godlike hero, yet he is also fragile, mistrustful and jealous, and very much of a conformist, both to his parents' wishes and to social opinion. These expectations, too, an Indian girl incorporates gradually into her inner world.

The legend of Nala and Damayanti provides a variation on the ideal of the good wife; Damayanti cheerfully accompanies Nala, her husband, into the forest after he has gambled away everything they own, including his clothes. And when he leaves her sleeping in the forest at night, taking away half of the only garment she possesses to clothe his own nakedness, Damayanti does not utter a single word of reproach as she wanders through the forest, looking for her husband. The 'moral' is the familiar one: 'Whether treated well or ill a wife should never indulge in ire.'

In another popular myth, Savitri, in spite of the knowledge that her chosen husband is fated to die within a year, insists on marrying him and renouncing the luxuries of her palace to join him in his poverty. When at the end of the year, Yama, the god of death, takes away her husband, Savitri follows them both. Although Yama assures her that she has loved her husband faithfully, that she need not sacrifice her own life but should return, Savitri replies that wherever her husband goes she must follow for that is the eternal custom: 'Deprived of my husband, I am as one dead!'[34]

In the Savitri myth, the ideal of fidelity to one man takes on an added dimension and categorical refinement: Exclusive devotion to one's husband becomes the prerequisite for the all-important motherhood of sons. Thus, as Savitri follows Yama to his country, the land in which all wishes come true, she refuses to accept his assurance that with her husband's death all her wifely obligations have expired. Only through her demonstration of wifely devotion, even after her husband's death, can she finally persuade Yama to revive him and grant her the boon of offspring: 'Of Satyavan's loins and mine, begotten by both of us, let there be a century of sons possessed of strength and prowess and capable of perpetuating our race.'[35]

To be a good wife is, by definition, to be a good woman. Thus Markandeya discourses to Yudhishthira of 'wives restraining all their senses and keeping their hearts under complete control. [They] regard their husbands as veritable gods. For women, neither sacrifice, nor *sraddhas* (penances), nor fasts are of any efficiency. By serving their husbands only can they win heaven.'[36] This is the ideal, purveyed over and over again, in numberless myths and legends, through which the Hindu community has tried to mould the character and personality of its female members. Moreover, a woman is enjoined that her devotion to her husband should extend also to his family members, especially to his parents. A married woman's duties have been nowhere more fully described than in Draupadi's advice to Satyabhama, Lord Krishna's wife:

Keeping aside vanity, and controlling desire and wrath, I always serve with devotion the sons of Pandu with their wives. Restraining jealousy, with deep devotion of heart, without a sense of degradation at the services I perform, I wait upon my husbands ... Celestial, or man, or Gandharva, young or decked with ornaments, wealthy or comely of person, none else my heart liketh. I never bathe or eat or

sleep till he that is my husband hath bathed or eaten or slept . . .
When my husband leaveth home for the sake of any relative, then
renouncing flowers and fragrant paste of every kind, I begin to undergo penances. Whatever my husband enjoyeth not, I even renounce
. . . Those duties that my mother-in-law had told me in respect of
relatives, as also the duties of alms-giving, of offering worship to the
gods . . . and service to those that deserve our regards, and all else
that is known to me, I always discharge day and night, without
idleness of any kind.[37]

I have quoted from the ancient texts in detail in order to emphasize
the formidable consensus on the ideal of womanhood which, in spite
of many changes in individual circumstances in the course of modernization, urbanization and education, still governs the inner imagery
of individual men and women as well as the social relations between
them in both the traditional and modern sectors of the Indian
community.

Together with this function as a more or less conscious ideal which
leaves indelible traces in the identity formation of every Hindu
woman, the Sita myth also plays an unconscious role as a defence
against the anxiety aroused by a young girl's sexual impulses, whose
expression would almost seem to be invited by the nature of family
life in traditional India. Freud has clarified for us the universal
themes of infantile psycho-sexual development in terms of the vicissitudes of the libido. He left it primarily to others to differentiate
among the social influences and cultural variations. Thus, sexual
development in Hindu daughters is *socially* influenced by the communal living pattern, the close quarters of the extended family and
the indulgent adult attitudes towards infant sexuality. In this intimate daily setting where constant close contact with many members
of the family of both sexes and several generations is part of a little
girl's early bodily experience; where the infant girl is frequently
caressed and fondled by the many adults around her; and where
playful exploratory activities of an explicitly sexual nature among
the many cousins living in the same house or nearby in the neighbourhood are a common early developmental experience, often
indulgently tolerated by the more or less 'permissive' adults—a promiscuous sexual excitation, as well as the fear of being overwhelmed
by it, looms large in the unconscious fantasies of an Indian girl.
Later, as she leaves childhood behind, the identification with Sita
helps in the necessary renunciation of these childhood fantasies, in
the concentration of erotic feeling exclusively on one man, and in

the avoidance of all occasions for sexual temptation and trans-gression. Sita sets the compelling example: Although Rama's emissary, the monkey-god Hanuman, offers to rescue Sita from her ordeal of imprisonment in Lanka by carrying her on his shoulders and transporting her through the air to her waiting husband, she must refuse the offer since it means touching Hanuman's body, and of her own free will she may, on no account, permit herself to touch any man except her husband. This enigmatic tension between the memory of intense and pleasurable childhood sexuality and the later womanly ideal which demands restraint and renunciation, between an earlier indiscriminate 'availability' and the later unapproachability, may account for that special erotic presence in Indian women which has fascinated the imagination of many writers and artists.

Perhaps the most striking mythological elaboration of the connection between the young girl's sexuality, in particular, her fantasied erotic wishes towards her father, and her later repudiation of these wishes by transforming them into their opposite, aloofness and chastity, is the myth of Arundhati, who, next to Sita, is the most famous chaste wife in Hindu mythology. I have reproduced the myth in detail not only to illustrate this aspect of feminine identity in India but also because of its special relevance for psycho-analytic theory, for it explicitly acknowledges the existence of infantile sexuality:

Brahma (the Creator) had displayed desire for his daughter, Sandhya (Twilight), as soon as she was born, and she had desired him. As a result of this, Brahma cursed Kama (Eros), who had caused the trouble, to be burnt by Siva. When everyone had departed, Sandhya resolved to purify herself and to establish for all time a moral law: that new-born creatures would be free of desire. To do this, she prepared to offer herself as an oblation in the fire. Knowing of her intention, Brahma sent the sage Vasistha to instruct her in the proper manner of performing *tapas*. Vasistha disguised himself as a *brahma-carin* with matted locks and taught her how to meditate upon Siva. Siva then appeared to her and offered her a boon. She said, 'Let all new-born creatures be free of desire, and let me be reborn as the wife of a man to whom I can just be a close friend. And if anyone but my husband gazes upon me with desire, let his virility be destroyed and let him become an impotent eunuch.' Siva said, 'Your sin has been burnt to ashes, purified by your *tapas*. I grant what you ask; henceforth, creatures will only become subject to desire when they reach youth, and any man but your husband who looks upon you with desire will become impotent.' Then Sandhya, meditating upon the chaste Brahmin for her husband, entered the sacrificial fire. Her body became the oblation, and she arose from the fire as an infant girl, named Arundhati. She grew up in a sage's hermitage and married Vasistha.[38]

Another version of the myth offers a diametrically opposite resolution of the conflict. Here the 'plot' works to lift the repression of childhood memories and to remove defences against erotic impulses and guilt feelings, and, according to the principle of the identity of opposites, the daughter of Brahma is reborn not as the most chaste of women, but as Rati, the incarnation of sexuality and the goddess of sexual pleasure. The unconscious fantasy elaborated in this version belongs of course to adolescence rather than to the oedipal years of childhood.

On still another level, the identification with Sita contributes to the Hindu woman's adaptation to married life in her husband's extended family and to the maintenance of this family as a functioning unit. Such a family, composed as it is of other men besides her husband, affords the Hindu wife temptations and opportunities for sexual transgression, the indulgence of which would destroy the necessary interdependence and co-operation of the Indian family. At some level of consciousness, every Hindu couple is aware, for instance, of Sita's exemplary behaviour towards Rama's brother Lakshman during the fourteen years of their exile together. There exist, of course, elaborate codes and rituals of social behaviour and discretion between the male and female members of an extended family, such as the injunction that the elder brother never directly address his younger brother's wife (nor enter her room when she is alone). Like most taboos, these are broken in fantasy. In a Bengali folk-song, for example, a woman expresses her desire for amorous relations with the elder brother of her husband, regretting that he is not the younger brother so that her desire might be gratified.[39] These taboos are designed to preclude intolerable jealous passions and disruptive rivalries; the reigning presence of Sita in the Indian inner world, in all her serene forbearance, is an important psychological reinforcement of these special codes.

The short description of daughterhood and the elaboration of the Sita ideal of womanhood cannot fully account for an Indian woman's emotional preparation for motherhood. Her chronological and developmental stage of life at marriage, her experiences and relationships within her husband's family, and the meaning of childbirth in her particular personal and social setting: these factors too are paramount; taken together, they are the 'psycho-social matrix of infancy' in India.

Life stage at marriage

An Indian girl is usually married during early adolescence, between the ages of twelve and eighteen; the average age of a Hindu bride is fifteen to sixteen.[40] In urban areas, or among higher castes, where daughters are more likely to receive some kind of formal education, the age may be somewhat higher. The traditional ideal holds that a girl should be married soon after her first menstrual period, for it is feared that 'if she remains long a maiden, she gives herself to whom she will'. The custom of early marriage, it seems, recognizes and is designed to guard against the promiscuous resurgence in adolescence of a girl's playful childhood sexuality and the threat this would pose to Hindu social organization. To marry one's daughters off propitiously is considered one of the primary religious duties of Hindu parents. Indeed, 'Reprehensible is the father who gives not his daughter at the proper time.' If married at eleven or twelve, the girl may remain in her parents' home for another three to four years before moving away to live with her husband. In any case, when she joins her husband's family, she is still a young adolescent and vulnerable to the universal psychological problems of this age.

First of all, before her departure for her husband's family and household, a very special relationship tends to develop between an Indian girl and her mother,[41] who becomes at this time her daughter's confidante and counsellor in the bewildering turmoil of adolescence and the newness of the prospect of marriage. Although the relationship between daughter and mother is surely characterized by the tension between the conflicting modalities of 'getting away' and 'coming nearer', the daughter none the less seeks to recreate the emotional closeness to the protective mother of her childhood. She has also formed intimate attachments to girl friends of her age in the village or neighbourhood among whom the secret fears and delights concerning the physical changes of puberty are shared, and fantasies about men and marriage are collectively evoked as each girl tries to envision and secure a clear sense of herself as a woman. These processes—the renunciation of dependency on the 'pre-oedipal' mother, the integration of what she was as a girl with the woman she is now suddenly becoming, and the acceptance of her inevitable marriage to a stranger—all these require time, her mother's

6

support and love, the reassuring exchange of confidences with peers, and the 'trying out' of new, as yet unexperienced identities in fantasy. This whole process of feminine adolescent development is normally incomplete at the time an Indian girl gets married and is transplanted from her home into the unfamiliar, initially forbidding environment of her in-laws.

The alien, often threatening, and sometimes humiliating nature of the setting in which an Indian girl's struggle for identity and adult status takes place cannot be stressed enough. In much of northern India, for example, the exogamous rule, that the bride comes from a village which does not border on the groom's village, strictly applies. In some other parts of the country, marriage customs are governed by a further rule which stipulates that a man who lives in a *gotra* village—that is, a village which is predominantly composed of a related caste group—is unacceptable as a potential bridegroom for any daughter of the village. In his study of social life in a village in Delhi, Oscar Lewis found that the 266 married women of the village came from 200 different villages, a pattern repeated by those who married outside this, their native village.[42] Consequently, this small village of 150 households was linked with over 400 other villages in its region; at the same time, no woman in the village could call for company, or in a moment of crisis or loneliness, on a friend or neighbour or relative known to her from childhood.

Whatever the contribution of these marriage rules to the integration of Indian society, and it is considerable, this integration is ultimately based on the insistence that women not only renounce their erotic impulses and primary loyalties to their parents—a universal developmental requirement—but also sever their attachments, in fact and in fantasy, to all the other boys and men they have known during their early lives who inevitably belong to one of the forbidden extended kinship or village groups. Instead, upon marriage, an Indian woman must direct her erotic tenderness exclusively towards a man who is a complete stranger to her until their wedding night, and she must resolve the critical issues of feminine identity in unfamiliar surroundings without the love and support of precisely those persons whom she needs most. Little wonder that the themes of the young girl pining for her parental home, her grief at separation from her mother, constantly recur in popular folk-songs and ballads.[43] The staunch presence of ideal feminine figures like Sita and Savitri is crucial to making the traumatic transition which an Indian girl undergoes at precisely the most sensitive and vulnerable period of her development.

Status within her husband's family: not wife but daughter-in-law

An Indian girl's entry into the married state and the new world of social relations within her husband's family thus does not take place under auspicious psychological conditions. In spite of her inner ideals and conscious resolutions to be a good wife and an exemplary daughter-in-law, a bride comes into her husband's family with a tremendous burden of anxiety and nostalgia, with a sense of antagonism towards her mother-in-law who has, after all, usurped the place of her own sorely missed and needed mother, with a mixture of shy anticipation and resentment towards her husband's sisters and other young female relatives who have presumed to replace the sisters and cousins and friends at home, and with ambivalent feelings of tenderness and hostility towards the unknown person who is now her husband and claims her intimacy.[44] And if her husband turns out to be unworthy, she knows that there is no recourse for her. Manu enjoins: 'Though destitute of virtue or seeking pleasure elsewhere, or devoid of good qualities, yet a husband must be constantly worshipped as a god by a faithful wife.'[45] And: 'By violating her duty towards her husband, a wife is disgraced in this world, [after death] she enters the womb of a jackal and is tormented by the punishment of her sin.'[46] These precepts, in spirit if not in these precise words, have been instilled into Hindu girls from the age of earliest understanding. For, as mentioned above, although treated with indulgence and demonstrative affection in the years immediately before her marriage, an Indian girl is so indulged partly because of her status as a guest in her own house. Her 'real' family is her husband's family. Whatever her future fortunes, when she marries an Indian girl knows that, in a psychological sense, she can never go home again.*

In the social hierarchy of her new family, the bride usually occupies one of the lowest rungs. Obedience and compliance with the wishes of the elder women of the family, especially those of her mother-in-law, are expected as a matter of course. Communication with the older men is minimal (if it exists at all) since they, as mentioned earlier, are traditionally expected to maintain a posture of

*Literally, of course, she may return to visit her family and village of origin; this is particularly likely in the case of a new, young wife at the time of confinement and childbirth.

formal restraint in the presence of the newcomer. Unflinchingly and without complaint, the new daughter-in-law is required to perform some of the heaviest household chores, which may mean getting up well before dawn and working till late at night. Any mistakes or omissions on her part are liable to incur sarcastic references to her abilities, her looks or her upbringing in her mother's home. For it must be noted once again that the new bride constitutes a very real threat to the unity of the extended family. She represents a potentially pernicious influence which, given family priorities, calls for drastic measures of exorcism. The nature of the 'danger' she personifies can perhaps best be suggested by such questions as: Will the young wife cause her husband to neglect his duties as a son? As a brother? A nephew? An uncle? Will social tradition and family pressure be sufficient to keep the husband–wife bond from developing to a point where it threatens the interests of other family members? Will 'sexual passion' inspire such a close relationship in the bridal couple that the new girl becomes primarily a wife rather than a daughter-in-law and her husband transfers his loyalty and affection to her rather than remaining truly a son of the house?

These are, of course, not either/or choices; however, custom, tradition and the interests of the extended family demand that in the realignment of roles and relationships initiated by marriage, the roles of the husband and wife, at least in the beginning, be relegated to relative inconsequence and inconspicuousness. Any signs of a developing attachment and tenderness within the couple are discouraged by the elder family members by either belittling or forbidding the open expression of these feelings. Every effort is made to hinder the development of an intimacy within the couple which might exclude other members of the family, especially the parents. Oblique hints about 'youthful infatuations', or outright shaming virtually guarantee that the young husband and wife do not publicly express any interest in (let alone affection for) each other; and they are effectively alone together only for very brief periods during the night. If women's folk-songs are any indication, even these brief meetings are furtive affairs; there is hardly a song which does not complain of the ever-wakeful *sas* (mother-in-law) and *nanad* (sister-in-law) preventing the bride from going to her husband at night. Madhav Gore's study of a sample of Indian men of the Agarwal community further confirms that these constraints, masterminded by the older women, usually succeed in their aims: 56 per cent of the men described themselves as being closer to their mothers than to their wives, while only 20 per cent felt they were closer to their wives.[47]

I do not intend to imply that marriage in India lacks intimacy— that mutual enhancement of experience within culturally determined patterns of love and care which is the commonly held criterion of a 'good marriage' in the West. Rather, in India, this intimacy develops later in married life, as both partners slowly mature into adult 'householders'. Ideally, parenthood and the shared responsibility for offspring provide the basis for intimacy, rather than the other way around as in the West. This postponement of intimacy is encouraged by the family, for in the years of middle age the husband–wife bond no longer seems to threaten the exclusion of other family members, but incorporates or rather evolves out of the responsibility to take care of the next generation. Thus it is not antithetical to communal and family solidarity but, in its proper time, a guarantor of it.

Has the newly-married girl's situation in her husband's family no redeeming, or even relieving, features? I have neglected to point out that an Indian girl prepares for the harsh transition of marriage for some time before her actual departure for her husband's household. Stories, proverbs, songs, information gleaned from conversations with newly-married friends who come back home on visits, all more or less 'prepare' her for her role as an obedient daughter-in-law. Moreover, as in many other parts of the world, puberty rites such as seclusion during her menstrual period, or fasting on certain days, are designed to separate the young girl, both physically and symbolically, from her parents and to enable her to tolerate 'oral deprivation', for in her husband's household, at any meal, she will be the last one to eat.

These and other procedures bring the Indian girl to the end of childhood and introduce her, in a measured, ritual way, to the realities of womanhood. If married *very* young, the bride's initiation into her new life and family is gradual, interspersed with long visits to her parents' home where much of the accumulated loneliness and resentment can be relieved by the indulgent love showered on her by everyone, and particularly by her own mother's constant presence as a sympathetic listener and a gentle mentor. The young wife's isolation in her husband's home, moreover, is not necessarily as extreme as I have implied. She often develops relationships of informal familiarity and friendly consolation with certain younger members of her husband's family; and it usually happens that one or another of the many children in the family forms a strong attachment to her. But above all, it should be emphasized that the suspicion and hostility towards her rarely degenerate into deliberate oppression. This reflects a cultural tradition of restraint and prudence, which manifests itself in the Hindu conscience. Respect for and protection of the female members of society are a prime moral duty, the neglect of which arouses anxiety and a sense of being judged and punished. Manu the law-giver, a misogynist by modern standards, leaves no doubt about the virtuous treatment of the female members of the family: 'Where women are honoured, there gods are pleased; but where they are not honoured, no sacred rite yields rewards ; . . . Where the female relations live in grief, the family soon wholly perishes; but that family where they are not unhappy ever prospers . . . The houses on which female relations, not being duly honoured, pronounce a curse, perish completely, as if destroyed by magic.'[48] Thus, the head of the family, or other elder males who feel themselves entrusted with the family's welfare, gently but firmly seek to mitigate the excesses of the mother-in-law and the elder women. On balance, however, the conclusion is unavoidable that the identity struggle of the adolescent Indian girl is confounded by the coincidence of marriage, the abrupt and total severance of the attachments of childhood, and her removal from all that is familiar to a state of lonely dependency upon a household of strangers.

Pregnancy and the anticipation of motherhood

The young Indian wife's situation, in terms of family acceptance and emotional well-being, changes dramatically once she becomes pregnant. The prospect of motherhood holds out a composite solution for many of her difficulties. The psychological implications of her low social status as a bride and a newcomer; the tense, often humiliating relationships with others in her husband's family; her homesickness and sense of isolation; her identity confusion; the awkwardness of marital intimacy, and thus, often, the unfulfilled yearnings of her sexual self—these are tangled up in a developmental knot, as it were. With the anticipation of motherhood, this knot begins to be unravelled.

The improvement in an Indian wife's *social* status once she is pregnant has been universally noted by cultural anthropologists.[49]

Elder family members, particularly the women, become solicitous of her welfare, seeing to it that she eats well and rests often. Many irksome tasks, erstwhile obligations and restrictions are removed, and gestures of pride and affection towards her as a daughter-in-law of the house increase markedly.

The growing feeling of personal well-being throughout the course of pregnancy is also reinforced by social customs. Thus, in many parts of India, the expectant mother goes back to stay at her own mother's house a few months before the delivery. This stay helps her to strengthen her identification with her mother, a prerequisite for her own capacity for motherhood. The anticipation of the birth itself, in spite of the primitive medical facilities available, does not. seem to provoke strong anxiety or fears of dying since she knows her own parents, the all-powerful protectors, will be constantly at her side during labour. Once having given birth, the new mother can bask in her delight in her child and also in her satisfaction with herself, all of this taking place in a circle of greatly pleased and highly approving close kin.

This unambiguous reversal in an Indian woman's status is not lost on her; moreover, the belief that pregnancy is a woman's ultimate good fortune, a belief that amounts to a cultural reverence for the pregnant woman, is abundantly broadcast in the favourite folk-tales and familiar myths of Hindu tradition. Thus, this passage from a Bengali tale: 'Suddenly it seemed that God had taken notice of the prayer. The youngest queen, Sulata, was expecting. The king was overjoyed at the happy news. His affection for Sulata grew even more. He was always looking after her comforts and attending to her wishes.'[50]

The roots of this solicitous respect for the pregnant woman lie deep in a religious and historical tradition which equates 'woman' with 'mother', and views the birth of a male child as an essential step in the parents' and the family's salvation. 'To be mothers women were created, and to be fathers men,' Manu states categorically.[51] Further on in the *Laws*, appraising the status of motherhood, he adds, 'The teacher is ten times more venerable than the sub-teacher, the father a hundred times more than the teacher, but the mother is a thousand times more than the father.'[52] 'She is a true wife who hath borne a son,' Shakuntala tells Dushyanta as she reminds him of his forgotten marriage vows, for wives who produce children are 'the root of religion and of salvation. They are fathers on occasions of

religious acts, mothers in sickness and woe.'[53] And the goddess
Parvati, with divine disdain for convention, remarks: 'Among all the
pleasures of women, the greatest pleasure is to unite with a good
man in private, and the misery that arises from its interruption is not
equalled by any other. The second greatest misery is the falling of
the seed in vain, and the third is my childlessness, the greatest sorrow
of all.'[54]

Numerous passages in legends and epics vividly describe the suf-
ferings of the souls of departed ancestors if a couple remain childless
and thus unable to guarantee the performance of the rituals prescribed for salvation. 'Because a son delivers his father from the hell
called *put*,' Manu says, 'he was therefore called *put-tra* [a deliverer
from *put*] by the self-existent himself.'[55] Hindu society is of course not
unique in revering motherhood as a moral, religious, or even artistic
ideal,[56] but the absolute and all-encompassing social importance of
motherhood, the ubiquitous variety of motherhood myths, and the
function of offspring in ritual and religious (not to mention economic)
life all give to motherhood in Indian culture a particularly incontro-
vertible legitimacy.

Subjectively, in the world of feminine psychological experience,
pregnancy is a deliverance from the insecurity, doubt and shame of
infertility: 'Better be mud than a barren woman', goes one proverb.
Moreover, until very recently, in Hindu society, as among the Jews,
Muslims and certain West African tribes, a childless wife could be
repudiated (even if not divorced) by her husband who was permitted
then to take another wife. On the positive side, pregnancy marks the
beginning of the psychological process which firmly establishes a
Hindu woman's adult identity. The predominant element in this
identity, the ideal core around which it is organized, is what Helene
Deutsch has called 'motherliness'.[57] Its central emotional expressions
are those of *tenderness, nurturing* and *protectiveness*, directed towards
the unborn child. Many of the other psychic tendencies generally
associated with the young woman's life-stage now become subordinate. The need for emotional closeness with her 'pre-oedipal' mother
and the wish to be loved can be transformed into the wish to love;
hostility, especially towards her new surroundings, can be directed
towards the protection of her child from the environment; the
longing of her reawakened sensuality can be temporarily sublimated,
given over to physical ministrations to her child.

To be sure, the development of motherliness as the dominant mode in a Hindu woman's identity and its harmony with other personality traits vary among individual women. Nonetheless, a Hindu woman's 'motherliness' (including manifestations of maternal excess) is a relatively more inclusive element of her identity formation than it is among western women. Given her early training and the ideals of femininity held up to her, motherhood does not have connotations of cultural imposition or of confinement in an isolating role.

For an Indian woman, imminent motherhood is not only the personal fulfilment of an old wish and the biological consummation of a lifelong promise, but an event in which the culture confirms her status as a renewer of the race, and extends to her a respect and consideration which were not accorded to her as a mere wife. It is not surprising that this dramatic improvement in her social relations and status within the family, the resolution of her emotional conflicts and the discovery of a way of organizing her future life around the core of motherliness tend to be experienced unconsciously as a gift from the child growing within her. The unborn child is perceived as her saviour, instrumental in winning for its mother the love and acceptance of those around her, a theme which recurs in many legends and tales. Thus Rama repents and is ready to take Sita back from her exile in the forest after he sees his sons for the first time; Dushyanta remembers and accepts Shakuntala as his legitimate wife after he comes face to face with his infant son; while in the two Bengali folk-tales of Sulata and Kiranmala, it is through their children's instrumentality that the injustice done to the mothers is redressed and they assume their rightful places as queens. In the case of a Hindu woman, at least in the imagery of the culture, maternal feelings of tenderness and nurturance occur in combination with a profound gratitude and the readiness for a poignantly high emotional investment in the child.

The 'Good Mother'

Although in the usage of pediatrics and medicine 'infant' refers to a child who cannot yet walk, the actualities of childhood and identity development in India suggest that the psycho-social *quality* of infancy extends through the first four or five years of life, the entire span of time in which feeding, toileting and rudimentary self-care, as well as walking, talking and the initial capacity for reasoning, become matters of course. This extension of the definition is not arbitrary. As we shall see, in India, the first developmental stage of childhood, characterized by a decisive, deep attachment to the nurturing mother, by dependence upon her for the necessities and the pleasures of succour and comfort, and by the 'crisis' of trust in the benign intentions of others towards oneself, is prolonged in such a way that the second and third developmental stages seem not to take place sequentially but are compressed into one. Thus, it is not until between the ages of three and five that an Indian child moves away (in a psychological sense) from the first all-important 'Other' in his life, his mother. And it is at this time that he[58] confronts simultaneously the developmental tasks of separation and individuation, of autonomy and initiative, of wilful self-definition and oedipal rivalry, and moves as it were from 'infancy' to 'childhood' all at once.

During this period of prolonged infancy, the Indian child is intensely and intimately attached to his mother. This attachment is an exclusive one, not in the sense of being without older and younger siblings close in age who claim, and compete for, the mother's love and care, but in that the Indian child up to the age of four or five exclusively directs his demands and affections towards his mother, in spite of the customary presence in the extended family of many other potential caretakers and 'substitute mothers'.[59] Nor does the father play a significant caretaking role at this time.

This attachment is manifested in (and symbolized by) the *physical closeness* of the infant and his mother. Well up to the fifth year, if not longer, it is customary for Indian children to sleep by their mother's side at night. During the day she carries the youngest, or the one most needing attention, astride her hip, the others within arm's reach, as she goes about on visits to neighbours, to the market, to the fields and on other errands. At home, if not suckling or nestling in his mother's lap, the infant is playing on the floor or resting in a cot nearby. Constantly held, cuddled, crooned and talked to, the Indian infant's experience of his mother is a heady one, his contact with her is of an intensity and duration that differentiate it markedly from the experience of infancy in western worlds. At the slightest whimper or sign of distress the infant is picked up and rocked, or given the breast and comforted. Usually it is the infant's own mother who swiftly moves to pacify him, although in her occasional absence on household matters it may be a sister or an aunt or a grandmother who takes him up to feed or clean or just to soothe with familiar physical contact. It is by no means uncommon to see an old grandmother pick up a crying child and give him her dried-up breast to suck as she sits there, rocking on her heels and crooning over him. The intensity of the infantile anxiety aroused by inevitable brief separations from the mother is greatly reduced by the ready availability of the other female members of the extended family. Hindu cultural tradition enjoins women not to let their infants cry, and maternal practice in India anticipates the findings of contemporary empirical research on infancy which attributes infant distress, when a baby is not hungry, cold or in pain, to separation from the mother (or her substitute).

From the moment of birth, then, the Indian infant is greeted and surrounded by direct, sensual body contact, by relentless physical ministrations. The emotional quality of nurturing in traditional Indian families serves to amplify the effects of physical gratification. An Indian mother is inclined towards a total indulgence of her infant's wishes and demands, whether these be related to feeding, cleaning, sleeping or being kept company. Moreover, she tends to extend this kind of mothering well beyond the time when the 'infant' is ready for independent functioning in many areas. Thus, for example, feeding is frequent, at all times of the day and night, and 'on demand'. And although breast feeding is supplemented with other kinds of food after the first year, the mother continues to give her breast to her child for as long as possible, often up to two or three years: in fact, suckling comes to a gradual end only when there is a strong reason to stop nursing, such as a second pregnancy. Even then, weaning is not a once-and-for-all affair, for an older child may also occasionally suckle at his mother's breast. It is not uncommon to see a five- or six-year-old peremptorily lift up his mother's blouse for a drink as she sits gossiping with her friends, an event which is accepted as a matter of course by all concerned.

Similarly, without any push from his mother or other members of the family, the Indian toddler takes his own time learning to control his bowels, and proceeds at his own pace to master other skills such as walking, talking and dressing himself. As far as the mother's and the family's means permit, a young child's wishes are fully gratified and his unfolding capacities and activities accepted, if not always with manifest delight, at least with affectionate tolerance.

The predisposition of an Indian mother to follow rather than lead in dealing with her child's inclinations and with his tempo of development does not spring from some universal component of maternal pride. In part, it reflects the cultural conception of and respect for the specific 'inborn' individuality of every child. In part it has been influenced by the facts of life in traditional India; given the infant mortality rate which used to range above twenty per cent, a surviving child was accorded by his mother the most deferential care, for he would become the parents' source of economic support in later life, and through his participation in the rituals of death and mourning, their guarantee of *religious* merit and of righteous passage into the next life. But above all, this quality of deference and indulgence in Indian motherhood has *psychological* origins in the identity development of Indian women. As I have described above, in daughterhood an Indian girl is a sojourner in her own family, and with marriage she becomes less a wife than a daughter-in-law. It is only with motherhood that she comes into her own as a woman, and can make a place for herself in the family, in the community and in the life cycle. This accounts for her unique sense of maternal obligation and her readiness for practically unlimited emotional investment in her children. These are the cultural, social, religious and developmental threads which are woven together in the formation of conscious attitudes and unconscious images in the mother which, in turn, give Indian infancy its special aura and developmental impact.

Given the experience of his mother's immediacy and utter responsiveness, an Indian generally emerges from infancy into childhood believing that the world is benign and that others can be counted on to act in his behalf. The young child has come to experience his core self as lovable: 'I am lovable, for I am loved.' Infancy has provided him with a secure base from which to explore his environment with confidence. This confidence in the support and protection of others, together with the memory traces of maternal ministrations, provide the basic modality for his social relations throughout the life cycle. In other words, Indians are apt to approach others with an unconscious sense of their own lovability and the expectation and demand that trustworthy benefactors will always turn up in times of difficulty. Suspicion and reserve are rare. Many character traits ascribed to Indians are a part of the legacy of this particular pattern of infancy: trusting friendliness with a quick readiness to form attachments, and intense, if short-lived, disappointment if friendly overtures are not reciprocated; willingness to reveal the most intimate confidences about one's life at the slightest acquaintance and the expectation of a reciprocal familiarity in others; and the assumption that it is 'natural both to take care of others . . . *and to expect to be cared for*'.[60] Considering the oppressive economic environment in which most Indians live, I find no other explanation than the emotional capital built up during infancy for the warmth that is abundantly and unreservedly given and received in the most casual encounters, for the bouts of spontaneous laughter (and crying), and for the glow of intimacy and vitality that characterizes social relations.

Setting aside our consideration of the unconscious for a moment, we can observe that an Indian child tends to experience his mother almost totally as a 'good mother'. The proportion of Indian men who express or experience an active dislike, fear or contempt for their mothers at a conscious level is infinitesimally small. This is strikingly apparent in clinical work; in initial interviews and in the early stages of psychotherapy, patient after patient invariably portrays his mother as highly supportive and extremely loving. In studies of family relations, sociologists and anthropologists confirm the existence of a very close mother–son relationship of the 'good mother' variety in different regions and social classes throughout India.[61]

Literary evidence further corroborates her sentimental prevalence. Thus, short stories and novels by Indian writers such as Sarat Chandra and Premchand tend to portray the mother in her benign and nurturing aspect, with a nostalgia uncomplicated by the slightest trace of hostility or guilt. Nor do autobiographical accounts deviate from this psychological stance of conscious devotion to the 'good mother'. Nehru, recalling his mother, writes, 'I had no fear of her, for I knew that she would condone everything I did, and because of her excessive and undiscriminating love for me, I tried to dominate over her a little.'[62] And Yogananda recollects, 'Father . . . was kind, grave, at times stern. Loving him dearly, we children yet observed a certain reverential distance. But mother was queen of hearts, and taught us only through love.'[63]

It needs to be noted here that this idealized image of the 'good mother' is largely a male construction. Women do not sentimentalize their mothers in this way. For daughters, the mother is not an adoring figure on a pedestal: she is a more earthy presence, not always benign but always *there*.

I have so far described the core of Indian personality in terms of confidence in the safeguarding supportiveness of others and trust in the fundamental benevolence of the environment. Mythological and religious representations of the 'good mother' as she is personified in the widely worshipped goddesses, Lakshmi, Sarasvati, Parvati or Gauri, allow us to elaborate on the Indian experience of this 'basic trust'. In Hindu mythology we find that the specifically oral aspect of maternal nurturing is represented by very minor deities such as Annapurna, portrayed as a fair woman standing on a lotus holding a rice bowl, or by the heavenly cow Surabhi who gives an eternal fountain of milk. But the central feature of the 'good mother', incorporated by every major goddess in the Hindu pantheon and dramatized either in her origins or in her function, is not her capacity to feed but to provide life-giving reassurance through her *pervasive presence*. Thus Lakshmi, the goddess of prosperity and good fortune, comes to *dwell* with men, while those in adversity are spoken of as being *forsaken* by her. Sarasvati, the goddess of learning, is identified as *Vak* (speech)—the mother soothing, consoling, talking to her infant. And Parvati, according to one of the Puranic accounts, came into existence to protect the gods against the distress caused by the demon Andhaka (born of Darkness), the representation of one of the elemental fears of childhood. The reassurance provided by the goddesses Sarasvati and Parvati against the terrific estrangements of infancy reminds me of Freud's account of the child who called out of a dark room, 'Auntie, speak to me! I'm frightened because it's so dark!' His aunt answered him, 'What good would that do? You can't see me.' 'That does not matter,' replied the child, 'if anyone speaks, it gets light.'[64]

This emphasis on a nurturing, fear-dispelling presence as the fundamental quality of the 'good mother' is unmistakable in the descriptions of the appearance of these goddesses: They *shine* 'with pearl and golden sheen', *glow* 'with splendour, bright as burnished gold' and *gaze* with faint smiles upon the worshippers.[65] Erikson has called this the 'numinous element, the sense of hallowed presence'.[66] This is the 'good mother', in earthly mothers and in maternal divinities, smiling down on the dependent infant, or on the devoted believer, who, each in his own way, yearns to be at one with that gracious presence. Shiva's lament at the loss of Parvati evokes the sense of intactness the mother's presence gives, as well as the dread of separation or abandonment: 'With thee I am almighty, the framer of all things, and the giver of all bliss; but without thee, my energy, I am like a corpse, powerless and incapable of action: how then, my beloved, canst thou forsake me? With smiles and glances of thine eyes, say something sweet as *amrita*, and with the rain of gentle words sprinkle my heart which is scorched with grief . . . O mother of the Universe! arise.'[67] The theme of isolation and its transcendence, as we have seen in Chapter II, constitutes the core of the *moksha* ideal. This theme has its ontogenetic source in the specific form and quality of the interactions between mothers and infants in Indian society; and it is vividly elaborated in Hindu mythology as the persistent nostalgic wish for the benevolent presence of the 'good mother' as she was experienced in infancy.

The preoccupation with the themes of loneliness and separation, together with the strong unconscious desire for the confirming presence of the 'good (M)Other', stays with the individual in India throughout the course of his life. This is in striking contrast to most western cultures in which the yearning for a loved one and distress caused by her or his absence are often held to be 'childish' and 'regressive'. But as Bowlby, marshalling impressive evidence from clinical, empirical and ethological research, has demonstrated, the tendency to react with fear to the threat of being left alone is a natural one which has developed out of a genetically determined bias in man and has the character of an instinctive response.[68]

.Yet in western culture on the whole, and especially in psychotherapy, ' . . . little weight is given to the component of "being alone". Indeed in our culture for someone to confess himself afraid when alone is regarded as shameful or merely silly. Hence there exists a pervasive bias to overlook the very component of fear-arousing situations that a study of anxious patients suggests is most important!'[69] When a patient's suffering stems from certain phobias, or even when it involves free-floating anxiety, clinicians resort all too readily to complex explanations hinging on 'internal dangers'; no other anxiety-provoking situation is overlooked or camouflaged, either by the patient or by the clinician, as is the common fear of isolation and separation. In India, on the other hand, patients openly allude to, and even insist upon, the fear of being cut off from 'attachment figures' and the consequent threat of loneliness. This fear is acknowledged by family and society in India (however negligible it is to the clinician trained in the West); it has a cultural legitimacy which reinforces its vicissitudes in the course of an individual neurosis and hence merits serious consideration by clinicians. Indeed, in India the fear of isolation is projected on to the Creator himself: In one of the

Hindu myths we are told that Creation began because Purusha, the soul of the universe, was alone and 'hence did not enjoy happiness'.[70]

The yearning for the confirming presence of the loved person in its positive as well as negative manifestation—the distress aroused by her or his unavailability or unresponsiveness in time of need—is the dominant modality of social relations in India, especially within the extended family. This 'modality' is expressed variously but consistently, as in a person's feeling of helplessness when family members are absent or his difficulty in making decisions alone. In short, Indians characteristically rely on the support of others to go through life and to deal with the exigencies imposed by the outside world. Some western as well as Indian social scientists have chosen to interpret this as a 'weakness' in the Indian personality, the price to be paid for the indulgence enjoyed in infancy and early childhood. Statements like, 'Training in self-reliance and achievement are conspicuous by their absence. Children are not encouraged to be independent. They, like adults, are expected to seek aid in difficulty,'[71] or, 'Family life tends to develop an acute sense of dependence with a strong sense of security, and a clear sense of responsibility without an accompanying sense of personal initiative or decision,'[72] are the rule in studies which touch on the developmental aspects of Indian character. And this invariably carries with it the general value implication that independence and initiative are 'better' than mutual dependence and community. But it depends, of course, on the culture's vision of a 'good society' and 'individual merit', whether a person's behaviour in relationships approaches the isolation pole of the fusion–isolation continuum, as postulated by the dominant cultural tradition in the West today, or the fusion pole as maintained in traditional Indian culture. To borrow from Schopenhauer's imagery, the basic problem of human relations resembles that of hedgehogs on a cold night. They creep closer to each other for warmth, are pricked by quills and move away, but then get cold and again try to come nearer. This movement to and fro is repeated until an optimum position is reached in which the body temperature is above the freezing point and yet the pain inflicted by the quills (the nearness of the other) is still bearable. In Indian society the optimum position entails the acceptance of more pain in order to get greater warmth.

The Indian resolution of the tension between the coldness of distance and the price (in dependency) of nearness is not 'deviant', nor are the consequences in patterns of social behaviour 'regressive'.

Even in the West, as Bowlby points out, a consensus is emerging among clinicians of many theoretical persuasions that emotional maturity includes the capacity to rely trustingly on others, and that true self-reliance is not only compatible with the capacity for mutual dependence but grows out of it and is complementary to it.[73] The capacity to be truly alone is greatest when the 'Other', originally equated with the accepting, giving 'good mother', has become a constant and indestructible presence in the individual's unconscious and is fused with it in the form of self-acceptance. We have seen in an earlier chapter that this paradox also underlines the Indian guru's meditation, his striving towards the attainment of *moksha*, wherein he attempts to reach the *sine qua non* of autonomy through the total introjection of the 'Other', the not-self. And, as ever, the imagery of Hinduism is uncompromising: Shiva, arch-ascetic and epitome of lonely self-sufficiency, is often portrayed in such close embrace with Shakti, the 'mother of the universe', that they are one, inseparable for the duration of a world-age.

The 'Bad Mother'

I have suggested above that much of the so-called dependent behaviour observed in individuals and in social relations in India is a manifestation of the universal wish to avoid isolation and the need to share the responsibility for one's life with others. The apparent ubiquity of these needs in India, and their open, undisguised expression, reflect not so much a regressive striving or an 'oral fixation' as the cultural acceptance and even encouragement of such needs and behaviour, an acceptance that is itself rooted in an ideal model of human relationships which diverges sharply from the corresponding ideal in the West. Yet even if we can transfer the larger part of 'dependent' behaviour from the domain of the 'infantile' to that of the 'normal', the fact remains that anxiety around the theme of separation is much more common and intense in India than in western cultures. However, it is inappropriate to attribute the neurotic warp of an otherwise normative element in Indian identity to a prolonged infancy characterized by affectionate care. This theory of 'spoiling', which often crops up in discussions of personality development and psychopathology in India, rests on an uncritical acceptance of Freud's contention that an excess of parental love serves to magnify for the child the danger of losing this love, and

7

renders him in later life incapable of either temporarily doing without love or accepting smaller amounts of it.[74] In spite of the widespread popularity of this hypothesis and its dogged influence on studies of character formation, there is little evidence to support it. In fact, all the available data[75] point in the opposite direction, namely, that a child becomes anxious and clinging if parental affection is insufficient or unreliable.

In India the anxiety that may fester around the theme of separation stems at least partly from that moment in later infancy when the mother may suddenly withdraw her attention and her presence from her child. And indeed, retrospective accounts of adults as well as anthropological observations of child-rearing practices suggest that this is a widely used method of disciplining young children in India. 'I don't remember my mother ever scolding me or hitting me. If I became too much for her she would become sad and start crying and would refuse to speak to me.' Or: 'She often told me that she would go away and leave me. If I was especially bothersome, she would say that the ghost living in the mango tree outside our courtyard would take me. I still cannot pass that mango tree without shivering a little inside.' These are typical recollections of patients in a culture where frightening a child with ghosts or goblins, or locking him up alone in a dark room—in short, threats of abandonment and isolation—are deemed the most effective methods of socialization. These are the apprehensions that make an Indian child 'be good'; yet if these punishments are threatened or carried out in a context of reliable mothering and family affection they do not immobilize development, but recede into the depths of the psyche, a flickering trace of the dark side of the Indian inner world.

If there is dis-ease in the mother–infant relationship (with its probable consequences in the formation of the Hindu psyche) it stems not so much from styles of maternal reprimand and punishment, and not from the duration or the intensity of the connection between mother and infant, but rather from the danger of inversion of emotional roles—a danger which all too frequently becomes a reality particularly in the case of the male child. By inversion of emotional roles I mean this: An Indian mother, as we have shown, preconsciously experiences her newborn infant, especially a son, as the means by which her 'motherly' identity is crystallized, her role and status in family and society established. She tends to perceive a son as a kind of saviour and to nurture him with gratitude and even reverence as well as with affection and care. For a range of reasons, the balance of nurturing may be so affected that the mother unconsciously demands that the child serve as an object of her own unfulfilled desires and wishes, however antithetical they may be to his own. The child feels compelled then to *act* as her saviour. Faced with her unconscious intimations and demands, he may feel confused, helpless and inadequate, frightened by his mother's overwhelming nearness and yet unable (and partly unwilling) to get away. In his fantasy, her presence acquires the ominous visage of the 'bad mother'.

Before I elaborate on the specific form the 'bad mother' theme takes in Hindu psyche and culture, it is necessary to emphasize that the 'bad' aspect of the mother is not unique to India. The 'bad mother' lives at the opposite pole from the 'good mother' in the fantasies of all of us. As Erich Neumann has shown in an analysis of the myths of ancient cultures, and as clinical reports have demonstrated in contemporary society, a generative, nurturing and compassionate femininity has always had its counterpoint in the demanding, destroying and devouring maternal image.[76] And, in unconscious fantasy, the vagina as the passage between being and non-being is not only perceived as a source of life and equated with emergence into light, but also shunned as the forbidding dark hole, the entrance into the depths of a death womb which takes life back into itself. At this most fundamental level of the psyche, no one is entirely free from ambivalent feelings towards the mother. The theme of the 'bad mother' merits particular attention in the Indian context not just because it exists, but because it is characterized by a singular intensity and pervasiveness. Considered from this angle, the idealization of the 'good mother' doubtless betrays the intensity of emotion aroused by her during infancy and suggests a secondary repression of the anxious and hostile elements of these feelings.

Images of the 'bad mother' are culturally specific. To a large extent they are a function of the relationship between the sexes in any society. In patriarchal societies, moreover, they reflect the nature of the mother's own unconscious ambivalence towards the male child. Thus, for example, aggressive, destructive impulses towards the male child are a distinct probability in societies which blatantly derogate and discriminate against women. Traditional psycho-analytic theory compresses the abundant variety of affect and fantasy deriving from the basic duality of the sexes into the concept of penis envy, claims for it a stubborn prominence in the feminine unconscious, and concludes that this prevents women from finding the satisfaction of emotional and psycho-sexual needs in marriage and predisposes them to seek this satisfaction from their infant sons. The invariability of these propositions in individual lives is questionable; however, it is more than likely that erotic feelings towards the child will be more intense and closer to consciousness in a society such as India where a woman is expected and encouraged to find emotional fulfilment primarily in her relationship with her children.

In all societies the image of the 'bad mother' combines both the aggressively destroying and the sexually demanding themes. The question as to which of the two aspects, in any society, casts a longer shadow over the infant's earliest experience and thus contributes to the formation of a culturally specific image of the 'bad mother' depends upon the position and status of women within the society and also upon the means and circumstances of socially sanctioned feminine expression of aggressive and erotic impulses. It goes without saying that in this analysis I am speaking of the imagery that informs a collective fantasy of the 'bad mother', and necessarily setting aside individual variations, attributable to the life-historical fates of individual mothers within a given culture.

In Indian society as a whole, for reasons suggested earlier, the aggressive dimension of maternal feeling towards the male child is comparatively weak. Rather, it is in the sphere of unsatisfied erotic needs, a seductive restlessness, that the possibility of disturbance lies. By this I do not mean to imply that Indian women are without feelings of envy and hostility for the males among them; the castration fantasy of turning all men into eunuchs in the Arundhati myth, however much a patriarchal projection, is but one illustration of the ambivalence that governs relations between the sexes. Given the overwhelming preference in Indian society for the birth of male offspring, it would indeed give the psycho-analytic interpreter pause if such envy were non-existent or totally repressed. However, for the purposes of elaborating the imagery of the 'bad mother' in Indian personality development, we must shift our attention from the 'aggressive' sphere of rivalry and rage to the 'erotic' sphere of love and longing. We must attend to the outcome of female psycho-sexual development in traditional Indian society.

The fate of an Indian girl's sexuality is a socially enforced progressive renunciation. The birth of a child does not change this prescription; in fact, maternity often demands an even greater repudiation of a woman's erotic impulses. The familial and social expectation that she now devote herself exclusively to her child's welfare, the long periods of post-partum taboo on sexual intercourse in many communities, her increasing confinement to female quarters—these are a few of the social factors which dispose a young mother to turn the full force of her eroticism towards an infant son.

Here, it must be remembered that a mother's inner discontents are conveyed to her infant, wordlessly, in the daily intimacy of her contact with him, and that the relief of his mother's tension may become as important to the child as the satisfaction of his own needs. And indeed, clinical experience has consistently and convincingly demonstrated that the displacement of a woman's sexual longings from her husband to her son poses one of the most difficult problems for a boy to handle. At a certain point, the mother's touch and stimulation, whether or not her ministrations are deliberately seductive or overtly sexual, together with the unconscious erotic wishes that infuse her caretaking arouse an intensity of feeling in the male child which his still weak and unstructured ego cannot cope. The surge of unbidden and uncontrollable affect seems to threaten to engulf him while at the same time it arouses acute anxiety. The son's predicament is extreme: although he unconditionally needs the physical tending and emotional sustenance that at first only his mother provides,* he is profoundly wary of the intensity of his feelings for her (and of hers for him) and unconsciously afraid of being overwhelmed and 'devoured' by her. As the infant boy grows—cognitively, psycho-sexually and socially—as he develops the capacity to 'put it all together', he senses that he cannot do without his mother nor remove himself from her presence, but at the same time he is incapable of giving her what she unconsciously desires. 'Realizing' his inadequacy in this regard, he also begins to fear his mother's anger and the separation which her disappointment in him seems to forebode. In his fantasy, the mother's body and especially her genitals may assume an ominous aspect. As Philip Slater in his interpretation of child-rearing in ancient Greece has expressed: 'In so far as the child receives a healthy, non-devouring love from the mother he will regard the female genitalia as the source of life. But in so far as he fails to receive such love, or receive it at the price of living solely for

*As we have noted on p. 80, the mother's primacy and the potential for a psychological 'clinch' between mother and son is prolonged well into childhood —and indeed into the whole life cycle.

the satisfaction of maternal needs, he will regard the female genitalia as threatening to his very existence.'[77]

In the child's fantasy, the menace implicit in the female genitalia may become concrete, magnified in horrific imagery—a chamber full of poison, causing death in the sexual act—or jaws lined with sharp teeth—the so-called *vagina dentata*. This ferocious motif, which occurs frequently in Indian legends and myths, is vividly illustrated in the following myth from the *Kalika Purana*: 'During a battle between the gods and the demons, Sukra, the guru of the demons, was able to revive all the demons who were slain. Siva knew that Sukra could not be killed because he was a Brahmin, and so he resolved to throw Sukra into the vagina of a woman. From Siva's third eye there appeared a horrible woman with flowing hair, a great belly, pendulous breasts, thighs like plantain tree trunks, and a mouth like a great cavern. There were teeth and eyes in her womb. Siva said to her, "Keep the evil guru of the demons in your womb while I kill Jalandhara [the chief of the demon army], and then release him!" She ran after Sukra and grabbed him, stripped him of his clothes and embraced him. She held him fast in her womb, laughed and vanished with him.'[78]

Whereas the Sukra myth is a symbolic dramatization of the child's helplessness in the face of the dreadful mother, another Siva myth from the *Matsya Purana* manages to incorporate the child's own sexual excitement and his fantasied revenge through the complementary motif of *penis aculeatus*—the sharp phallus: Siva once teased Parvati about her dark skin, and she resolved to perform *tapas* to obtain a golden skin. As Parvati departed, she said to her son Viraka, 'My son, I am going to do *tapas* [ascetic practices], but Siva is a great woman-chaser, and so I want you to guard the door constantly while I am gone, so that no other woman may come to Siva!' Meanwhile, Adi, the son of the demon Andhaka, who had resolved to kill all the gods to revenge his father's death, learned that Parvati had gone to do *tapas*. Adi did *tapas* and won from Brahma the boon that he would only die when he had transformed himself twice. Then he came to Siva's door and seeing Viraka there, he changed himself into a serpent to delude him, forgetting the stipulation about the manner of his death. Once inside the house, he took the form of Parvati in order to deceive Siva, and he placed teeth as sharp as thunderbolts inside her vagina, for he was determined to kill Siva. When Siva saw him he embraced him, thinking him to be Parvati, and Adi said, 'I went to do *tapas* in order to be dear to you and lovely, but I found no pleasure there so I have returned to you.' When Siva heard this he became suspicious, for he knew that Parvati would not have returned without completing *tapas*, and so he looked closely for signs by which to recognize her. When he saw that the illusory Parvati did not have the mark of the lotus on the left side of her body, as the true Parvati did, he recognized the magic form of the demon, and he placed a thunderbolt in his own phallus and wounded the demon with it, killing him.[79]

The figure of the mother is indeed omnipresent in the psyche of Indian men. Yet what these typical myth fragments make clear is the ambivalence with which she is regarded in fantasy: she is both nurturing benefactress and threatening seductress. The image of the 'bad mother' as a woman who inflicts her male offspring with her unfulfilled, ominous sexuality is not just a clinical postulate, supported by mythological evidence; it is indirectly confirmed by the staunch toboos surrounding menstrual blood and childbirth throughout traditional India.[80] A menstruating woman may not prepare food, nor make offerings, nor participate in family feasts. She is forbidden to go into the temple, into the kitchen, into the granary or to the well. Men have a mortal horror of being near a woman during the time of menstruation. As with many other customs in India, the menstruation taboos have a hoary tradition. Manu is customarily blunt on the subject: 'The wisdom, the energy, the strength, the might and the vitality of a man who approaches a woman covered with menstrual excretions utterly perish.'[81]

Thus, underlying the conscious ideal of womanly purity, innocence and fidelity, and interwoven with the unconscious belief in a safeguarding maternal beneficence is a secret conviction among many Hindu men that the feminine principle is really the opposite—treacherous, lustful and rampant with an insatiable, contaminating sexuality. This dark imagery breaks through in such proverbs as, 'Fire is never satisfied with fuel, the ocean is never filled by the rivers, death is never satisfied by living beings and women are never satisfied with men.' In mythology, when Shiva destroys Kama, the god of sexual desire, Kama's essence enters the limbs of Devi, the great mother-goddess and archetypal woman. Or, the women in the Pine Forest, in their efforts to seduce Shiva, quote from a text which appears in several Upanishads and Brahmanas: 'The Vedas say, "Fire is the woman, the fuel is her lap; when she entices, that is the smoke, and the flames are her vulva. What is done within is the coals, and the pleasure is the sparks. In this Vaisvanara fire, the gods always offer seed as oblation." Therefore have pity. Here is the sacrificial altar.'[82]

The anxiety aroused by the prospect of encountering female sexuality is also evident in the mildly phobic attitude towards sexually mature women in many parts of India. Dube's observations in a Hyderabad village—'Young people have a special fascination for adolescent girls "whose youth is just beginning to blossom." Young men who succeed in fondling "the unripe, half-developed breasts" of a girl and in having intercourse with one "whose pubic hair is just beginning to grow" easily win the admiration of their age-group . . . Success—real or imaginary—with an adolescent girl is vividly described'[83] illustrate the widespread preference for immature girls and the concomitant fear of mature female sexuality. The fantasy world of Hindu men is replete with the figures of older women whose appetites debilitate a man's sexuality, whose erotic practices include, for example, vaginal suction, 'milking the penis'. These fantastic women recall the Hindu son's primitive dread of the maternal sexuality that drains, devours and sucks dry. Here we may note that the common term of abuse, 'Your mother's penis', whose meaning puzzles Dube, stems from precisely this dark side of the Hindu male's emotional imagery of maternity; as Karen Horney has shown, the attempt in male fantasy to endow the woman with a penis is an attempt to deny the sinister female genitals—in India, those of the mother.[84]

The latent sexual dread of the mature female is also the main *psychological* reason for the unusual disparity in age between men and women at the time of marriage in India, although this difference in age rarely approaches the number contemplated by Manu as right and proper: namely, sixteen to eighteen years! Yet even a girl bride gets older, of course. She becomes an adult woman who, especially after childbirth, moves dangerously close to the sexually intimidating mother of infancy in her husband's unconscious fantasy. The most direct expression of this (generally unconscious) association in the male psyche is the myth of Skanda, the son of Shiva and Parvati: 'When Skanda killed Taraka [a demon who had been terrorizing the gods], his mother, Parvati, wished to reward him, so she told him to amuse himself as he pleased. Skanda made love to the wives of the gods, and the gods could not prevent it. They complained to Parvati, and so she decided she would take the form of whatever woman Skanda was about to seduce. Skanda summoned the wife of Indra [the king of gods], and then the wife of Varuna [the wind-god], but when he looked at each one he saw his mother's form, and so he would let her go and summon another. She too became the image of his mother, and then Skanda was ashamed and thought, "the universe is filled with my mother", and he became passionless.'[85] On the other side of the coin, the counterphobic attitude, the conscious seeking out of what is unconsciously feared, is expressed in the following passage from the *Yogatattva Upanishad*: 'That breast from which one sucked before he now presses and obtains pleasures. He enjoys the same genital organs from which he was born before. She who was once his mother, will now be his wife and she who is now wife, mother. He who is now father will be again son, and he who is now son will be again father.'[86]

One of the likely psycho-sexual consequences of this anxiety-provoking process of association in unconscious fantasy is a heightened fear, or the actual occurrence, of impotence. And indeed this is a phenomenon to whose ubiquity Indian psychiatrists as well as their traditional counterparts—the *vaids* and *hakims* to whom a majority of Indians turn with psychosomatic complaints—can bear witness. This anxiety is plainly in evidence in the advertisements for patent medicines plastered or painted on the walls enclosing the railway tracks in any of the larger Indian towns. Together with cures for barrenness, the major worry of Indian women, these remedies hold out the promise of sexual rejuvenation for men. Psycho-sexual development and problems of intimacy between Indian men and women suggest the vicious circle that spirals inward in the Indian unconscious: mature women are sexually threatening to men, which contributes to 'avoidance behaviour' in sexual relations, which in turn causes the women to extend a provocative sexual presence towards their sons, which eventually produces adult men who fear the sexuality of mature women.

Given the concurrence of these phenomena, we must conclude that the sexual presence of the 'bad mother' looms large in the unconscious experience of male children in India and is therefore critical to an understanding of the Hindu psyche. And indeed, as I attempt to show below, the mine of collective fantasy around this theme is unusually rich. Certainly all societies call upon witches, vampires, ghosts and other spectres to symbolize the forbidding, negative aspect of a real mother; these phantoms, along with other mother surrogates such as a stepmother and evil goddesses, are infused with meanings derived from archaic early childhood fears of the mother's emotional needs and fantasied threats. These are familiar figures in individual and collective fantasy across cultures, and the *dayans, jinns,* and *bhoots* who people the Indian night and the Hindu imagination in such profusion are unexceptional. Female vampires who suck the blood from the toe of a sleeping man suggest (even without an analysis of the obvious sexual symbolism) the fantasied rapacious mother as graphically as Ghitachi, Menaka, Rambha, Urvasi, Chitralekha and all the other *apsaras,* or 'heavenly damsels', who lure men from their practice of 'rigid austerities' and deprive them of their 'spiritual' life substance.

A vivid illustration of the collective male fantasy of the child's encounter with the sexual mother is the mythical meeting of Arjuna, a hero of the epic *Mahabharata,* with the *apsara* Urvasi, which is one of the most popular and frequently enacted subjects in Indian dance drama. As described in the *Mahabharata,* the episode has a dreamlike quality. It begins with the child's pleasurable feeling of wonderment at his mother's beauty and his desire for her presence, a tender expectancy which gradually changes into its opposite—anxiety about his inadequacy to fulfil her sexual needs. The conflict is resolved through a self-castration which appeases the mother. In fantasy, the mother takes the initiative and approaches the child: 'And when the twilight had deepened and the moon was up, that *Apsara* of high hips set out for the mansions of Arjuna. And in that mood, her imagination wholly taken up by thoughts of Arjuna, she mentally sported with him on a wide and excellent bed laid over with celestial sheets, and with her crisp, soft and long braids decked with bunches of flowers, she looked extremely beautiful. With her beauty and grace, and the charm of the motions of her eyebrows and of her soft accents, and her own moonlike face, she seemed to tread, challenging the moon himself. And as she proceeded, her deep, finely tapering bosoms, decked with a chain of gold and adorned with celestial unguents and smeared with fragrant sandal paste, began to tremble. And in consequence of the weight of her bosom, she was forced to bend slightly forward at every step, bending her waist exceedingly beautiful with three folds. And her loins of faultless shape, the elegant abode of the god of love, furnished with fair and high and round hips, and wide at their lower part as a hill, and decked with chains of gold and capable of shaking the saintship of anchorites, being decked with this attire, appeared highly graceful. And her feet with fair suppressed ankles, and possessing flat soles and straight toes of the colour of burnished copper and high and curved like a tortoise back and marked by the wearing of ornaments furnished with rows of little bells, looked exceedingly handsome. And exhilarated with a little liquor which she had taken and excited by desire, and moving in diverse attitudes and expressing a sensation of delight, she looked more handsome than usual.'

Urvasi enters Arjuna's palace. 'Upon beholding her at night in his mansion, Arjuna, with a fear-stricken heart, stepped up to receive her, but from modesty, closed his eyes. And Arjuna said, "O thou foremost of the Apsaras, I reverence thee by bending my head down. O lady, let me know thy commands. I wait upon thee as thy servant." ' Without the circumlocution and hyperbole so dear to the Hindu, Urvasi expresses her sexual desire for Arjuna frankly and directly. But—'Hearing her speak in this strain, Arjuna was overcome with bashfulness. And shutting his ears with his hands, he said, "O blessed lady, fie on my sense of hearing, when thou speakest thus to me. For, O thou of beautiful face, thou art certainly equal in my estimation unto the wife of a superior. Even as Kunti [his mother] of high fortune or Sachi the queen of Indra [King of gods] art thou to me, O auspicious one . . . O blessed Apsara, it behoveth thee not to entertain other feelings towards me, for thou art superior to my superiors, being the parent of my race." ' Urvasi, however, insists, and Arjuna expresses the increasing helplessness of the child who desires the mother's comfort and care but instead is confronted with her sexuality: 'Return, O thou of the fairest complexion: I bend my head unto thee, and prostrate myself at thy feet. Thou deservest my worship as my own mother and it behoveth thee to protect me as a son.' The conflict now crescendos, for thus addressed, 'Urvasi was deprived of her sense by wrath. Trembling with rage, and contracting her brows, she cursed Arjuna saying that since he disregarded a woman who is pierced by shafts of Kama, the god of love, " . . . Thou shalt have to pass thy time among females unregarded, and as a dancer and destitute of manhood and scorned as a eunuch." '

As in all Hindu myths and legends, there is a benevolent power in the background who comes forward to mitigate the extreme consequences of the curse. In striking contrast to ancient Greek mythology with its blood-thirsty homicides, mutilations and castrations, in

Indian fantasy the murderous impulses of parents towards children or of children towards their parents do not result in permanent injury or death. Even in the rare instance when an actor goes beyond the attempt to actual fulfilment, there is always a good figure, a god or goddess or ancestral spirit, who helps to undo the act that has been committed. Thus, Arjuna must live only one year in the castrated state as eunuch, a solution with which he 'experienced great delight and ceased to think of the curse'.[87]

The renunciation of masculine potency and prowess, mythically depicted in Arjuna's transient fate, is one of the principal unconscious defences of the male child against the threat posed by the mother's sexuality. This 'typical' defence is cartooned in yet another, less well-known myth: 'The demon Ruru with his army attacked the gods, who sought refuge with Devi. She laughed and an army of goddesses emerged from her mouth. They killed Ruru and his army, but then they were hungry and asked for food. Devi summoned Rudra Pasupati (Siva by another name) and said, "You have the form of a goat and you smell like a goat. These ladies will eat your flesh or else they will eat everything, even me." Siva said, "When I pierced the fleeing sacrifice of Daksa, which had taken the form of a goat, I obtained the smell of a goat. But let the goddesses eat that which pregnant women have defiled with their touch, and newborn children and women who cry all the time." Devi refused this disgusting food, and finally Siva said, "I will give you something never tasted by anyone else: the two balls resembling fruits below my navel. Eat the testicles that hang there and be satisfied." Delighted by this gift, the goddess praised Siva.'[88] Here, in spite of commendable efforts to dilute the elements of disgust and dread at the heart of the fantasy by adding such details as the multitude of goddesses, the goat, and so on, that maternal threat and the defence of self-castration are unmistakable, although perceived and couched in the rapacious oral imagery of earliest infancy.

The fantasied renunciation of masculinity is but one resolution which the male child may resort to in his helplessness in this dilemma. Hindu mythology gives dramatic play to others—such as the unsexing of the 'bad mother'. Consider the myth of Surpanakha, sister of the demon-king Ravana. The giantess, 'grim of eye and foul of face', tells Rama that he should

> This poor misshapen Sita leave
> And me, thy worthier bride, receive.

Look on my beauty, and prefer
A spouse more like me than one like her;
I'll eat that ill-formed woman there,
Thy brother, too, her fate shall share.
But come, beloved, thou shalt roam
Through our woodland home.[89]

Rama staunchly refuses her advances. Thinking Sita to be the chief obstacle to her union with him, Surpanakha is about to kill her, but is forcibly prevented from doing so when Rama's brother cuts off Surpanakha's nose. In accordance with the well-known unconscious device of the upward displacement of the genitals, this becomes a fantasied clitoridectomy, designed to root out the cause and symbol of Surpanakha's lust.

Another 'defence' in the mythological repertoire against the sexually threatening 'bad mother' is matricide followed by resurrection and deification. Philip Spratt, summarizing the legends of twenty-nine popular goddesses locally worshipped in the villages of southern India, points out that nineteen of the women who were eventually deified had met first with a violent death; moreover, in fourteen of these legends the woman's forbidden sexual activity is the central theme.[90] Thus: 'Podilamma was suspected of sexual misconduct. Her brothers, who were farmers, threw her under the feet of their oxen. She vanished, and all they could find was a stone. Her spirit demanded that they [the villagers] worship the stone.' Or: 'A widow named Ramama had immoral relations with her servant. Her brother murdered them both. Cattle-plague broke out, and the villagers attributed it to her wrath and instituted rites to pacify her spirit.'[91] On the one hand, the fantasy underlying these legends aims to accomplish and gratify the sexual wishes of the mother, while on the other, the child revenges himself upon her for putting him, with his own unsettling 'wishes', his inexperience and his woeful lack of mature genital equipment, in this hopeless predicament. By the 'murder' of the sexual mother, however, the child's source of affirmation, protection and motherly love is also eliminated, thus arousing an unbearable sense of longing and guilt. To reclaim the filial relationship, to restore the forfeited mutuality, the mother must be resurrected as no less than a goddess.

Yet another defence in the male child's struggle against the 'bad mother' is the fantasy of having been born of a man, in which case one's existence has nothing whatsoever to do with the mother and is thus unquestionably masculine. This fantasy is expressed in one version of the birth of Ganesha, one of the most popular deities in the Hindu pantheon. Ganesha is usually portrayed as a short, corpulent god with an elephant's head and a large belly. His image, whether carved in stone or drawn up in a coloured print, may be found in almost any Hindu home or shop. Important matters of householding, whether in the sphere of the family or of business, whether the task at hand is the construction of a house or embarking on a journey or even writing a letter, are not undertaken without an invocation to Ganesha. In the particular version of his birth I have in mind here from the *Varaha Purana*, it is related that gods and holy sages, realizing that men are as liable to commit bad acts as good ones, came to Shiva and asked him to find a way of placing obstacles in the path of wrongdoing. While meditating on this request, Shiva produced a beautiful youth with whom all the heavenly damsels fell in love and who was charged by his father with the task of hindering evil. But Shiva's wife, the great mother-goddess Uma (also known as Durga, Parvati or Gauri), became extremely jealous of the youth's immaculate conception and incomparable beauty, and so she cursed him with a large belly and the head of an elephant.

Other accounts in Hindu mythology of the origin of Ganesha's incongruous physiognomy reflect the strikingly different sequential 'editions' of unconscious fantasy that inform infantile psycho-sexual development. Thus, in the version of the *Brahmavaivarta Purana*, it is narrated that Parvati who was very desirous of having a child was finally granted her wish after a long period of penance and prayer. All the gods come to Shiva's house to congratulate the couple and to admire the newborn. But Sani, the ill-omened Saturn, refuses to look at the baby, and keeps his gaze firmly fixed on the ground. When asked the reason for this discourtesy, Sani replies that he is cursed and that any child he looks upon will lose its head. Parvati, however, forces Sani to look at the infant, whereupon Ganesha's head is severed from his body and flies off. Parvati's pitiful lamentations over her son's decapitation attract the sympathy of Vishnu who intercedes and finds an elephant's head which he joins to the infant's trunk. Thus Ganesha is resurrected.

In the sequence of developmental time within the individual psyche, these two versions of the Ganesha myth exist in close proximity. Without elaborating on the unconscious equation of genitals and head so prominent in Hindu fantasy, it is clear that each version of

Ganesha's genesis threatens the son, symbolically, with the loss of his penis at the behest of the 'bad mother'. Moreover, when Ganesha's head is restored, we witness one of the psyche's marvellous compensations, for the replacement is not an ordinary human head, but the head of an elephant, with a trunk for good measure!

In the third version of the Ganesha story, which is from the *Shiva Purana*, the variation of the fantasy is more advanced; it condenses and reflects the dominant themes of a later, oedipal, stage of development. A new conflict arises out of the intrusive presence of the father, his claims on both mother and child, and the threat this poses to their earlier symbiosis. In this version of the myth, Siva has nothing to do with Ganesha's birth. Rather, the infant is said to have been fashioned solely by Parvati from the impurities of her own body and brought to life by being sprinkled with 'maternal water' from the holy river Ganges. Charged by Parvati to stand at the door and guard her from intruders while she is bathing, Ganesha refuses to let his father enter. In his anger at being kept from his wife, Shiva cuts off Ganesha's head. But when Parvati tells Shiva that her son was only carrying out her orders and when she proves inconsolable at the loss of her son, Shiva restores Ganesha to life by taking the head of a passing elephant and fitting it to the child's headless body.

The oedipal struggle in this version of the myth and the way the son resolves it, through castration by the father, is not my main concern here. I merely want to indicate, and stress, the various sequential transformations of fantasy from stage to stage in psychological development and their co-existence in the unconscious. Moreover, this may occur in relation to a *single* mythological figure, who thus comes to represent a plurality of psychic propensities. The enormous popularity enjoyed by Ganesha throughout India, a phenomenon of considerable puzzlement to Indologists, can thus be partially explained if we recognize Ganesha as a god for all psychic seasons, who embodies certain 'typical' resolutions of developmental conflicts in traditional Hindu society.

These, then, are the legendary elaborations of the Indian boy's encounters with the 'bad mother'. The evidence of popular myths, religious customs and anthropological observations converges to suggest that the modal resolution of the conflict is a lasting identification with the mother.[92] This process of identification contrasts with the earlier grateful incorporation of the 'good mother' into the infant's budding ego in that it contains an element of hostility, for the source of anxiety, the mother, is only eliminated by being taken inside oneself.

In psycho-sexual terms, to identify with one's mother means to sacrifice one's masculinity to her in order to escape sexual excitation and the threat it poses to the boy's fragile ego. In effect, the boy expresses his conviction that the only way he can propitiate the mother's demands and once again make her nurturing and protective is to repudiate the cause of the disturbance in their mutuality: his maleness. In myths, we witnessed this process in Arjuna's encounter with Urvasi, in Shiva's offer of his testicles, in Ganesha's losing his head because of Parvati's jealousy.[93] In the ancient and medieval tales collected, for example, in *Hitopadesha*, *Vikramaditya's Adventures* and *Kathasaritsagar*, the cutting off of one's own head (symbolic of self-castration) as an act of sacrificial worship to the mother-goddess occurs frequently. Western readers may recollect Thomas Mann's treatment of the Indian tale, in *The Transposed Heads*, in which two friends caught in a sexually tempting and dangerous situation repair to the goddess Bhavani's temple and cut off their heads.

In its purely sexual sense, the puerile identification with the mother is even more explicit in the story of King Bhangaswana in the *Mahabharata*, who, after being transformed into a woman by Indra, wished to remain in that state. Refusing Indra's offer to restore his masculinity, the king contended that a woman's pleasure in intercourse was much greater than a man's.[94] Philip Spratt's painstaking collection of anthropological evidence—traditional village ceremonies in which men dress as women, the transvestite customs of low-caste beggars in Bellary, the possession of men of the Dhed community in Gujarat by the spirit of the goddess Durga, the simulated menstrual period among certain followers of Vallabhcharya— need not be further catalogued.[95] And although we may be tempted to view these phenomena as aberrant, as extreme manifestations of marginal behaviour, we must nevertheless acknowledge the possibility that, just as the 'sick' member may act out the unconscious conflict of the whole family, thereby permitting other family members to remain 'normal', so these marginal groups disclose the governing emotional constellations within Hindu society as a whole. Nor is this to deny that transvestism, like any aspect of behavioural style, is 'overdetermined'. As a re-enactment of a powerful infantile conflict, rituals such as these represent not only the boy's attempt to identify with his mother but also the man's effort to free himself from her domination. By trying to be like women—wearing their clothes, acquiring their organs, giving birth—these men are also saying that they do not need women (mothers) any longer. The counterpart of such extreme 'femininity' rituals among men are those rites, common in many parts of the world, in which men behave in a rigid, symbolic masculine way. Both extremes suggest a family structure in which the mother is perceived by the male child as a dangerous, seductive female presence during his early years. However compelling the sexual idiosyncrasies spawned by this childhood identification with the mother may be, our main concern is the broader question of its consequences on the evolution of Indian identity.

Infancy and Ego: Origins of Identity in a Patriarchal Culture

We have seen that minimal demands are placed on the Indian infant to master the world around him and to learn to function independently of his mother. The main emphasis in the early years of Indian childhood is avoidance of frustration and the enhancement of the pleasurable mutuality of mother and infant, not encouragement of the child's individuation and autonomy. By and large, an Indian child is neither pressed into active engagement with the external world, nor is he coerced or cajoled to master the inner world represented, temporarily at least, by his bodily processes. Thus, with respect to elimination, the toddler in India is exempt from anxious pressure to learn to control his bowel movements according to a rigid schedule of time and place. Soiling of clothes or floor is accepted in a matter-of-fact way and cleaned up afterwards by the mother or other older girls or women in the family without shame or disgust.

This does not of course mean that no attempts of any kind are made at training toddlers in cleanliness. A child may indeed be taken outside in the morning, seated on a hollow made by his mother's feet and coaxed to relieve himself. What is relevant here is that such attempts are not a matter of systematic instruction or *a priori* rules; therefore they rarely become occasions for a battle of wills in which the mother suddenly reveals an authoritarian doggedness that says her nurturing love is, after all, conditional. More often than not, an Indian child gradually learns to control his bowels by imitating older children and adults in the family as he follows them out into the fields for their morning ablutions. This relaxed form of toilet-training, as Muensterberger (among others) has observed,[96] can contribute to the formation of specific personality traits such as a relative feeling of timelessness, a relaxed conscience about swings of mood and a certain low-key tolerance of contradictory impulses and feelings not only in oneself but in others as well. Indians do tend to accept ambiguity in emotions, ideas and relationships, with little apparent need (let alone compulsion) to compartmentalize experience into good/evil, sacred/profane—or inner/outer, for that matter.

In India the process of ego development takes place according to a model which differs sharply from that of western psychologists. Indian mothers consistently emphasize the 'good object' in their behaviour. They tend to accede to their children's wishes and inclinations, rather than to try to mould or control them. Hindu children do not have a gradual, step-by-step experience of the many small frustrations and disappointments which would allow them to recognize a mother's limitations harmlessly, over some time. Rather her original perfection remains untarnished by reality, a part of the iconography of the Hindu inner world. Thus, the detachment from the mother by degrees that is considered essential to the development of a strong, independent ego, since it allows a child almost imperceptibly to take over his mother's functions in relation to himself, is simply not a feature of early childhood in India. The child's differentiation of himself from his mother (and consequently of the ego from the id) is structurally weaker and comes chronologically later than in the West with this outcome: the mental processes characteristic of the symbiosis of infancy play a relatively greater role in the personality of the adult Indian.

In these, the so-called primary mental processes, thinking is representational and affective; it relies on visual and sensual images rather than the abstract and conceptual secondary-process thinking that we express in the language of words. Primary-process perception takes place through sensory means—posture, vibration, rhythm, tempo, resonance, and other non-verbal expressions—not through semantic signals that underlie secondary-process thought and communication.[97] Although every individual's thinking and perception are governed by his idiosyncratic mixture of primary and secondary processes, generally speaking, primary-process organization looms larger in the Indian than the western psyche.[98] The relative absence of social pressure on the Indian child to give up non-logical modes of thinking and communication, and the lack of interest or effort on the part of the mother and the family to make the child understand that objects and events have their own meaning and consequences independent of his feelings or wishes, contribute to the protracted survival of primary-process modes well into the childhood years.

Compared with western children, an Indian child is encouraged to continue to live in a mythical, magical world for a long time. In this world, objects, events and other persons do not have an existence of their own, but are intimately related to the self and its mysterious moods. Thus, objective, everyday realities loom or disappear, are good or bad, threatening or rewarding, helpful or cruel, depending upon the child's affective state; for it is his own feelings at any given moment that are projected onto the external world and give it form and meaning. Animistic and magical thinking persists, somewhat diluted, among many Indians well into adulthood. The projection of one's own emotions onto others, the tendency to see natural and human 'objects' predominantly as extensions of oneself, the belief in spirits animating the world outside and the shuttling back and forth between secondary and primary process modes are common features of daily intercourse.

The emphasis on primary thought processes finds cultural expression in innumerable Hindu folk-tales in which trees speak and birds and animals are all too human, in the widespread Hindu belief in astrology and planetary influence on individual lives, and in the attribution of benign or baleful emanations to certain precious and semi-precious stones. The Indian sensitivity to the non-verbal nuances of communication—all that is perceived with the 'sixth sense' and the 'inner eye'—has been noted not only by western psychiatrists but also by western writers such as Hesse, Kipling and Forster with fascination or horror or both.

Traditionally, moreover, Indians have sought to convey abstract concepts through vivid concrete imagery. Whether we consider the instruction in political science by means of the animal fables of *Panchatantra*, or the abundance of parables in Upanishadic metaphysics, a good case can be made that symbolic imagery rather than abstract concepts, and teleology rather than causality, have historically played a prominent role in Indian culture. Causal thinking has never enjoyed the pre-eminence in Indian tradition that it has in western philosophy.

Clinically, the persistence of primary processes in an individual's thinking and perception has been associated with psychopathology, in the sense that it suggests the persistence in adult life of an 'infantile' mode of behaviour. As Pinchas Noy has pointed out, however, in many kinds of normal regression (such as reveries and daydreams), artistic activity and creative endeavour, primary processes govern in the sphere of thought without signs of regression in other aspects of the individual's life.[99] And though the supremacy of primary processes in an individual's mental life may indeed lead to distorted perceptions of outside reality or to an impaired ability to grasp the 'real meaning' of external events and relationships, these processes serve a fundamental human purpose, namely, preserving the continuity of the self in the flux of outer events and maintaining one's identity by assimilating new experiences into the self. Throughout our lives, we must deal not only with an outer world but also an inner one, and whereas the secondary processes of logical thought and reasoning govern our mastery of the outside world, the primary processes of condensation, displacement and symbolization—the language of children, dreams and poetry—contribute to the unfolding and enrichment of the inner world.

The western cultivation of secondary processes, by and large at the expense of primary processes, contributes (almost inevitably) to a sense of disorientation among westerners who confront Indian culture for the first time. This confusion has often resulted in a foreclosure of experience and explicit or implicit negative value judgements of the Indian mode of experiencing the world, rather than in a questioning of the basic cultural assumption. As Noy remarks:

The ability to represent a full experience, including all the feelings and ideas involved, is a higher achievement than merely operating with abstract concepts and words, and the ability to transcend time limits and organize past experiences with the present ones is a higher ability than being confined to the limitations of time and space . . . The schizophrenic, for example, tries to deal with reality by his primary processes, and accordingly tries to organize reality in terms of his own self. The obsessive-compulsive does the opposite—he tries to assimilate and work through his experience with the aid of secondary processes. He tries to 'understand' and analyse his feelings in terms of logic and reality. Both fail because you cannot deal with reality by self-centred processes nor can you deal with your self by reality-oriented processes.[100]

The different emphases placed by western and Indian cultures on one or the other of the two basic modes thus reflect two diametrically opposed stances to the inner and outer worlds.

We can now appreciate that certain elements of the Hindu world image are strikingly consistent and reciprocal with the ego configuration generated in the developmental experience of Indian childhood. The widespread (conscious and pre-conscious) conviction that knowledge gained through ordering, categorizing, logical reasoning, is *avidya*, the not-knowledge, and real knowledge is only attainable through direct, primary-process thinking and perception; the imperative that inspires the yogi's meditation and the artist's *sadhana*, namely, that to reach their avowed goals they must enlarge the inner world rather than act on the outer one; the injunction inherent in the *karma* doctrine to accept and use outer reality for inner development rather than to strive to alter worldly realities; the indifferent respect given to eminent scientists and professionals, compared with the unequivocal reverence for Sai Baba, Anandamai, Tat Baba, Mehr Baba and the innumerable shamanic gurus who act as spiritual preceptors to Hindu families: these are a few of the indicators of the emphasis in Hindu culture on the primary processes of mental life.

Unless the social organization makes some special provision for it, however, no group can survive for long if its members are brought up to neglect the development of those secondary processes through which we mediate and connect outer and inner experience. An 'underdeveloped' ego in relation to the outer world is a risky luxury except under the most bountiful and utopian of natural conditions. Indian social organization traditionally 'took care' of the individual's adaptation to the outer world. That is, traditionally, in the early years, the mother serves as the child's ego, mediating his most elementary experiences, well into the years of childhood proper, until around the age of four. The ego's responsibility for monitoring and integrating reality is then transferred from the mother to the family-at-large and other social institutions. Thus, when making decisions based on reasoning through the pros and cons of a situation, the individual functions as a member of a group rather than on his own. With the help of traditional precedents and consensual (as opposed to adversary) modes of decision-making, based on the assumption that no two people have identical limits on their rationality, Indians cope effectively with their environment (if it does not change too fast). Similarly, as far as the environment of relationships is concerned, the myriad, detailed rules and regulations governing social interaction and conduct define the individual Hindu's interpersonal world in most conceivable situations and spell out appropriate behaviours. By making social interactions very predictable, these norms make it unnecessary (and usually imprudent) for each individual to assess the exigencies of a particular encounter or circumstance on his own, and encourage him to respond according to a tried-and-true traditional pattern.

The highly structured and elaborated social organization that seems oppressive to many westerners is functional in the sense that it strengthens and supplements the individual's basic ego fabric in which the world of magic and animistic projection looms large. In Indian society, this complementary 'fit' between ego and social organization remains functional only so long as the process of environmental change is a slow one, as it has been in the past, affording enough time for gradual, barely perceptible evolution of cultural ideals, social institutions and generational relationships. Difficulties arise when the pace of change quickens. Today, the outer world impinges on the Indian inner world in an unprecedented way. Harsh economic circumstances have resulted in higher social and geographical mobility, which has meant, in turn, that dealings with the outer world are more and more on an individual, rather than a social, footing. Under these 'modern' conditions, an individual ego structure, weak in secondary and reality-oriented processes and unsupported by an adequate social organization, may fail to be adaptive.

I have discussed the influence of the protracted intimacy between mother and infant in India—subsuming childhood, as it does—on the entrenchment of primary mental processes in the Hindu inner world. These processes, as we have seen, are supported by the structures of Hindu social organization and traditional cultural mores. The second lifelong theme in the Indian inner world (more actual for men by far than for women) that derives from the special psychosocial features of Indian motherhood is the simultaneous, often unintegrated presence in fantasy of images of the 'good' and the 'bad' mother.

These contradictory aspects of the maternal presence can coexist in the very young child's psyche without disturbing each other, for it is a feature of primary mental processes characteristic of infancy that contradictions do not cause urgent conflicts pressing for resolution. It is only later, when the ego gains strength and attempts to synthesize and integrate experience, that conflicts erupt and ambivalence comes into own, and that the negative, threatening aspects of earliest experience may be forcibly repressed or projected onto the external world.

Taken into the child's ego, the 'good mother's' maternal tolerance, emotional vitality, protectiveness, and nurturing become the core of every Indian's positive identity. Alongside this positive identity, however, and normally repressed, is its counterpart: the negative identity that originates in experiences with the demanding, sometimes stifling, all too present mother. Whatever the contours of the negative identity, they reflect certain defences against the 'bad mother' who may have been most undesirable or threatening, yet who was also most real at a critical stage of development.[101] In conditions of psychological stress and emotional turmoil, the negative identity fragments tend to coalesce in a liability to a kind of psychological self-castration, in a predisposition to identify with rather than resist a tormentor, and in a longing for a state of perfect passivity.

Although the inner world of Indian men is decisively influenced by both the 'good' and the 'bad' versions of the maternal-feminine, the adult identity consolidation of men is of course not to be cast exclusively in these terms. For identity is constituted not only out of early feminine identifications but also from later masculine ones, all of them rearranged in a new configuration in youth. Normally, the biological rock-bottom of maleness limits the extent to which a boy can or will identify with his mother as he grows up. The view advanced here, namely, that the length, intensity and nature of the mother–infant relationship in India, together with the sexualized nature of the threat posed by the mother to the male child in fantasy, contribute to the Hindu male's strong identification with his mother and a 'maternal-feminine' stance towards the worldly world, only makes sense in the light of these self-evident reservations. The expression of the maternal-feminine in a man's positive identity is, however, neither deviant nor pathological, but that which makes a man more human. Its presence precludes that strenuous phallicism which condemns a man to live out his life as half a person, and it enhances the possibility of mutuality and empathic understanding between the sexes. Of course, in its defensive aspect, the maternal-feminine identification of men may serve to keep the sexes apart and may even contribute to discrimination against women. A precarious sense of masculine identity can lead to a rigid, all-or-nothing demarcation of sex roles; this kind of rigid differentiation is a means of building outer bulwarks against feared inner proclivities.

The seeds of a viable identity, if they are not to mutate into plants of a 'false self', require the supportive soil of a compatible family structure and a corresponding set of cultural values and beliefs. In India, the child learns early that emotional strength resides primarily in his mother, that she is 'where the action is'. The cultural parallel to the principal actuality of infancy is the conviction that mother-goddesses are reservoirs of both constructive and destructive energy. The very word for energy, Shakti, is the name of the supreme mother-goddess. And although the spirit of the godhead is one, its active expression, worshipped in innumerable forms ranging from parti-cular local village goddesses to the more or less universal manifesta-tions of Mahadevi ('great goddess'), is decisively female. The male gods of the Hindu pantheon, Shiva, Vishnu, Brahma, may be more dignified beings, but the village deities, earthy, mundane, attuned to the uncertainties and troubles, the desires and prayers of daily life, are generally female. In south India, as Whitehead has shown, village deities are almost exclusively feminine; and the exceptional male gods, such as Potu-Razu in Andhra Pradesh, are not worshipped in their own right, but in conjunction (as brother or husband) with the local village goddess, the position of the male gods being often subordinate if not outright servile.[102]

Hindu cosmology is feminine to an extent rarely found in other major civilizations. In its extremity (for example) in Tantric beliefs, god and creation are unconditionally feminine; in *Mahanirvana Tantra*, even the normally male gods Vishnu and Brahma are portrayed as maidens with rising breasts. The essence of this deepest layer of Hindu religiosity is conveyed in the following prayer to the goddess Durga:

O thou foremost of all deities, extend to me thy grace, show me thy mercy, and be thou the source of blessings to me. Capable of going everywhere at will, and bestowing boons on thy devotees, thou art ever followed in thy journeys by Brahma and the other gods. By them that call upon thee at daybreak, there is nothing that cannot be attained in respect either of offspring or wealth. O great god-dess, thou art fame, thou art prosperity, thou art steadiness, thou art success; thou art the wife, thou art man's offspring, thou art knowledge, thou art intellect. Thou art the two twilights, the night sleep, light, beauty, forgiveness, mercy and every other thing. And as I bow to thee with bended head, O supreme goddess, grant me protection. O Durga, kind as thou art unto all that seek thy protection, and affectionate unto all thy devotees, grant me protection![103]

The most striking illustration of the cultural acceptance and outright encouragement of the passive feminine aspects of identity in Indian men is the *bhakti* cult associated with Lord Krishna. Its appeal, as we shall see in detail in Chapter V, is dramatically simple. Renouncing the austere practices of yoga, the classical Hindu means of attaining *moksha*, the Krishna cult emphasizes instead the emotional current in religious devotion. Personal devotion to Lord Krishna absorbs a devotee's whole self and requires all his energies. Depending on individual temperament and inclination, this devotional emotion—*bhava*—may express itself in a variety of modes: *santa*, awe, humility, a sense of one's own insignificance; *dasya*, respect, subservience and pious obedience; *vatsalya*, nurturing, protective (maternal) feelings of care; and so on.

The most intensely and commonly desirable feeling towards the godhead, a rudimentary prerequisite for the state of pure bliss, is held to be *madhurya bhava*, the longing of a woman for her lover, of the legendary *gopis* for their Lord. In an interview with Milton Singer, a Krishna devotee in the city of Madras articulates the systematic cultivation of this feminine-receptive stance and its transformation into a religious ideal:

The love of a woman for her husband or for her lover is very much more intense than any other sort of love in the world, and I mentioned the gopis, Radha, Rukmini, Satyabhama, and so forth, as instances in point. Their love was indeed transcendent. Even when the husband or lover is a man the woman's love for him is of a very high order and when the Lord Supreme is the husband or lover of a woman, you can find no other love excelling or surpassing this love. The ladies mentioned above can therefore be said to be the most blessed in the world. If we concede this, we can ourselves aspire for this kind of supreme love for God. We can imagine ourselves to be those women or at any rate ordinary women, imagine that the Lord is our husband or lover and bestow the maximum love on Him . . . Think constantly that you are a woman and that God is your husband or lover, and you will be a woman and God will be your husband or lover . . . You know the philosophy here that all men and women in the world are spiritually women, and the Lord alone is male—the Purusa. The love of the gopis, Radha, Rukmini, and Satyabhama explains the principle of the human soul being drawn to the Supreme Soul and getting merged in it.[104]

Fragments from the life history of the widely revered nineteenth-century Bengali saint, Sri Ramakrishna, further highlight the respect and reverence Indian society pays to the ontogenetically motivated, religiously sublimated femininity in a man. As a child, it is related, Ramakrishna often put on girl's clothing and sought to mimic the village women as they went about their daily chores. In adolescence, he would imagine that he was a forsaken wife or child-widow and would sing songs of longing for Krishna. In his quest for union with the godhead, he systematically practised *madhurya bhava*. For six months during his youth, he wore women's clothes and ornaments, adopted women's gestures, movements and expressions, and 'became so much absorbed in the constant thought of himself as a woman that he could not look upon himself as one of the other sex even in a dream'.[105]

If interpreted solely from an individual developmental viewpoint, Sri Ramakrishna's behaviour would seem deviant, the eruption of negative elements latent in Indian masculine identity. Yet the meaning of any thematic event or behaviour cannot be grasped in one dimension only. What appears to be an episode in Ramakrishna's life of 'psychopathological acting out' is, when viewed culturally and historically, an accepted, representative phenomenon in the tradition of Krishna worship. It is profoundly consistent with the basic 'mood' of all schools of Hindu miniature painting and of the *bhajan, kirtan* and even *dadra* forms of vocal music. Finally, the feminine stance is consistent with the life style of certain specialized religious groups, and its aim dramatizes a cultural ideal of the whole society, namely, a receptive absorption rather than an active alteration and opposition.

To conclude, the primary themes of Indian identity, emerging from the infant's relationship with his mother, are inextricably intertwined with the predominant cultural concerns of Hindu India. These concerns, both individual and social, govern, inform and guide the Indian inner world in such a way that they reverberate throughout the identity struggles of a lifetime.

CHAPTER IV
Families and Children

The preceding chapter explored the legacy of Indian infancy and its implications for identity both in its manifest varieties and in the hidden wishes, fantasies and fears that characterize the unconscious recesses of the inner world of the psyche. Given the primacy of the mother in early childhood in India, we have dwelt at length on her role in the evolution of the inner world and postponed our consideration of the psycho-social outcomes of the traditional form of family organization in India: the extended family. Just as the initial crystallization of the infant's inner world cannot be properly understood without an exploration of the intra-psychic, social and cultural forces that shape Indian motherhood, the period of childhood, the next step in the evolution of Indian identity, can only be interpreted in the context of the family relationships within which it occurs.

Psycho-social Matrix of Childhood:
The Extended Family

Most Indians grow up in an *extended* family, a form of family organization defined by social scientists as one in which brothers remain together after marriage and bring their wives into their parental household.[1] Brothers are expected not only to continue to live together after they marry, but more important, to remain steadfast to their parents in devotion and obedience. This ideal of filial loyalty and fraternal solidarity is the rationale for the extended family which then stipulates common residence and common economic, social and ritual activities. The brothers, their parents and their own wives and children share a single house or compound, eat meals prepared in a single kitchen and pool their income for distribution by the head of the family. In addition to this core group, there may be others who are either permanent or temporary residents in the household, widowed or abandoned sisters and aunts, or distant male relatives somewhat euphemistically known as 'uncles' who have no other family to turn to. In practice, there are variations of this pure model: in particular, the *joint* family with two or more married brothers living together with their wives and children but without their parents and the *generational* family consisting of the parents and only one of their married children and his spouse and children. I am using the term *extended* family loosely here; I intend to include all its traditional variations, and specifically to differentiate it from the nuclear family pattern dominant in the West.

In the last few years, sociologists have been engaged in a lively debate as to whether the extended family system in India is as widespread (today, or even in the past) as is commonly believed. Unfortunately, neither census returns nor empirical research has contributed much to the discussion; nor can we hazard a guess, let alone measure conclusively, whether the nuclear family has begun to replace the extended family during the last twenty-five years. One survey of two hundred Calcutta families, one hundred from a poor district and one hundred from a rich district, concludes that 80 per cent of the families in the rich district and 57 per cent in the poor are joint; these statistics suggest that urbanization does not necessarily produce a sharp increase in nuclear families. Similar figures have been reported from small towns and villages of Gujarat, and from sampling a large city in Madhya Pradesh. Conversely, a Bombay study found the proportion of joint families in a sample of 1022 families to be only 13.7 per cent.[2]

The conclusions of studies such as these depend upon the criteria of 'jointness' and the rigour with which they are applied. For example, the criterion of pooling income may not be fulfilled by many families which qualify by every other measure as an *extended* family. Because of frictions arising out of real or imagined inequities in the distribution and consumption of food, some extended families may have discarded the common kitchen. In other instances, brothers and their families may live in adjacent houses rather than in a single residence and yet share family life and householding responsibilities as a single family unit. The definition of the extended family used by some sociologists, that it consists only of patrilineally related persons, excludes families which contain one or more relatives of the mother or of the brothers' wives.

If we move beyond these definitional issues to consider the evolution of individual families, it is clear that a family cannot continue adding the families of sons and of sons' sons without reaching a 'stopping point' imposed by space and household efficiency, at which time the extended family necessarily breaks up into smaller units, each with a new head-of-household: Brothers may separate upon the death of one or both parents; the brothers' sons traditionally do not feel the same obligation to live together as the brothers (their fathers) themselves. Moreover, in recent times, migration to cities and towns in search of economic opportunity has contributed to the dissolution of extended families. Yet even in these instances of temporary or permanent transition, a social (as distinguished from a residential or logistical) 'jointness' generally continues to operate. When a brother from the village family moves to the city, his wife and children frequently continue to live with the village family while he himself remits his share to the family income; or if he takes his family with him, they return 'home' as often as they can. The ideal of the extended family is so strong in India that even in the face of seemingly insurmountable economic odds, a constant effort is made by all family members to preserve the characteristic Indian 'jointness', at the very least, in its social sense.

The point I wish to make here, and to emphasize, is that regardless of minor variations in definition or the historical and economic dislocation of adults in the family, most Indians spend the formative years of early childhood in an extended family setting. In part, the 'demography of childhood' in India reflects Indian marriage patterns. Most couples marry in adolescence[3] and have neither the economic nor the psycho-social resources to set up an independent household. Separation from the extended family, if it does take place, comes later when the children are older and well into the middle years of childhood. Even grown children who nominally live in a nuclear family make long and frequent visits to members of the extended family. Thus it is not surprising that uncles, aunts and cousins, not to mention grandparents, figure prominently in the childhood recollections of all Indians. In short, although at any given time, adults may find themselves in a period of familial transition, and households may not always be extended or joint, most people in India spend at least their childhood (and often their old age) in an extended family.[4]

The psychological 'actuality' of the extended family in an Indian child's early years, as well as the highly differentiated nature of a child's relationships within it, are dramatized in the sphere of language. Morris Lewis has identified six basic nursery sounds as a universal baby language used by infants all over the world with only slight variation from one society to another.[5] These 'words' are repeated combinations of the vowel 'ah' preceded by different consonants— 'dada', 'mama', 'baba', 'nana', 'papa' and 'tata'. Infants repeat these or other closely related sounds over and over, in response to their own babbling and to their parents' modified imitations of their baby sounds. In most western countries, only a few of these repetitive sounds, for example, 'mama', 'dada' or 'papa' are 'recognized' and repeated by the parents and thus reinforced in the infant. In India, on the contrary, just about *all* of these closely related sounds are repeated and reinforced since each one is the name of various closely related kin with whom the infant is in close contact from his earliest years. Thus, for example, in my mother tongue, which is Punjabi, *ma* is mother, *mama* is mother's brother, *dada* is father's father, *nana* is mother's father, *chacha* is father's younger brother, *taya* is father's eldest brother, *masi* is mother's sister, and so on. This transformation of the basic baby language into names for kinship relations within the extended family is characteristic of all Indian languages; it symbolizes as it activates a child's manifold relationships with a range of potentially nurturing figures in the older generations. By way of contrast, the ideal of fraternal solidarity (and its socio-economic importance) within each generation has usually resulted in only one word for one's own brothers or first or second cousins: *bhapa.*

Let us turn then to a review of the organization of relationships in the extended family and the social norms and values this family organization confirms and generates. The extended family is the immediate 'society' encountered by the Indian child as he grows up. This range of typical childhood encounters prefigures, as it informs, the identity of adult Indians.

Family structure

The extended family is, in one sense, a large group, its members engaged in the manifold activities necessary to maintain the group as a cohesive, co-operative unit, to enable its survival and promote the individual and, especially, collective welfare of its members and to protect it from the incursions of the outside world. It must deal with problems confronted by any other organization: determining an acceptable division of labour, articulating the roles and role relationships between and among family members, and co-ordinating their efforts in the service of family objectives. As in other organizations, these problems are resolved in the Indian family on the basis of the hierarchical principle; the difference is that the hierarchy of roles within an extended family is legitimated by the tradition and the social sanction not of generations but of centuries, so that for an Indian, superior and subordinate relationships have the character of eternal verity and moral imperative. In other words, an Indian's sense of his relative familial and social position—which is superior to some and subordinate to others—has been so internalized that he qualifies, in Dumont's phrase, as the original *homo hierarchicus.*[6] Regardless of personal talents or achievements, or of changes in the circumstances of his own or others' lives, an Indian's relative position in the hierarchy of the extended family, his obligations to those 'above' him and his expectations of those 'below' him are immutable, lifelong. Already in childhood he begins to learn that he must look after the welfare of those subordinate to him in the family hierarchy so that they do not suffer either through their own misjudgement or at the hands of outsiders, and that he is reciprocally entitled to obedience and respectful compliance with his wishes.

The ordering principles of this hierarchical system are age and sex. Elders have more formal authority than younger persons—even a year's difference in age is sufficient to establish the fact of formal superiority—and men have greater authority than women. Consider some of the relationships within the extended family. Among brothers, authority attends seniority, so that men and boys, while deferring to their father as his sons, owe some of the same respectful compliance to their elder brothers. The eldest brother, as future head of the family, holds an especially powerful position, for on his accession to family leadership he assumes not only moral authority and ritual prominence in family life but also the economic responsibility for the family's survival and welfare. His younger brothers and their wives and children are then obliged to transfer to him the allegiance and obedience once commanded by the father. Thus, the obligations of respect and obedience of nephews and nieces towards the uncle who is the head of the family customarily supersede filial duty to their own father.

A woman's authority usually depends on her husband's position in the household. The wife of the head of the family is supreme in household affairs, subject only to the countervailing authority of her mother-in-law. Relationships among brothers' wives mirror the prerogatives and duties of the brothers themselves. The wife of an elder brother is entitled to issue orders to the wife of a younger brother but she is also responsible for the well-being of her younger sister-in-law. In cross-sex relationships the authority associated with age is considerable but carries less weight than in same-sex relationships. A son or a daughter owes less formal deference to the mother than to the father; an elder brother has greater authority over a younger sister than an elder sister over a younger brother. In short, ideally 'the oldest male of the highest generation is supposed to receive the most respect and obedience, the female at the opposite pole, the most protection and care.'[7]

As in any other institution, there is a good deal of discrepancy between the traditional model of social relations within the extended family and the actual everyday politics of family life. The informal organization, depending on region, caste, age and economic circumstances of the family, may deviate considerably from the normative pattern. Moreover, individual differences in personality, temperament and ability—the earning power of a younger brother, the reliability and courtesy of a daughter-in-law—invariably modify the traditional blueprint.

The outstanding example of the discrepancy between traditional norm and the actuality of daily life is the common fact that the powerful role played by the older women in the family—mothers and grandmothers—bears little resemblance to the Hindu ideal of the deferential *pativrata* (ever-loyal to husband) wife. Although the classical dictum is that 'By a girl, by a young woman, or even by an aged one, nothing must be done independently, even in her own house. In childhood a female must be subject to her father, in youth to her husband; when her lord is dead, to her sons; a woman must be never independent',[8] the plain truth is that this is (and perhaps always was) a masculine wish-fulfilment rather than an accurate description of the 'real life' of older Indian women. Although the wife of the family patriarch may indeed pay a formal, and often perfunctory deference to her husband, especially in front of strangers, she may exercise considerable domestic power, not merely among the other women of the household, but with her husband, and she often makes many of the vital decisions affecting the family's interests. The fact that women gain a powerful voice in family affairs as they age, that seniority holds out enormous rewards not just in status but in actual decision-making, is one of the factors that contribute to the conservatism of Indian women, their tenacious resistance to any separatist and divisive tendencies in the extended family and their indifference to egalitarian ideologies of social change.

Authority in family and other forms of social organization

The principle of a hierarchical ordering of social dependencies extends beyond its home base in the extended family to every other institution in Indian life, from the *jajmani* system to corporate business, from the *guru–chela* relationship in religious education to department staffing in an Indian university, from village *panchayat* politics to the highest reaches of government bureaucracy. Elsewhere, in a content analysis of primers used to teach Hindi and English in Indian schools, I have shown that in a total of thirty-one stories depicting authority situations, there is not a single instance of an egalitarian authority relationship cast in a fraternal or democratic mode.[9] This study suggested that Indians view the ideal superior as one who acts in a nurturing way so that his subordinates either anticipate his wishes or accept them without questioning.[10] He receives compliance by taking care of his subordinates' needs, by providing the emotional rewards of approval, praise and even love, or by arousing guilt. On the other hand, the same study showed that high-handed attempts to regulate behaviour through threat or punishment, such as personal rejection or humiliation, are likely to lead to open defiance or devious evasion on the part of the subordinate. Thus, although family relationships are generally hierarchical in *structure*, the *mode* of the relationship is characterized by an almost maternal nurturing on the part of the superior, by filial respect and compliance on the part of the subordinate, and by a mutual sense of highly personal attachment.

As we know, in stable societies there is a psycho-social reciprocity between the institutions that govern and organize adult lives and the culture's characteristic modalities of child-rearing. We would then expect that the hierarchical actuality of extended family life in India, based primarily on *age* status, legitimated by an enduring *moral tradition*, and sustained through the complementary modes of *nurturing* and *succouring*, is extrapolated to all other social institutions as the normative form of organization. This is not surprising, for we know that if a child is praised and loved for compliance and submission, and subtly or blatantly punished for independence, he can-

9

not easily withdraw from the orbit of family authority during child-hood, nor subsequently learn to deal with authority other than sub-missively.

The hierarchical principle of social organization has been central to the conservation of Indian tradition, but it can only be a source of stagnation in modern institutions whose purpose is scientific inquiry or technological development. Such institutions require a more flexible, egalitarian structure in which the capacity for initiative as well as seniority governs role relationships, in which competence rather than age legitimates authority, and in which the organizational mode is non-coercive and fraternal. In such modern institutions, younger people may have a voice in the decision-making councils; however, their say is a limited one. Like children in the extended family, their concerns are tolerantly listened to but their serious at-tempts to initiate or influence the strategic policy decisions of the institution are dismissed, if they are heard at all. Confrontations 'on the issues' simply do not occur; younger professionals have from childhood internalized the 'hierarchical tradition', so any discrepancy between the criteria of professional performance and the prevailing mores of the organization does not produce either a confrontation with the older men or the persistent, critical questioning necessary to effect change. The aggression inevitably aroused in the younger generation is blocked from expression in outright anger; instead, the conflict between intellectual conviction and developmental 'fate' manifests itself in a vague sense of helpless and impotent rage. The anxiety triggered by the mere possibility of losing the nurturing patronage of powerful figures usually prevents any deviation from the safer compliant stance. Gradually, the younger organization men resign themselves to waiting until they become seniors in their own right, free to enjoy the fruits and the delayed gratification that age brings with it in Indian society. The suspicion is unavoidable, how-ever, that psychologically, the fruits of seniority mean the chance to 'turn passive into active', that is, to do unto the upcoming young pro-fessionals what was once done to oneself.

Family Bond

The psychological identification with the extended family group is so strong that even the loosening of the family bond, not to mention an actual break, may be a source of psychic stress and heightened inner conflict. A separation from the family, whatever the necessity or reason for such a step, not only brings a sense of insecurity in a worldly, social sense, it also means the loss of 'significant others'[11] who guarantee the sense of sameness and affirm the inner continuity of the self. Psychiatric observations in India on the occurrence of certain kinds of mental disturbances following a break from the extended family amply bear this out.[12]

There are, of course, other than psychological explanations for the importance of the family in an individual's life; economic realities and social considerations of prestige, status and reputation all reinforce the family tie. Economically, in a country without large government programmes of social security, unemployment compensation and old-age benefits, it is the extended family, if anyone, that must provide temporary relief when a man loses work, a young mother is ill, or the monsoon destroys the harvest. The extended family provides the only life insurance most Indians have. Socially, a man's worth and, indeed, recognition of his identity, are bound up in the reputation of his family. Life-style and actions—how a man lives and what he does—are rarely seen as a product of individual effort, aspiration or conflict, but are interpreted in the light of his family's circumstances and reputation in the wider society. Individual initiative and decisions make sense only in a family context. To conform is to be admired; to strike out on one's own, to deviate, is to invite scorn or pity. 'How can a son of family X behave like this!' is as much an expression of contempt as 'How could she not turn out well! After all she is the daughter of family Y!' is a sign of approval.

An individual's identity and merit are both enhanced if he or she has the good fortune to belong to a large, harmonious and closely knit family. When a man or a woman approaches a major life transition, particularly marriage, the character of the family weighs heavily in the scales of his or her fate. To illustrate this through an anecdote: I vividly remember a distant aunt coming to my grandmother for advice regarding a prospective son-in-law. After all his individual qualifications—age, earnings, education, physical appearance and future prospects—had been duly discussed and approved, the man was rejected on the grounds that his family was too small. 'If my daughter made such a marriage,' the aunt remarked somewhat regretfully, 'their child would be at a great disadvantage.' By this she meant that a large and harmonious family helps to safeguard a child's future, to advance him in life, because more people are helping him along, contributing to the decisions that will affect his future, maximizing the number of connections that may be necessary to secure a job or other favours, coming to his aid in times of crisis and generally mediating his experience with the outside world. This conviction that a large, close family is an essential advocate and protector may be undergoing some revision among highly educated urban Indians, yet it remains fundamental to the Hindu world-view.

The family itself recurrently emphasizes and seeks to strengthen the family bond through the festive yet basically solemn celebration of the turning-points in the individual life cycle. These rituals not only commemorate the 'grand occasions' of birth, marriage, giving birth, and death, they also celebrate many small climaxes such as a boy's first hair-cut, a girl's first menstrual period. These traditional ceremonies, major and minor, performed within the benevolent circle of the extended family, are the punctuation of the life cycle. They celebrate the individual's place and importance in his particular family, they are the ritual reassurance that he *belongs*, and as such, they not only affirm individual identity as a family member, they consolidate the child's and the adult's belief that family ties are the most moral, durable and reliable of all social relations. Moreover, the joint celebration of religious festivals and especially (in most castes) the performance of prescribed rites for the dead in which the participation of every family member is mandatory, attempt to extend the psychological reality of family membership beyond an individual lifetime and to remind the participants that family bonds are immutable, exempt from individual mortality.

Beyond family: caste (jati)

Second only to the extended family as a pervasive social dimension of identity in India is the institution of caste. Family and caste are the parameters of Indian childhood. By caste here, we do not mean *varna*, the four sweeping social categories of traditional Hinduism, Brahmin, Ksatriya, Vaisya and Sudra, but the Hindu institution of *jati*.[13] *Jati* is caste in all the immediacy of daily social relations and occupational specialization. Essentially, it is a social group to which an individual belongs by birth. Usually, a *jati* member participates in one of the *jati*'s several traditional occupations, and his marriage partner will almost certainly belong to his *jati*. His friendships with other *jati* members tend to be closer than those with persons of other *jatis*, with whom his relations are more formal, governed as they are by unwritten codes prescribing and proscribing relationships between *jatis*. Although some families of a particular *jati* may live in the same village, the *jati* itself extends beyond the confines of any single village; a large, prominent *jati* may include considerable geographical territory. The relationships and dealings between and among different *jatis* within a single village or in a larger region (which may comprise several hundred villages) are organized, as in the extended family, according to the hierarchical principle. Patterns of deference are defined by tradition and history, although in practice, again, the ranking order may be disputed locally whenever a particular *jati* demands higher ritual status than accorded by the going consensus. As Mandelbaum sums up the theory and practice of *jati* organization, 'Most villagers assume that there should be a ranked hierarchy of groups, even though they may disagree about the particulars of ranking.'[14]

Just as the extended family is the primary field and foil for an individual's developing sense of identity, the *jati* is the 'next circle' in his widening social radius. The *jati*'s values, beliefs, prejudices and injunctions, as well as its distortions of reality, become part of the individual's psyche as the content of the ideologies of his conscience. It is the internalized *jati* norms which define 'right action' or *dharma* for the individual, make him feel good and loved when he lives up to these norms, and anxious and guilty when he transgresses them.

Since individual anxiety reflects the latent concerns of a man's immediate society, knowledge of his *jati*, its aspirations and apprehensions, enriches clinical understanding of individual identity formation and/or identity conflict. For instance, the depressive reaction of a man from a lower *jati* to a career setback or failure is only partly a function of individual dynamics; in addition, his depression is bound up with his *jati*'s striving for upward mobility and improved status relative to other *jatis*. Another person's violent outrage provoked by an ostensibly minor slight (in the context of village society) not only betrays an individual problem in 'managing aggression', it also reflects the historical well of resentment shared by his *jati* as a whole and passed down from generation to generation as a part of *jati* identity.

As a part of the modernization process of the last twenty to thirty years, the campaign against the real and imaginary evils of the 'caste system' has fostered a wilful effort among educated Indians to banish from consciousness any sense of their *jati* affiliation and to repress its salience in individual identity formation. For westernized Indians, *jati* has become a dirty word to be mentioned only in a covert whisper. Yet the persistence of *jati* identity in an individual's inner world is often revealed in self-reflective moments. Thus Nehru, the epitome of a modern Hindu, acknowledges, without spelling it out in detail, the psychological 'presence' of his Brahminness: 'Perhaps my thoughts and approach to life are more akin to what is called Western than Eastern, but India clings to me as she does to all her children, in innumerable ways; and behind me lie, somewhere in the subconscious, racial memories of a hundred, or whatever the number may be, generations of Brahmins. I cannot get rid of either that past inheritance or my recent acquisitions.'[15] A highly-placed civil servant writes even more frankly of the influence of his *jati*, the Khatris, on his identity: 'As I could follow that Khatri was a derivation from Ksatriya, the warrior and princely class of the Vedic and classical age, I have always thought of myself belonging to a *Herrenvolk* when compared to other castes. I took pride in stories that they [the Khatris] did not intermarry or interdine with Aroras, said to spring from Vaisyas, the merchant class. I used to take pride in the fact that Khatris are, by and large, good-looking and have a fair complexion, without bothering about the fact that I possessed neither. I know I do not possess any attributes of the warrior class, yet I cling to the dogma of being a warrior type of yore, of being a ruling type with all the obligations of conduct that go with it.'[16]

Implicit in the organization of Indian society, in which each individual is part of a complex, hierarchically ordered, and above all stable network of relationships throughout the course of his life, is a psychological model of man that emphasizes human dependence and vulnerability to feelings of estrangement and helplessness. The core of emotional life is anxiety and suffering, *dukha* as the Buddhists would call it. Thus Hindu social organization accentuates the continued existence of the child in the adult and elaborates the care-taking function of society to protect and provide for the security of its individual members. We might also view traditional Indian society as a therapeutic model of social organization in that it attempts to alleviate *dukha* by addressing itself to deep needs for connection and relationship to other human beings in an enduring and trustworthy fashion and for ongoing mentorship, guidance and help in getting through life and integrating current experience with whatever has gone before and with an anticipated future. In the relatively more activist and task-oriented social organization of western countries, these dependency needs of adults are generally seen as legitimate only in moments of acute crisis or circumstances of 'sickness'. Shashi Pande has distinguished western and Indian social relations by suggesting that in the West, intimacy in a relationship develops out of some shared activity, as when a father takes his son on hunting and fishing trips as a means of developing (or proving) a mutual trust and camaraderie, whereas no such 'hidden agenda' is needed for the cultivation of a relationship in Indian society.[17] From the earliest years, the Indian child learns that the core of any social relationship, therapeutic, educational, organizational, is the process of caring and mutual involvement. What he should be sensitive to (and concerned with) are not the goals of work and productivity that are external to the relationship, but the relationship itself, the unfolding of emotional affinity.

Among those Indians closely identified with the process of modernization, the well-educated urban elite who hold positions of power in modern institutions, the psycho-historical fact of the primacy of relationships, of family loyalities, of *jati* connections, is often a source of considerable emotional stress. For although intellectually the Indian professional or bureaucrat may agree with his western counterpart that, for example, the criterion for appointment or promotion to a particular job must be objective, decisions based solely on the demands of the task and 'merits of the case', he cannot root out the cultural conviction that his *relationship* to the individual under consideration is the single most important factor in his decision. This conflict between the rational criteria of specific tasks and institutional goals rooted in western societal values, and his own deeply held belief (however ambivalent) in the importance of honouring family and *jati* bonds is typical among highly educated and prominently employed Indians. And among the vast majority of tradition-minded countrymen—whether it be a *bania* bending the law to facilitate the business transaction of a fellow *jati* member, or a *marwari* industrialist employing an insufficiently qualified but distantly related job applicant as a manager, or the clerk accepting bribes in order to put an orphaned niece through school—dishonesty, nepotism and corruption as they are understood in the West are merely abstract concepts. These negative constructions are irrelevant to Indian psycho-social experience, which, from childhood on, nurtures one standard of responsible adult action, and one only, namely, an individual's lifelong obligation to his kith and kin. Allegiance to impersonal institutions and abstract moral concepts is without precedent in individual developmental experience, an adventitious growth in the Indian inner world. Guilt and its attendant inner anxiety are aroused only when individual actions go against the principle of the primacy of relationships, not when foreign ethical standards of justice and efficiency are breached.

In summary, the psycho-social world encountered by Indian children as they reach the 'age of accountability' is governed by the principle of the inviolable primacy of family, and secondarily *jati*, relationships. This 'widening world of childhood'[18] employs religious tradition, ritual, family ceremony, social sanction and psychological pressure to shore up family and caste relationships against outsiders, and against the future. From the beginning, participation and acceptance in this world entail strict observance of a traditionally elaborated hierarchical social order and the subordination of individual preferences and ambitions to the welfare of the extended family and *jati* communities.

The Second Birth

In a psycho-social sense, the world of Indian childhood widens suddenly from the intimate cocoon of maternal protection to the unfamiliar masculine network woven by the demands and tensions, the comings and goings, of the men of the family. This 'entry into society' occurs in the fourth or fifth year of a child's life; for the male child especially, the abruptness of the separation from his mother and the virtual reversal of everything that is expected of him may have traumatic developmental consequences.

As in other societies, it is at this advanced stage of early childhood in India that cultural expectations of boys and girls begin to diverge although in psycho-dynamic terms, as we have seen, the configuration of maternal identity tends to produce a more intense, provocative mothering of male infants than of females. The Indian daughter, insulated from the full force of this maternal ambivalence, is not severed at the age of four or five from the company of her mother and the other women in the household, although like her brothers, she is given new, 'grown up' household tasks and responsibilities. But unlike her brothers, she continues to be cared for by her mother, albeit more casually than before, as she gradually learns to be like her mother by taking care of herself as well as the other younger children in the family. The rest of this chapter will attend almost exclusively to issues of masculine identity in India, for in the quintessential patriarchal world of traditional Hindu culture, the substance of girlhood is left to the private variations of individual relationships whereas the full weight of the prescriptive norms and traditional expectations falls fatefully on Indian boys.

Thus, it is the son who experiences the shock—and it is that, as countless vivid screen memories of events during this period of life attest—of maternal separation and entry into the man's world. Even more than the suddenness of the transition, the *contrast* between an earlier, more or less unchecked benevolent indulgence and the new inflexible standards of absolute obedience and conformity to familial and social standards is its striking feature. As an anthropological account of a Hyderabad village describes the male child's second birth: 'The liberty that he was allowed during his early childhood is increasingly curtailed. Now the accent is on good behaviour and regular habits. The child is more frequently spanked for being troublesome . . . As he grows older the discipline becomes more and more difficult. At first he was punished for being "troublesome" or for "crying without reason" but now he has to distinguish clearly between things to be done and things not to be done.'[19] And a north Indian proverb, addressed to men, pithily conveys what the boy has to now face: 'Treat a son like a *raja* for the first five years, like a slave for the next ten and like a friend thereafter.'

Whereas until this time, the male child is enveloped in, and often overpowered by, his mother's protective nurturing and love—a love abundantly lavished (and ideally unconditional)—whatever approval or appreciation he can hope to receive from the men in the family who now take responsibility for his care and instruction is much more qualified. Relationships become more businesslike, and affection is a token in each transaction. It is conditional upon the boy's behaviour, something he has to earn by learning the formalities of correct relationships with each member of the family according to his or her rank and status, and by conforming to the norms of family and caste behaviour. Without any preparation for the transition, the boy is literally banished from the gently teasing, admiring society of women into a relatively stern and unfeeling male world full of rules and responsibilities in which he cannot be quite so cocky. Little wonder that this transition, his 'second birth', is associated with intense bewilderment, uprootedness and misunderstanding.

This critical shift takes place, of course, in a psycho-social dimension; it is one of the emotional frontiers of the inner world of experience. In so far as the daily logistics of eating, playing, sleeping and taking care of himself are concerned, the four- or five-year-old Indian boy retains for a while longer the leeway to be with his sisters and to seek out his mother. Although he must spend even more time in the exclusive company of boys and men, going back to his mother less and less for reassurance, he begins to learn to dilute his need for emotional support and succouring and to turn for these things now to one of his grandparents perhaps, or to an uncle or aunt. This process of intimacy diffusion, the replacement of the exclusive nurturing attachment to the mother with a variety of less intense relationships with any number of others in the extended family circle, marks this stage of masculine personality development in India.

In spite of these 'extra-maternal' sources of comfort and guidance provided by the very structure of the extended family, psychoanalytically speaking, the Indian boy's loss of the relationship of symbiotic intimacy with his mother amounts to a narcissistic injury of the first magnitude. The consequences of the 'second birth' in the identity development of Indian men are several: a heightened narcissistic vulnerability, an unconscious tendency to 'submit' to an idealized omnipotent figure, both in the inner world of fantasy and in the outside world of making a living; the lifelong search for someone, a charismatic leader or a *guru*, who will provide mentorship and a guiding world-view, thereby restoring intimacy and authority to individual life. To understand these we must take a brief theoretical excursion into the problem of narcissism, as it has been clarified in the writings of Heinz Kohut.[20]

The primary narcissism of the human infant, that sense of original perfection and exclusive instinctual investment in the self, a state of being in which the whole world, including other people, is experienced as a part of the self and within one's spontaneous control, is a brief, transitory but fateful experience in human development. The inevitable limitations of maternal attention together with cognitive changes in infant development bring this stage of primary narcissism to a necessary conclusion. Yet the intensity plus the brevity of this original experience of narcissistic omnipotence serves as a powerful emotional magnet throughout life's developmental vicissitudes, pulling the individual back to beginnings and down into the unconscious in moments of confusion or panic. In his unconscious attempts to regain the lost paradise of narcissistic equilibrium, the child, according to Kohut, creates two narcissistic configurations, the *grandiose self* and the *idealized parental imago*. The grandiose self, with its central conviction, 'I am perfect', contributes, Kohut declares, to a 'broad spectrum of phenomena, ranging from the child's solipsistic world-view and his undisguised pleasure in being admired, and from the gross delusions of the paranoiac and the crudely sexual acts of the adult pervert, to aspects of the mildest, most aim-inhibited, and non-erotic satisfaction of adults with themselves, their functioning and their · achievement.'[21] The idealized parental imago is based in the conviction, 'You are perfect, but I am a part of you.' In the emotional imagery of this configuration, the omnipotence and perfection are now attributed to an idealized parental figure who is experienced as a part of the self, the so-called 'self-object' (to be distinguished from another person who is clearly perceived as separate from the self).

When psychological development proceeds soundly, both configurations gradually lose their power, become attenuated and are integrated into the personality. The grandiose self sheds its archaic characteristics and becomes the source of the instinctual energy that fuels the adult's ego-syntonic ambitions and activities, as well as the all-important 'mature' and realistic forms of self-esteem, while the idealized parental imago becomes part of the superego, consolidating an individual's guiding ideals and ethical sensibility. Massive narcissistic injury such as an abrupt separation from the mother or traumatic disappointment in the adults who count during the early, dependent stages of individual development can, however, thwart the integration of these narcissistic configurations into the 'mature' psychic structure. Thus, as a consequence of a narcissistic injury the grandiose self may continue 'at large' in the psyche, following its archaic aims and generating such narcissistic personality disturbances as a solipsistic clamour for attention, exhibitionism, hypochondria, or in the extreme of psychosis, a cold paranoid grandiosity. Similarly, when an individual is traumatically let down by one or both parents during the oedipal period of childhood, the developmental process of idealization of the superego—that is, the internalization of the parents' loving, approving aspects that give the psyche its positive goals and ideals—is disrupted and the idealized parental imago remains unaltered in the psyche as a self-object necessary foɩ providing the longed-for narcissistic nourishment. Here, personality disturbance may manifest itself in a compelling need for merger with powerful authority figures or in incoherent mystical feelings divorced from the transcendent experience or tradition of mature religiosity, while in psychosis the reactivation of the archaic parental imago may lead to delusions of the powerful persecutor, the omniscient mind reader or disembodied voices whose commands must be obeyed.

I would contend that among Indian men the process of integrating these archaic narcissistic configurations developmentally is rarely accomplished in the sense that it is among men in the West. This does not mean that Indians are narcissistic while westerners are not. Adapting one of Freud's metaphors, we might say that westerners have fewer 'troops of occupation' remaining at the home base of archaic narcissism, the bulk of the army having marched on—although under great stress they too may retreat. In contrast, Indians tend to maintain more troops at the narcissistic position, with the advance platoons poised to rejoin them whenever threatened or provoked.

The abrupt severance of the four- or five-year-old boy from the intimate company of a single paramount 'other' partly explains the narcissistic vulnerability of the male psyche in India. This second birth is as unpremeditated in the child as the first, and as traumatic; as such, it tends to foster both regression to an earlier 'happier' era and a tendency to consolidate one's identification with the mother in order to compensate for her loss. But we must anchor this hypothesis in a clear and complete picture of the Indian boy's developmental experience in the first three to four years of his life. In spite of the emotional 'riches' that a long and intense reciprocity with the mother may store up in the individual's inner world, this same intense exclusivity tends to hinder the growth of the son's autonomy, thereby leaving the psychic structure relatively undifferentiated, the boundaries of the self vague, and the inner convictions—'I am perfect' and 'You are perfect but I am a part of you'—more or less uncompromised in their primitive emotional orginality.

The ambiguous role of the father in Indian childhood is yet another factor that contributes to the narcissistic vulnerability of Indian men. For the narcissistic injury inherent in the abrupt dissolution of the mother–son bond can be tempered through the reinforcement provided by the boy's identification with his father. A father, as both Erikson and Fromn have emphasized, is not only the counterplayer of little Oedipus but the guardian and sponsor of the boy's separation from his mother at a time when his courage for such an autonomous existence is brand new. Indeed, 'the affirmation of the [father's] guiding voice is a prime element in a man's sense of identity.'[22] Given the intensity and ambivalence of the mother–son connection in the Indian setting, the need for the father's physical touch and his guiding voice becomes even more pressing, the necessity of oedipal alliance often outweighing the hostility of the Oedipus complex.

The guiding voice can become effective and the son's identification with his father can take place only if the father allows his son emotional access to him—that is, if he allows himself to be idealized at the same time that he encourages and supports the boy's own efforts to grow up. The generative responsibility of a father is not to withdraw from his son to a plane of aloof perfection or preoccupied authority, but to let the boy gradually detect his limitations as a father and as a man so that the child's identification becomes gently diluted into a developmentally cogent masculine identification with a *realistic* image of his father. Identification is a process, however; it requires that over the years the father be constantly available to his son in a psycho-social sense, a criterion fundamentally at odds with the rationale and structure of the Indian extended family. For the strength and cohesion of the extended family depend upon a certain psycho-social diffusion; it is essential that nuclear cells do not build up within the family, or at the very least, that these cells do not involve intense emotional loyalties that potentially exclude other family members and their interests. Thus, the principles of Indian family life demand that a father be restrained in the presence of his own son and divide his interest and support equally among his own and his brothers' sons. The culturally prescribed pattern of restraint between fathers and sons is widespread in India, sufficiently so to constitute a societal norm.[23] In autobiographical accounts, fathers, whether strict or indulgent, cold or affectionate, are invariably distant.

Behind the requisite façade of aloofness and impartiality, an Indian father may be struggling to express his love for his son. Fatherly love is no less strong in India than in other societies. Yet the fact remains that the son, suddenly bereft of the 'good' mother and needing a firm masculine model with whom to identify as a means of freedom from the 'bad' one, is exposed to bewildering contradictory messages of simultaneous love and restraint, emanating from his father's behaviour. He does not have that necessary conviction that his father is a dependable 'constant' to learn from, be loved by and emulate. In short, the Hindu son lacks the affirmation of that one guiding masculine voice, as it becomes diffused among many. To be sure, autobiographical accounts depict the Indian father as a sensitive man of love and charged with feelings for his sons, for he too grew up with similar needs and longings. Thus in *Autobiography of a Yogi*, Yogananda describes meeting his father after a long separation, 'Father embraced me warmly as I entered our Gurupur Road home. "You have come," he said tenderly. Two large tears dropped from his eyes. Outwardly undemonstrative, he had never before shown me these external signs of affection. Outwardly the grave father, inwardly he possessed the melting heart of a mother.'[24] And Gandhi has given us a moving account of asking his father's forgiveness for an adolescent transgression: 'I was trembling when I handed the confession to my father . . . He read it through, and pearl-drops trickled down his wet cheeks, wetting the paper. For a moment he closed his eyes in thought and then tore up the note. He had sat up to read it. He again lay down. I also cried. Those pearl-drops of love cleansed my heart, and washed my sin away. Only he who has experienced such love can know what it is . . . This sort of sublime forgiveness was not natural to my father. I had thought that he would be angry, say hard things, and strike his forehead. But he was so wonderfully peaceful.'[25]

Such public testimony to the father who is kind and affectionate *inside* belies the psycho-social distance and formal, often perfunctory daily social contact between sons and fathers in India. Psychotherapy and counselling often uncover a long-buried resentment against the father who somehow failed his son by not having been 'there' enough, by not having been a tangible solid presence to lean on, take hold of, and measure oneself against in order to stabilize and strengthen one's own psychic structure and masculine identity. The unconscious anger of sons against good but 'intangible' fathers, whose individual paternity is muffled in the impartiality required by the extended family, is one of the major themes in Hindu personality. Thus, the fact that almost eighty per cent of the adolescent Indian boys who were given the Thematic Apperception Test in a recent study[26] saw in the covered figure lying on the bed the father who is ill, dead or recovering from illness, not only reflects unconscious oedipal hostility in its narrow sense but also constitutes an expression of the boy's resentful anger against the father whose presence was a childhood blur.

I have tried to identify three culturally influenced psycho-social constellations that emphasize the narcissistic vulnerability and emotional self-absorption of the masculine psyche in India: first, the length and symbiotic nature of the mother–son relationship; second, the rupture of this connection at the age of four or five and the radical alteration of the child's 'life style'; and third, the little boy's disappointment when he perceives his father as more of an onlooker than an ally in his boyish struggle to cope with his new life-circumstances.

Ontogeny of homo hierarchicus

The significance of narcissistic vulnerability in the personality development of Indian men, its role in the aetiology of neurosis in the Indian setting,[27] and its cultural elaboration in rituals like the worship of the Shiva *linga* comprise but one of the psycho-social consequences of the second birth. The consolidation of the *homo hierarchicus* element in Indian identity is another vital feature stemming from the second birth. The two main psycho-dynamic elements of the *homo hierarchicus* identity—an accentuation of the homo-erotic impulse, especially in its passive form, and a relatively weak differentiation and idealization of the superego—are the emotional glue that has cemented the hierarchical principle securely in Indian social institutions. We must unearth and examine the childhood roots of both these constellations if we are to appreciate Indian patterns of authority and the emotional hold exercised by certain kinds of authority figures.

We have noted that the emissary of the culture demanding that the Indian boy relinquish his intimate status with his mother is not just the father but the whole assembly of elder males in the family. The boy's confusion and rage at being separated from his mother, all the more conflicted because it has been delayed, coincides with the oedipal stage in psycho-sexual development. But his fury is not directed towards his father alone; it is diffused against all the male authority figures who are collectively responsible for taking his mother away. It makes sense, symbolically, that in Indian mythology, Ravana, the abductor of the 'good mother', Sita, has not one but ten heads. Because it is diluted and diverted to include other elder males, oedipal aggression against the father, in its 'classical' intensity, on the whole, is not common in India. This varies, of course, from region to region and among different social groups.[28] In communities who emphasize manliness in its *machismo* elaboration and keep their women in the seclusion of purdah—for example, the Rajputs—and who thus exact from their sons a dramatic and total renunciation of the feminine world of mothers and sisters and aunts, the 'oedipal' dimension of boyish rage against the father and other males tends to be more pronounced than in communities where the second birth is a more relaxed or gradual process. Irrespective of the variable intensity of the oedipal conflict in different communities, the 'impacted' identification of the Indian son with his mother leads to a modal resolution of the conflict that differs from the western model. In the West, the oedipal conflict is usually resolved as the boy's aggressive stance towards his rival/father triggers anxiety that is in turn reduced by identification with the father. In India, however, carrying the weight of a strong pre-oedipal feminine identification and lacking a vivid, partisan father with whom to identify, the boy is more likely to adopt a position of 'non-partisan' feminine submission towards all elder men in the family. The son exchanges his active phallic initiative for an 'apprentice complex', as Fenichel called it,[29] in which he takes a passive-receptive stance towards male authority that one day will enable him to become a man in his own turn. In the sexualized imagery of the child, he is open to the phallus with its promise of masculine potency.

This resolution of the oedipal conflict by means of a submissive, apprentice-like stance towards elder men in the family leaves a psycho-sexual residue in the unconscious that influences the rest of a boy's life; in the identity development of Indian men, this has generated a passive-receptive attitude towards authority figures of all kinds. The psycho-dynamic contours of this traditional and nearly ubiquitous stance towards authority become markedly plain in situations that reactivate the childhood conflict. Thus, for example, whereas in the West the unconscious passive homosexual temptations of patients that emerge at certain stages of psycho-analytic therapy invariably provoke intense anxiety, analogous fantasies and dreams among Indian patients have a relatively easier, less anxious access to consciousness. The imagery conveyed in clinical terms like 'passive homosexual' or 'feminine submission' is vividly sexual—as the inner life of the child, the patient, the dreamer, bears witness. Yet I do not mean to emphasize the sexual dimension of these terms so much as their connection with the vicissitudes of aggression, with the conflict between dominance and submission.

The erect penis and the offer of the anus among human males, as among many other primates, are symbolic of an attempt to establish a hierarchical order in their relationships. The fantasy among Indian patients of anal assault by an authority figure reflects not so much the occult pleasure and guilt of anal erotism as it does the (relatively unconflicted) acceptance of the dominance of 'those in authority' and the wish to incorporate some of their power into oneself. The high frequency among adolescent boys and young men in India of swear-words with the general tenor, 'fuck you in the anus', is another index of the common masculine preoccupation with hierarchical status; that is, this usage reflects the fierce struggle to ascertain who is superior to whom in ambiguous social situations unclarified by the customary guidelines of age or sex, *jati* affiliation or position in the family.

The conflicts generated by the second birth and the modal Hindu resolution of the Oedipus complex also lead to a relatively weaker differentiation and idealization of the Indian superego. By this I mean that the categorical conscience, as a representative of the rights and wrongs, the prescriptions and prohibitions of Indian *dharma*, does not exist as a psychic structure sharply differentiated from the id and the ego, nor are its parts 'idealized' as they tend to be in western cultures. Much of the individual behaviour and adaptation to the environment that in westerners is regulated or coerced by the demands of the superego, is taken care of in Indians by a *communal conscience*. This comprises, from the beginning, not exclusive parental injunctions but family and *jati* norms. In contrast with the western superego, the communal conscience is a social rather than an individual formation: it is not 'inside' the psyche. In other words, instead of having one internal sentinel an Indian relies on many external 'watchmen' to patrol his activities and especially his relationships in all the social hierarchies.

The greater authority of the codes of the communal conscience, as opposed to the internalized rules of the individual superego, creates a situation in which infringements of moral standards become likely in situations 'when no one is looking'. Such situations normally arise when the individual is away from the watchful discipline of his family, *jati* and village groups. Thus, although Indians publicly

10

express a staunch commitment to traditional moral codes, privately, in relation to himself, an individual tends to consider the violation of these codes reprehensible only when it displeases or saddens those elders who are the personal representatives of his communal conscience.

The weaker differentiation of the superego has several important psycho-social consequences. First, Indians generally demonstrate a greater tolerance for the expression of ambivalence and aggression in situations where it is not explicitly forbidden by the communal conscience and hierarchical imperative. Though the social taboos on the expression of overt hostility are indeed strong, they are not matched by complementary superego controls. When these taboos break down or where they do not apply, the 'relaxed' controls permit a volatile aggressiveness which can quickly flare up and as suddenly die down.

A second consequence is the relative lack of tension between the superego and the ego in Indian personality; the inner life of most Indians is not crippled by the constant judgement or the compulsive categorization of fantasies, thoughts and actions into 'good' or 'bad'. There is thus much less pressure and guilt on the ego to appease the superego by means of productive activity and achievement in the outside world. An Indian can sit for hours doing nothing, without an inner voice condemning him as a 'do-nothing'. By contrast, western cultures seem to place a premium on a relatively high level of tension between ego and superego and then to channel the resulting feelings of guilt, shame and inferiority into a high potential for activity.[30] The goals of initiative and achievement so prominent in the western world-image function also as ego-defences designed to reduce psychic stress; this can become a social exploitation of individual dis-ease in which society encourages the individual to replace inner drivenness (after having generated it in the first place) with social, intellectual and economic productivity. Whatever the psychological price in neurosis for some, the adaptive value of this tension is of course considerable.

In addition to the relayed 'management' of aggression and the mutual accommodation of superego and ego, the Indian's bland, unassuming superego has a third consequence: a heightened dependence on external authority figures. The superego, as we know, is not only the prohibitory and punitive agency of the psyche, it also harbours the representations of an individual's ideals and standards.

Indian men tend to search for external figures to provide that approval and leadership not forthcoming from their own insufficiently idealized superegos. Relatively unintegrated into a weak superego, the narcissistic configuration of the *idealized parental imago* operates throughout life with much of its original intensity and many of its archaic aims. This results in a state of affairs in which the individual is perpetually looking for authority figures he can idealize whose 'perfection' and omnipotence he can then adopt as his own. Both these themes, the infinite potence attributed to idealized parental figures and the child's unconscious fantasy of incorporating this potence, are highlighted in the following Shiva myth:

Shiva and Parvati had made love for a thousand years and the gods were deeply worried. Any child born of such an embrace-between Shiva and the Great Mother was bound to be powerful enough to destroy all creation and topple the king of gods, Indra, from his throne. It was thus resolved that this embrace must be interrupted so that Parvati would not bear Shiva's child. Agni, the fire-god, was dispatched to disturb the divine coupling, and appeared in the form of a parrot in Shiva and Parvati's bedchamber. He was recognized by the couple, and Parvati, ashamed of having been observed during intercourse by the fire-god, averted her face. Thereupon Shiva ejaculated into Agni's mouth; his seed was so powerful that it split open the stomach of all the gods and flowed out to form a golden lake. Agni, however, could not bear the intense heat generated by the seed that remained within him and he spat it out into the Ganges. She too was unable to bear its intensity, and therefore placed it on her bank where it burnt as a blazing fire. The wives of sages came and warmed themselves against this fire. The seed entered the women through their buttocks and came out of their stomachs to form the six-headed Skanda, who later became the powerful general of the gods.

This myth has other versions; in one of them, the Ganges cannot bear the potence of Shiva's seed and throws it out in floods on a mountain which turns to gold and where the birth of Skanda takes place. The potence of Shiva's seed and Agni's swallowing it are, however, common to all the versions.[31]

The need to bestow *mana* on our superiors and leaders in order to partake of the *mana* ourselves, an unconscious attempt to restore the narcissistic perfection of infancy, 'You are perfect but I am a part of

you', is of course a universal tendency. In India, this automatic reverence for superiors is a nearly universal psycho-social *fact*. Leaders
at every level of society and politics, but particularly the patriarchal
elders of the extended family and *jati* groups, take on an emotional
salience independent of any realistic evaluation of their performance,
let alone acknowledgement of their all too human being. When it
comes to leadership in the larger social institutions of business and
government in India, charisma plays an unusually significant role.
The search for leaders of purity and authority, and their idealization,
is vividly manifest in the sphere of religion. Hindu spiritual leaders
or gurus, virtually by definition, embody every Indian's traditional
ideals as defined by the concepts of *moksha* and *dharma*. When
contemplating or confronting these holy men, as well as a few
political leaders such as Gandhi and Nehru, Indians are apt to be
overwhelmed by the propensity to idealize and to transmute the
commonplace into the miraculous, as 'objectivity' is swept away in
a flood of reverence. The follower partakes of the guru's 'perfection'
merely by being in his presence, through his *darshan*. Conversations between Yogananda and his guru provide a striking illustration of these emotional dynamics. Yogananda describes their first
meeting:

'O my own, you have come to me!' My guru uttered the words again
and again in Bengali, his voice tremulous with joy. 'How many years
I have waited for you!'
   We entered a oneness of silence; words seemed the rankest super-
fluities. Eloquence flowed in a soundless chant from the heart of
master to disciple. With an antenna of irrefragable insight I sensed
that my guru knew God and would lead me to Him. The obscuration
of this life disappeared in a fragile dawn of prenatal memories.
Dramatic time! Past, present and future are its cycling scenes. This
was not the first sun to find me at these holy feet!
   My hand in his, my guru led me to his temporary residence in the
Rana Mahal section of the city. His athletic figure moved with firm
tread. Tall, erect, about fifty-five at this time, he was active and
vigorous as a young man. His dark eyes were large, beautiful with
plumbless wisdom. Slightly curly hair softened a face of striking
power. Strength mingled subtly with gentleness.
   As we made our way to the stone balcony of a house overlooking
the Ganges, he said affectionately:
   'I shall give you my hermitages and all I possess.'
   'Sir, I come for wisdom and God-realization. Those are your
treasure troves I am after!'
   The swift Indian twilight had dropped its half-curtain before my

master spoke again. His eyes held unfathomable tenderness. 'I give you my unconditional love.'[32]

Later on, the new disciple gratefully accepts the guru's authority in every detail of his life, transferring the responsibility for his life to the divinity in the guru and then: 'A lifelong shadow lifted from my heart; the vague search, hither and yon, was over. I had found eternal shelter in a true guru.'[33]

Together with the search for the guidance of an ideal, ever-present father, the above encounter, socially accepted and culturally encouraged, also reveals the childhood antecedents of such a search. For the feeling-tone of this meeting between Yogananda and his guru is like that of the communion between mother and infant and of the later soothing of disappointments by the 'guru-mother's' love. Normally, the extended family itself (and even the *jati*) attempts to satisfy these unconscious longings. For social structures cannot neglect individual developmental concerns for long without generating unbearable tensions. In the Indian family, the hierarchical ordering of relationships, and their durability, even timelessness, provides some fulfilment of the individual's lifelong need for external authority figures; the maternal mode of family care salvages some of the continuity between the individual's early and later experiences, while the emphasis on the primacy of relationships seeks to counteract the individual's narcissistic orientation and self-absorption which, if unchecked, would seriously undermine social stability and co-operation.

CHAPTER V

Tracings: The Inner World in Culture and History

In the preceding pages, I have tried to identify the central psychological themes in Indian infancy and childhood and to interpret the long shadow they cast on the horizons of individual and cultural consciousness. Fears and anxieties as well as specific psycho-social strengths are rooted in the earliest 'pre-verbal' experiences and connections of life. As individual consciousness and personality are developed and articulated in successive stages of the life cycle, our early experience tends to be covered over, a 'forgotten' subterranean layer in the topography of the inner world. It is this residual dark soil of infantile experience that erupts in our psychopathology, that we mine in our myth-making, and that underlies the strivings and disappointments of everyday life.

In this chapter, I want to explore the traces of this infantile substratum in three different cultural/historical contexts: in two centuries-old religious cults that command the loyalty and devotion of millions of Indians; and in the life and work of one of the early prophets of a modern Indian identity.

Cult and Myths of Krishna

In a country of many religious cults and a variety of gods, Krishna is unquestionably the most popular. Worshipped throughout the subcontinent, among men and women of different castes and sects, among traditional orthodox Hindus as well as among modern 'secular' Indians, Krishna is the focus of Hindu devotionalism.

Krishna is usually portrayed as a blue-complexioned child full of pranks and mischief, or as a youthful cowherd wearing a crown of peacock feathers whose beauty entrances all who see him or hear the irresistible call of his flute. This is his present version. Two thousand years ago, when Krishna first moved into the Hindu pantheon, the god was a more sober and austere deity. In the *Mahabharata*, for instance, he is the wise adult and helpful teacher and counsellor. His nature began to undergo transformation around A.D. 500 in the *Harivamsa* (the genealogy of Hari or Krishna) which stressed Krishna's early years as a wilful, mischievous child and as the youthful, divine lover of the *gopis*, the cowherd girls. The later Krishna texts, *Vishnu Purana, Padma Purana*, and *Brahmavaivarta Purana*, are fascinated by, and focus upon, these aspects of the god: Krishna's freedom and spontaneity as the eternal child, the youth-Krishna's surpassing beauty and the seductive power of his haunting flute which breaks down human resistance to the appeal of the divine lover.[1]

The cult primarily associated with Krishna, with its stress on *bhakti* or devotional activity, has faithfully reflected the change in the nature of the god. Whereas the *bhakti* of *Mahabharata* and *Bhagavad Gita* is staid and pietistic, its devotion channelled through a life of discipline and strict adherence to ethical and social norms, in the medieval *bhakti* cults and down to the present day, *bhakti* is no longer a pale and austere affair but rather emphasizes intoxication and uninhibited response to the dark god, a release from the constraints and precepts of orthodox Hinduism.

Devotional activity, practised in groups composed of male and female devotees together, takes many forms. In festivals, processions, gatherings at temples and homes, the devotees sing, dance, enact the legends of Krishna's childhood and youth, and chant his glories with an emotional fervour radically different from the meditative contemplation and emotional asceticism enjoined by other traditional Indian methods of enhancing spiritual experience. Krishna *bhakti* is a vision of the divine that is free and spontaneous, boisterous and anarchical. As it happens, as I sit writing this late at night in an old section of Bombay, the open-air theatre next door is putting on a Krishna festival to the music of stringed instruments, drums and the voices of several hundred devotees. The festival is a ten-day affair that starts each day at around nine in the evening and continues well into the early hours of the morning. Fervent discourses on Krishna by learned pundits are interspersed with communal singing of songs of praise accompanied by an abandoned, mesmerizing drum beat. The whole effect, 'liturgical' and dramatic, is an intended one, perfected over the centuries to enhance the individual's *bhakti*. For as Krishna himself puts it:

Till the pores of the body do not spill over with joy, till the mind does not dissolve, till tears of bliss do not begin to flow and the mind does not dissolve in a flood of devotion, until then there is no possibility of purification for the devotee. He whose voice breaks with emotion, whose mind has dissolved and flows only in one direction, who does not stop crying for a moment yet sometimes breaks out in loud laughter, who leaving shame bursts into loud song and begins to dance, such a devotee not only purifies himself but the whole world.[2]

This invitation to abandon self-control and self-consciousness perfectly captures the ecstatic nature of the Krishna cult. For Krishna is not one of those father-gods who primarily evoke attitudes of filial reverence in their worshippers. Krishna invites the devotee to fuse with him: he gives permission for joy. In psychological terms, he encourages the individual to identify with an ideal primal self, released from all social and superego constraints. Krishna's promise, like that of Dionysus in ancient Greece, is one of utter freedom and instinctual exhilaration.

The psycho-social meaning of *bhakti* is that it provides for, and actually uses, 'democratic' fantasies in which the inner and outer repressions exacted by life in a rigidly structured and highly stratified social order are lifted. Traditional codes of conduct, and relationships between social groups, between generations, and especially between the sexes, are abrogated in Krishna worship. To illustrate this, I would like to quote passages from an anthropological report of the annual *Holi* festival in a north Indian village. *Holi* is of course an extraordinary celebration, a special ritual event. It does not represent the everyday ritual of Krishna devotees, and it is a vivid counterpoint of their chaste daily life. Or, perhaps, this 'obscene and depraved saturnalia' (as the disapproving British called *Holi*) illuminates Krishna devotion in much the same way that an individual's 'nervous breakdown' sheds light on his 'normal' personality, by revealing latent conflicts and laying bare the fundamental structure of the psyche.

McKim Marriott, the American anthropologist who did fieldwork in a village of Uttar Pradesh, captures *Holi*:

As the moon rose high, I became aware of the sound of racing feet: gangs of young people were howling '*Holi!*' and pursuing each other down the lanes ... Pandemonium now reigned: a shouting mob of boys called on me by name from the street and demanded that I come out. I perceived through a crack, however, that anyone who emerged was being pelted with bucketfuls of mud and cow-dung water. Boys of all ages were heaving dust into the air, hurling old shoes at each other, laughing and cavorting 'like Krishna's cowherd companions' —and of course, cowherds they were.³

As the day of *Holi* advances, the action becomes more frenzied, and at the same time subtly changes as the boundaries between the sexes dissolve. Women become the 'attackers' while the men turn into willing victims: the traditional roles of the one who pursues and the one who endures (and invites) pursuit are over-turned in that cathartic exuberance that often accompanies the breakdown of exaggerated repressive conventions: in this case, rigid sex-role differentiation:

As I stepped into the lane, the wife of the barber in the house opposite, a lady who had hitherto been most quiet and deferential, also stepped forth, grinning under her veil, and doused me with a pail of urine from her buffalo . . . I witnessed several hysterical battles, women rushing out of their houses in squads to attack me and other men with stout canes, while each man defended himself only by pivoting about his own staff, planted on the ground, or, like me, by running for cover . . .⁴

Moreover, the aggression inevitably pent up in an inner world whose social boundaries are defined by the intransigent hierarchical systems of caste and family finds some release in this 'festival of love':

Who were those smiling men whose shins were most mercilessly beaten by the women? They were the wealthier Brahman and Jat farmers of the village, and the beaters were those ardent local Radhas, the 'wives of the village', figuring by both the real and the fictional inter-caste system of kinship . . . The boldest beaters in this veiled battalion were often in fact the wives of the farmers' low-caste field labourers, artisans or menials—the concubines and kitchen help of the victims . . . Six Brahman men in their fifties, pillars of village society, limped past in panting flight from the quarter staff wielded by a massive young Bhangin, sweeper of their latrines . . .⁵

Nor do erotic impulses languish during the celebration of *Holi*, although the expression of eroticism is not always sexual in the sense of adult genital intercourse. Rather, the 'erotic' activity of *Holi* suggests the sexuality of the very young child. Obscene words and gestures, the smearing of loved ones with urine and dung, the throwing of mud, are as characteristic of the *Holi* festival as furtive, impetuous adultery. The ritual *Holi* dance in the Bundelkhand and Vraja areas of northern India in which two men respectively take the parts of a prostitute and an ascetic equipped with (what else!) a short crooked staff or horn, is harmless compared to many others shocking to even the most flamboyant imagination. In this particular village, 'There was one great throng of villagers watching an uplifted male dancer with padded crotch writhe in solitary states of fevered passion and then onanism; then join in a remote *pas de deux* with a veiled female impersonator in a parody of pederasty, and finally in telepathic copulating—all this to a frenzied accompaniment of many drums.'⁶

The *Holi* festival, then, with its exuberant polymorphous sexuality and insubordinate aggression momentarily obliterating all the established hierarchies of age, sex, caste and class, is an idealization and elevation of instinctuality and an apt celebration of Krishna who, of all the Hindu gods, is accorded the greatest permission for instinctual indulgence. To a psychologist who must necessarily forsake the mystical explanations of legends describing Krishna's sixteen thousand wives, his unrestrained amorous dalliance with the village *gopis*, his voracious childhood hunger for milk, butter and curds and his completely amoral attitude towards stealing them, as well as his general inability to bear any kind of frustration, Krishna is all impulse and appetite, a highly narcissistic being who incidentally benefits mankind while pursuing his own libidinous desires.⁷ The cult of Krishna affords his devotees all manner of fantasied instinctual gratification through an unconscious identification with him.

The popularity of the Krishna cult has not only a psychological but also a social rationale—namely, its promise of salvation to the dispossessed classes. By rejecting the conventional Hindu axiom that a person's birth, social status and caste membership govern his chances of reaching *moksha*, the Krishna cult actively welcomes and even recruits the participation of oppressed castes and classes in its devotions and ceremonies, an utterly unorthodox state of affairs. The sole criterion of merit in Krishna worship is the extent and intensity of devotion. As Krishna says in the *Bhagavata Purana*, the closest Indian equivalent to the New Testament, 'The practice of yoga, knowledge and science, living in *dharma*, prayer or ascetic renunciation are none of them as successful in obtaining me [the godhead] as is the daily increase in loving devotion',⁸ and, more specifically, 'I believe that even a Brahmin equipped with twelve qualities [wealth, family status, knowledge, yoga, intellect, etc.] who has turned his face away from the lotus feet of god [Krishna] is inferior to the *chandala* [outcaste] who has laid his mind, speech, work, wealth and life at god's feet; that *chandala* saves his whole family while the Brahmin, arrogant of his station, cannot even save himself.'⁹

Numerous other passages in the *Bhagavata Purana* are critical of the arrogance of high castes, and historically the Krishna cult has always drawn its support from the social and economic groups that were 'despised by the rest of society, but their poverty and distress made them naturally sympathetic to a devotional religion based on faith and simplicity'.¹⁰ Although its appeal to the oppressed classes would be seen as a particularly sinister form of opium by most Marxists, many other modern Hindus sympathize with a religion that implicitly rejects the traditional interpretation of *karma* in that it views members of socially and economically disadvantaged groups compassionately rather than as erstwhile sinners getting their just desserts. In any case, the democratic practices of the Krishna cult set it apart from other forms of Hinduism in which many holy men who preach other-worldly values seem to accept only the rich and the powerful into their company or their *ashramas* as favoured devotees, and rationalize the favour they show to the chosen few in terms of the workings of the impersonal *karma* principle.

Whereas I have so far explained the popularity of the Krishna cult in terms of its promise to release both the repressed instincts and the oppressed classes, a consideration of the *myths* surrounding Krishna's childhood leads us back to the world of psychological experience as it is magnified in cultural imagery, for the Krishna myths highlight the main themes in Indian inner life. Filtered through the decorous symbolism of art and folk-tale, these myths present modal psychic conflicts and their fantasied resolutions in a socially congenial form. As Jacob Arlow has pointed out, whereas an individual's dreams are meant to be forgotten after they have performed their nightly task of relieving instinctual pressure, myths are designed to be remembered and repeated in order that the sharing of unconscious fantasies may confirm and consolidate the mutual identification of members of the society to whom the myths appeal.¹¹ In myths, the terrific wishes and impulses of unconscious fantasy are defused by the very fact of the fantasy's becoming collectively shared rather than remaining an individual burden, and by the simple device of its being externalized and projected onto mythical heroes and heroines.

In the Indian family, as we have emphasized, the male child's early experience diverges significantly from his sister's. So too, we find, do the myths of a single god such as Krishna, who is equally popular with both men and women, diverge; there are 'masculine' and 'feminine' Krishna legends. In spite of certain elementary features in common, all Krishna myths do not serve equally as a projective vehicle for the unconscious fantasy of both men and women. Whereas the cult in its rituals and festivals extends a promise of freedom and parity, both social and sexual, to both men and women, and indeed often has an even stronger appeal for women given the confined and constrained life that is their lot, the mythology surrounding a truly universal god must also appeal to both sexes. The enduring claim of the god Krishna to the devotional love of both sexes reflects in part the fact that, unlike others in the Hindu pantheon, Krishna enjoys a more explicit 'dual mythology'. In addition to the legends that elaborate the inner world of Indian men, the god of love is surrounded by lore that evokes, and responds to, the longings of Hindu women. This differentiation of 'masculine' and 'feminine' myths about a single god-hero is rarely made in psychological analyses, embedded as they are in a venerable patriarchal tradition of myth-interpretation that simply ignores women in such undertakings. The Krishna myths, however, show both faces; the myths of Putana, Kaliyanag, Agasur and the lifting of Mount Govardhan are predominantly masculine in their orientation and appeal, while the Krishna–Yasoda and Krishna–Radha legends seem to be primarily, though not exclusively addressed to women.

Krishna, the reincarnation of Vishnu, the Preserver of the Hindu trinity, is said to have been born to rid the earth of the tyranny and oppression of King Kamsa. According to legend, Kamsa, informed of the prophecy that the eighth child of his uncle's daughter would one day slay him, confined his cousin and her husband in a prison and killed all their offspring as soon as they were born. But Krishna, the eighth child, was smuggled out of the prison and taken to live with foster parents in another part of the kingdom. Kamsa, learning of the infant Krishna's escape and yet ignorant of his exact whereabouts, instructed the demoness Putana to kill all the boys born in the kingdom during the month in which his cousin had expected the birth of her child. Putana went around the kingdom, obediently carrying out her master's orders. Transformed into a beautiful woman, with a deadly poison smeared on her nipples, she finally came to the house where Krishna lived in the remote region of

Gokula. Pretending an upsurge of maternal love and relief that she had at last found him, she took Krishna from his foster mother and gave him her poisoned breast to suckle. Krishna sucked so hard that he not only drank all the milk Putana had to give, he also sucked her life away. The maternal monster swooned, with Krishna's mouth still at her breast, and as she fell dead, she resumed her original hideous form. The legend concludes that Putana nevertheless attained *moksha* since she had acted as a mother, albeit a malevolent one, to the infant-god.

The Putana myth contains several themes, such as the attempt to kill the infant god, that occur in the mythologies of other civilizations.[12] Krishna's suckling feat has a parallel in the ancient Greek account of Heracles sucking so hard at Hera's breast that she throws him off in agony, the milk spurting out of Heracles' mouth to form the Milky Way.[13] Yet the psychologically critical thematic items in the Putana myth that are perhaps unique to Hindu culture are the poisoned breast, the fight for survival between the malevolent mother and the voracious infant, and the capital punishment and subsequent redemption of the 'bad mother'.

The secret fantasy of poisoned milk, of nourishment that kills, originates early in life when the separation between child and mother begins.[14] The elevation of this fantasy, which is occasionally encountered clinically, to the status of myth for a whole culture indicates the intensity of inner conflict associated with this separation in the Indian setting. On the one hand, the poisoned breast symbolizes the child's loss of the familiar protection and nurturing of his mother, an experience of 'overall loss' and alienation intensified by the physical fact of the final weaning that may take place as late as the third or fourth year of a child's life, thus coinciding with the 'second birth'. If this coincidence is attended by the birth of a new baby, the psychological injury is likely to be compound. The 'favoured son' finds himself a small, awkward involuntary novice subjected to a peculiar form of exile among the older boys and grown men of his own family. His emotional hunger for the milk of love, which but lately flowed in abundance, can become physically unbearable. His (confused) rage is necessarily projected outward onto the mother who is thus transformed in fantasy into a hostile and threatening figure, while the boy's own voracious need is also projected onto the 'oral image' of the devouring mother. This archaic mechanism of projection—'It is not I who wants to kill my mother for frustrating me, but she who wants to destroy me for my ravenous need for her'—is part of the unconscious fantasy that 'feeds' the symbol of the poisoned breast. The child's need to repair the severance and restore the nurturing is, however, only one aspect of the conflict between his need for his mother and his anger at her. For he is also subject to a biologically-rooted developmental push towards becoming an independent and 'individuated' person, separate from his mother. Putana's poisoned breast thus symbolizes the Indian boy's critical psycho-social dilemma: how to receive nurturing without being poisoned by it, how to enjoy his mother's love and support without crippling his own budding individuality. This universal developmental dilemma is aggravated in the Indian setting (it creates an insoluble conflict for some Hindu men) because of the profound, often unconscious reluctance of the Hindu mother to 'release' the male child, to let him go in an emotional sense, for as we have seen, he is the psycho-social guarantor of her own identity.

In this regard, the fantasy of poisoned milk or poisoned breast resembles the 'double bind' in certain cases of schizophrenia in which the mother is perceived by the child to have given a contaminated love.[15]That is, unconditional maternal love and empathy, responsive to the child's needs, are missing; the price of the mother's nurturing being that the child remain an extension of her person and a fulfiller of *her* needs. The legendary Putana thus represents the dangerous 'schizophrenagenic' mother who has her son in an emotional clinch in which neither can let go; the mother wields the weapons of 'love', maternal solicitude and self-sacrifice, with an unconscious virtuosity that keeps the son in ambivalent emotional thralldom. Yet we must remember that although the imagery of the poisoned breast reflects the dark side of the legacy of the prolonged, intense mother–son relationship in India, this same relationship is decisive in rooting Hindu personality in the rich soil of trust and devotion and sensual care. After all, Krishna not only survives, he positively thrives.

The Putana myth underplays the sexually threatening aspect of the 'bad mother' discussed in Chapter III. Although secondary to the theme of poisoned maternal love, the theme of maternal sexuality and its impossible aims is by no means absent. For we need not subscribe to the view that the killing of maternal monsters is always a disguised form of incestuous intercourse[16]to recognize that Krishna's avid fastening of his mouth to Putana's nipple, not releasing it till Putana falls down lifeless, is an act of oral sexual violence that combines both the infant's excitement and his anger. This image may be construed as a fantasied fulfilment of the mother's sexual demands and at the same time a grim revenge on her for making such demands at all.

Those who would reject this interpretation as a far-fetched 'wish fulfilment' concocted by a psycho-analytic interpreter irreverently predisposed to locate sexuality everywhere will no doubt be taken aback by the following rendition of the Putana legend by Kanhaiyalal Munshi, a devout Hindu writer on philosophical and religious themes who cannot even remotely be suspected of conscious awareness of the sexual content of the suckling scene:

She (Putana) found her heart bounding in joy. In a transport of ecstasy, she hugged Krishna again. Her repressed maternal instinct burst out, as if it was a roaring flood. And she felt that her skin had become wet. Milk—in that moment of sudden transport—had oozed out of her generous breasts. Her bodice was drenched.

Her body and mind and soul were now craving for this child. Wild ill-assorted thoughts ran beneath her transport. She must take this lovely boy to her breasts . . .

The insistent promptings of her heart were: 'Take this lovely boy to your breast. You are a wicked, miserable woman. You have never seen joy before, joy which thrills your whole body and mind with mad delight. This is your moment—the moment for which your life and the lives of your husband and children can be staked. Take this boy to your breast!' Putana had no command over herself. Torn by ecstatic longing for the boy and forgetful of the poison which she had applied to her breasts, she took Krishna on her lap. He struggled to wriggle out, laughing all the time. She lost control of herself . . .

She felt as if her mind was stopping. Was she swooning with delight? Yes, all she wanted was that Krishna, Yashoda's boy, should suck this milk, her life, her hope and her all, if he so chose. 'Yes, I give you all, my beloved child.' The thought flashed across her mind: 'I am yours.'[17]

Krishna's destruction of Putana and her subsequent redemption as a 'purified' being, represents one solution of the son's conflict. By killing the 'bad' mother in fantasy, the son obliterates the overweening and sexually ravenous maternal imagos in his psyche and leaves the benign, protective one intact. This is the only way he can survive as an individual, for libidinal as well as aggressive energy must be ransomed before he can engage in adolescent or adult relationships of intimacy; the 'bad mother' must die in order that the son's capacity for individuation and for sexualizing (and loving) others, may emerge. In the Putana myth, this emptying of the 'bad' mother of her life-giving sensuality and sexual vitality, as well as the necessary establishment of boundaries between her and her son, is condensed into a single, pungent image. As Putana falls down lifeless, her hideous demonic body suddenly begins to emit a pleasing perfume, the exciting smells that infuse the maternal embrace, the odour of her skin and sweat, the smell of milk around her nipple are neutralized, transformed, and rendered benign.

The myths of Agasur and Kaliyanag are variations on one or the other of the themes in the Putana myth. The monster Agasur lies in wait, its huge mouth open and ready to swallow the child Krishna and his friends as they innocently walk into its mouth; Krishna kills Agasur by bursting out of its throat. The gaping-jawed monster of the legend is a symbolic projection of the child's own hunger for sustenance while its murder presents the elimination of these intense infantile needs, the end of orality.

The myth of the serpent Kaliyanag is a more 'developed' version of this fantasy, in the sense that here the passions projected onto the 'bad mother' are not annihilated but appear capable of being tamed and controlled. Like all serpent myths,[18] the myth of Kaliyanag of the poisonous pool lends itself to interpretation at many different levels. The story goes that Kaliyanag, the king of the cobras, lived with his wives and brood in a pool of water so poisoned that anyone drinking it immediately fell dead. The child Krishna dived into the poisoned pool, and swimming towards the serpent, lassoed its hood with a rope. The serpent put up a furious struggle but was finally subdued. As Krishna triumphantly dragged the serpent out onto the shore, he was followed by the king cobra's wives and children who pleaded with the child-god to spare the life of their husband and father. Krishna explained that he did not wish to kill Kaliyanag but simply to subdue him and cleanse the pool of his poison.

In this myth, Krishna represents the Hindu ideal of the strong ego, one that must struggle with instinctual drives in order to contain and transform them rather than make futile attempts to destroy and deny them. One must, the legend seems to say, dive into the unconscious pool of instinctuality and confront its awesome nature, an instruction from the ancestors reminiscent of the yogic injunction to plumb the depths of the waters of *chitta* in order to know the self. At another level, Kaliyanag represents the mother's passions, or, more accurately, the son's own anxieties and affects triggered by his (conscious and unconscious) perceptions of her, anxieties that must be laid to rest without destroying the life-giving maternal imago in the psyche. The subjugation of the serpent represents a resolution of this dilemma, by means of which the son takes a developmental step forward towards adulthood and 'genitality', relatively free from the 'poisonous' incestuous passions of infancy.

The Putana, Agasur and Kaliyanag myths may be seen as a cultural elaboration of 'pre-genital' fantasy. That is, these myths incorporate collective infantile wishes and anxieties common and paramount during the first two or three years of the infant's life. By contrast, the lifting up of Mount Govardhan represents the later, oedipal stage of psycho-sexual development when the male world, represented by the father and the other men in the family, first intrudes upon the dyadic intimacy of Hindu son and mother. In this myth, the child Krishna tries to convince the villagers of Vrindavana that their annual rites to placate Indra, the king of the gods, are a shameful act of submission and cowardice, and that they should instead have a festival that celebrates the fields, rivers, trees—mother earth—and that pays homage especially to Gaumata ('Mother-cow'), who is their main source of livelihood and sustenance. With much trepidation and fear of the father-god's wrath, the villagers finally accept Krishna's suggestion. Incensed at this show of disrespect and the turn to the 'mother', Indra lets loose his fury on the hapless cowherds. The sky explodes with thunder and lightning and torrents of rain descend on the village, threatening to wash away the villagers and their livestock. The child Krishna lifts up the mountain Govardhan on his little finger and holds it above the earth as a protective roof till Indra's anger is spent and he becomes reconciled to the new festival.

The Govardhan myth lends itself to a straightforward oedipal interpretation; the male child, although frightened, withstands the veritable thunder and lighting of the father's presumed anger, survives the fantasied threat of being drowned in the huge urethral flood which that giant certainly seems capable of letting loose, and emerges from the contest victorious, ready to retrieve and celebrate intimacy with the mother. There are other corroborative elements that point to the myth's ontogenetic origin in the little boy's proud oedipal fantasies about his newly discovered tumescence, such as the phallic impudence of lifting up a mountain on one's little finger.

11

But once again, in Hindu mythology even oedipal legends close with a characteristic gentle benevolence: neither of the parties to the conflict is blinded, maimed, castrated or killed. Since fathers of Hindu families have never been perceived as terrible avengers, that final, irrevocable act of violence is simply not germane.

The rebellion and dark passions that characterize the myths of Putana, Agasur and Kaliyanag are missing from those Krishna myths that I have called 'feminine'. Some of these legends recount the tricks played by Gopal, the Babe-Krishna, on his foster-mother Yasoda, her anger at his mischief and ultimate forgiveness in an orgy of hugs, kisses and the inevitable 'overflowing of maternal milk'. On one occasion the *gopis* come to complain of Krishna's pranks:

O Yasoda! This boy of yours has become much too mischievous. He sets the calves free even when it's not time to milk the cows. When we scold him, he only laughs out loudly. He not only steals our curds and milk for himself, but feeds them to the monkeys. He breaks our pots. When he does not find anything to eat in our houses he teases our children and makes them cry. Even if we hide our milk pots, he always seems to know the hiding place and when we are busy elsewhere in the household, he comes and steals the milk and curds. Not content with his brazen stealing, he pees all over our freshly swept houses. Look at him standing there, pretending to be such an innocent![19]

But even while the *gopis* complain, they cannot take their eyes off the child's lotus face; they are fascinated by his beauty. A flood of affection and joy rises in Yasoda's heart as she sees their admiration of her son, and she begins to laugh, unable to scold, let alone chastise, the boy.

The rest of the legends, celebrated in centuries of devotional poetry, deal with Shyam, the Youth-Krishna, and his love-play with the *gopis*, especially Radha, his chosen consort, whose love for the youthful god is so great that she flouts parental prohibitions and social disapproval to be together with her god-lover. The love of Radha and Krishna, which has been one of the central features of the cult from the eleventh century A.D. to the present, is celebrated in legends and poems as an idyllic affair beyond the norms of traditional courtship. It is full of playfulness and joy, of mock quarrels and passionate reconciliations in which Radha often takes the initiative. Thus in the following passage from the *Rasikapriya*:

Radha came smilingly to Krishna and sang him a tale of love. She then asked him to explain to her the meaning of some of the sequences in the story: the simultaneous partaking by the lovers of the nectar of each other's mouths, and other parts of the body which in consequence suffered amorous injuries by nails and teeth. Enclosing him in an embrace, she also asked him, on an oath, what mode of embracing the lovers in the tale had adopted. Thus did Radha herself make up her quarrel with her lover today.[20]

In another poem by Kaviranjana, Radha sets aside traditional feminine modesty and takes the active part in their love-making:

Her massive locks are dishevelled. She is the goddess of amorous sports embodied and incarnate. Their passionate love is excessive. So the girl behaves as a man . . . Her vase-shaped breasts are turned upside down, as if the god of love is pouring out the nectar of love. Over them the hands of the dearest [lover] have been placed, as if [a pair of] *chakravakas* are sitting over [a pair of]lotuses. Bangles and bells at her girdle are jingling, as if the band of joy has been struck by the company of the god of love.[21]

One of the central features of the 'feminine' Krishna legends is the infantilization of the god and, implicitly, of the ideal male by Indian women. In striking contrast to the masculine identification with Krishna, Hindu women perceive and experience him primarily as an ideal son—mischievous, irresponsible and intrusive in a delightful, almost thrilling way. At the same time, Krishna's very playfulness reflects the deep sensual comfort and security of the idealized bond of intimacy between Hindu mother and son. In contrast with the ripe sexuality stimulated in fantasy and exaggerated in certain rituals and festivals of his cult (such as *Holi*), Krishna, the god of the legends, is the saviour of women not as an adult male and lustful partner but as the son who is vital to the consolidation and confirmation of a Hindu woman's identity around the core of motherliness. The legends of Youth-Krishna as the lover of Radha do not alter the intensity of the Indian woman's emotional investment in her son but rather serve simply, elegantly, to incorporate the fantasied fulfilment of her sexual desire for him. For we must remember that Radha was years older than Krishna and fell in love with him when she was already at the age of marriage, while he was still only a young boy. Radha–Krishna legends are thus illustrative of the Hindu woman's unconscious fantasy of her son as her lover and the complementary male fantasy, incorporated in Putana and other myths, of the sexually ravenous mother. The masculine and feminine myths of Krishna thus neatly dovetail to highlight the dominant concerns and fantasies of both Hindu men and women.

Shiva and Narcissus

Here I want to focus attention on another provocative player on the stage of the inner world, Shiva, the Destroyer in the Hindu trinity. Psychologically, the ubiquitous cult of Shiva is a cultural phenomenon that strikingly illustrates the narcissistic orientation of Indian men. By narcissism I do not mean a developmental stage, a sexual perversion, or a specific mode of object choice—the different contexts in which the term has been used in early psycho-analytic literature—but a concentration of mental interest on the self with its correlative central problem of maintaining self-esteem; the term itself deriving from the Greek myth of Narcissus who, on seeing his image reflected in a pool of water, fell in love with himself.

Next only to Krishna, Shiva is perhaps the most widely worshipped god in the densely populated Hindu pantheon. Although Shiva's origins have been traced back to the Sumerian and Egyptian civilizations and images and emblems of him and his power have been found in the excavations of Mohenjodaro, Shaivism proper, the creed in which Shiva is the supreme God, first appears in the early hymns of the Rigveda. In these hymns some of the features associated with Shiva, the personification of nature's destructive powers, are depicted in the Vedic deity, Rudra. He is called by the name Shiva (auspicious) in the latter portion of the Veda, as he comes to be represented as the patron of ascetics and described as the great god (*mahadeva*). The distinctive features of his creed—*moksha,* attainable through loving devotion (*bhakti*),and god's grace (*prasad*)—are prominent in certain sections of the *Mahabharata*. Today, the original theism of the Shiva cult is found principally among the Shaivite sects of south India. In other sects, especially in central and eastern India, the original conception has been adulterated by many parochialisms such as the priority of the female goddesses associated with Shiva, the ritual importance of rivers, cremation grounds and the use of drugs.[22]

The Shaivites, who are found mostly among the non-Brahmin peasant castes are estimated to number anywhere from thirty to forty million devotees. They are spread all over India and are especially numerous in the south. In Karnataka, for example, the Lingayats, sometimes called Virasaivas, or strict Shiva devotees, number almost 4.5 million, the single largest caste group.

In popular lithographs, available in the bazars of towns and cities throughout India and decoratively displayed in hundreds of thousands of Indian homes and shops, Shiva is usually shown as a meditating ascetic sitting cross-legged on a platform of craggy rock somewhere deep within the snow-covered vastness of the Himalayas. Garlanded with hissing cobras, his matted locks ornamented with the crescent moon, his loins girdled with a dark antelope or elephant hide: thus he sits, the supreme ascetic and great renunciator, *digambara* or 'sky-clad'.

The worship of Shiva, however, is not focused on a human representation of the god, as it is with other Hindu gods and goddesses, but on his symbol, the *linga*, or phallus. In Banaras, the holy city intimately identified with Shiva worship, a stone or metal phallus dominates the altar of the inner sanctum in innumerable temples. And in towns and villages throughout India, crude phalluses daubed with auspicious red powder stand erect at shrines within a hundred yards of each other, to which devotees bow in passing or pause with eyes and hands folded in a moment of silent homage.*

Phallus worship is of course not unique to the Indian cult of Shiva. Both phallic symbolism and phallus worship, not to mention the 'penis envy' among men jealous of their genital prowess and ever pitting it in fantasy against that of other men, are found in other cultures thoughout history. Whereas the anatomy of the penis allows the alternation of periods of detumescent repose with the potent sensuality of erection, the symbol of the phallus transcends the human limitations of the penis and incorporates the very essence of manhood. As Thorkil Vanggaard puts it, 'For the boy, the phallus represents the grown man's greatness, strength, independence, courage, wisdom, knowledge, mastery of other men and possession of desirable women, potency—and everything else a boy may look up to in men and desire for himself.'[23] Thus, as the boy lives on in the man, men everywhere and of all ages are phallus worshippers, although most societies have not institutionalized this universal male propensity into anything like the phallic cult of Shiva worship.

Our attention is drawn to phallus worship in India not because Hindu culture holds a monopoly on it, but because the intensity of devotion of millions of linga devotees, the formal institutionalization of phallic worship into a vigorous cult, and its legitimacy as one of India's principal forms of spiritual activity all combine to give a

---

*The contradiction between Shiva's two aspects—the ascetism of the god and the eroticism of his symbol—has always puzzled Indologists. We will come back to this contradiction later.

unique cultural stamp and confirmation to a more or less universal masculine psycho-sexual actuality. The symbolic linga of Shiva not only incorporates the little boy's desire and striving for the strength and 'agentic' ability of manhood by identifying with the anatomical reality and functional capacity of the erect male genital, it also serves a defensive function, psycho-analytically speaking, in that an identification with the great phallus is a bulwark against the anxiety triggered by the separation from the mother during the time of the second birth.

Psycho-analytic experience has abundantly demonstrated that a traumatic event in early childhood, such as the Indian boy's second birth, shatters his primitive, pleasurable confidence in himself and his powers. His sense that the world is subject to the wish of his infantile self is fundamentally shaken, if not completely destroyed.[24] In the childhood setting of the Indian extended family, the boy's ensuing feelings of helpless rage and anxiety, unmitigated by the active presence of a helpful father, represent the prototypal narcissistic injury, one that requires militant psychological effort to repair. Actual or threatened violations of self-esteem in later life invariably evoke some version of the pattern of restitutive measures cast in childhood, namely, that earliest reparation in which the boy turns away from the disappointing external world and seeks comfort and a sense of control in such defensive manoeuvres as 'I do not need anyone', 'I am sufficient unto myself', and 'I am perfect'. This compensatory activation of the grandiose self finds its mythological counterpart in the very conception of Shiva—remote from the world, isolated and self-sufficient in his mountain hideout of Kailasha.

In the young boy's inner life, the compensatory restitution of self-assurance and control is expressed primarily in a fantasied overvaluation of his body, its strength, intactness, invincibility, and especially of his penis. For in the inner world of the small boy, the self, the body and the penis are often interchangeable, with the phallus a miniature representation not only of the body but of the 'total ego'.[25] As we know, in the unconscious layers of the psyche this equation persists well into adulthood. Deep down, the penis remains a major focus of a man's narcissistic concern, such that any lapse in sexual potency is accompanied by a general loss of self-esteem and a dreadful intimation of collapse in every sphere of activity and livelihood. The fantastic image of a towering, universally admired penis is a powerful compensation for the Indian boy's expulsion from the

. maternal 'paradise'; the Shiva linga with which the adult devotee identifies, thereby 'possessing' its attributes, incorporates the boy's twin restitutive themes of bodily perfection and psychic invulnerability.

The fantasy becomes collective in the vivid portrayals and mythical elaborations of the linga found in the epics and the Puranas, which form the Shiva devotees' catechism and inspiration. For example, in the *Mahabharata*, Krishna praises Shiva: 'His lingam is fixed and immovable for all time. He is for this reason called *sthanu* . . . Because his lingam always observes the vow of continence, therefore all the worlds adore it . . . The *rishis* [sages], the gods, the gandharvas [heavenly singers], the apsaras [heavenly nymphs], adore that lingam of his which is ever erect and upraised.'[26]

Many Shiva myths also incorporate the theme of phallic grandiosity. Thus it is related that Brahma and Vishnu, Shiva's counterparts in the Hindu trinity, once started arguing as to which of the two was a greater god. As they stood there, each one boasting of his attributes, a flaming phallus materialized before them. The phallus was so huge that neither its beginning nor its end was visible. Greatly intrigued, the two gods decided to investigate, one of them diving towards its roots, the other taking off into the air. But no matter how far they went, neither Brahma nor Vishnu could reach the extremities of Mahadeva's linga.

In a second version of the same myth, the fantasy of the great phallus is explicitly related to a wound to Shiva's self-esteem. 'Brahma and Vishnu asked Rudra [Shiva] to create. He said, "I will do it," and then he plunged into water for a thousand years. Brahma and Vishnu began to worry, and Vishnu said, "There is not much time left. You must make an effort to create, for you have the ability and I will give you the female creative power." Brahma then created all the gods and other beings, and when Siva emerged from the water, about to begin creation, he saw that the universe was full. He thought, "What will I do? Creation has already been achieved by Brahma, and therefore I will destroy it and tear out my own seed." He released a flame from his mouth, setting the universe on fire, but eventually Brahma propitiated Siva who broke off his linga, saying, "There is not much use for this linga except to create creatures." He threw the linga upon the earth, and it broke through the earth and went down to hell and up to the sky. Vishnu and Brahma failed to find the top and bottom of it, and they worshipped it.'[27] In yet another legend, the combined efforts of all the gods in the Hindu pantheon could not subdue a fiery, leaping linga till the mother-goddess came along and held it within her vagina; here, the myth incorporates not only the theme of phallic grandiosity but also the wish to regain the lost symbiosis with the mother.

We find the second theme, psychic invulnerability achieved by means of identification with the 'ever erect and upraised linga', in numerous legends in which the devotee achieves *moksha* by merging with the phallus. Thus, King Jalpa of Assam, who was steadfast in his devotion to the linga, heard a voice coming from inside the phallus forgiving his sins and drawing him into the linga.[28] Sculpted reliefs on the faces of Hindu temples often depict a boy holding fast to the linga from which Shiva emerges to slay Yama, the god of death and the harbinger of the ultimate narcissistic injury, annihilation of the self.

Let us turn now to a uniquely Hindu amendment to the symbolism of phallic worship. The manifest narcissistic obsession with the penis and the pervasive masculine self-doubt and ego-fragility underlying it become even more pronounced in the Hindu embellishment of the linga—the Gauripatta or *yoni*—the vulva-like base from which the phallus juts out. For in spite of fantasies of phallic grandeur, the penis itself is of course situated *outside* the body, exposed and vulnerable to injury from without, just as the outgoing self is ever susceptible to the outer world's encroachments. In situations of aggravated anxiety, the fantasy of the grand invulnerable phallus may not be a sufficient dam against the threat to self-esteem. The solution to the threat is a symbolic withdrawal of the overcathected penis into one-self, into an internal organ, the vagina, where the phallus (and the ego) is safe and beyond harm.

Thus, in addition to the representation of masculine potency and the defensive fantasy of the grandiose self condensed in a single phallic image, the linga of Shiva arising from the *yoni* also includes the unconscious idea of bisexuality as a means of narcissistic self-sufficiency. Narcissistic bisexuality finds its cultural expression not only in the impacted symbol of the *linga–yoni*, but also in Shiva's form as *Hara–Gauri* or *ardhanarishwara*, the deity who is half-man and half-woman, one of the most popular subjects in Hindu art, particularly in the Tantric schools. Here, the god is divided vertically, male on one side and female on the other. The classical dancers who depict Shiva in this form, one half of the body executing vigorous 'male' movements while the other half simultaneously carries out flowing 'feminine' ones, splendidly convey not only the imagery but the emotion of bisexuality. Such mythopoetic expressions of Indian culture are not vestiges of a grotesque antiquity; they express powerful living forces in the individual unconscious—dark, ambivalent forces, repressed by most of us, that only the deviant, by means of consummate artistry, or intense mental anguish, dare to 'act out'.

In spite of their obviously limited representativeness, cases from Indian psycho-analytic practice vividly illustrate the correspondence between a cultural symbol, Shiva and his *linga*, and a modal childhood fantasy, bisexuality in the service of narcissism. Thus, a patient believed that strange changes had taken place in his body as a result of his love affair with the daughter of his superior in the cotton mill where he worked. The man was convinced that his left hand had become soft and delicate like his girl friend's while his right hand had become strong and muscular like his boss's hand, and that he alternately was transformed into Shiva and Shiva's female counterpart.[29] In a second case, reported by T. C. Sinha, an unmarried thirty-year-old man avoided heterosexual activity because of his fantastic dread of the dangers of pregnancy and delivery. The homosexual activity and fantasies to which he turned were not reassuring. Taking the feminine role, he could not trust the male partner to withdraw before ejaculation; nor was masturbation in the female role satisfactory to him. So he conceived of having a penis inside a vagina, thereby ensuring himself both 'feminine' pleasure and 'masculine' control. Moreover, there was no possibility of his becoming pregnant, since the penis would be thrust not into the vagina, but outside it. Not only did this fantasy allow him the feminine gratification he sought, but he imagined that 'people would come to offer flowers and water to it [the penis] for worship as they do in the case of the Shiva linga'. Another, somewhat older patient fantasied the similarly gratifying idea of possessing a penis inside the anus, and sometimes, a penis inside the vagina; in both instances, these bisexual arrangements meant he was able to gratify himself all by himself without the dependency implicit in intercourse or the social stigma associated with passive homosexuality.[30]

In a sublimated form, the androphile current implicit or manifest in the cases reported above is an important modal psychic tendency among Indian men. There is a greater acceptance of the homoerotic element in relationships between men in India, not as an inversion, in the sense of sexual preference among men who are neither attracted to nor genitally potent with women, but as the presence of erotic feelings, fantasies and impulses among men who are otherwise normal in their erotic attitude towards women.

We are now in a better position to resolve the paradox in the fact that Shiva, the renunciator and arch-ascetic, claims the erect phallus with all its erotic connotations as his particular symbol. Many Hindu texts have simply accepted this duality without attempting to offer an explanation: 'The yogi who thinks of Siva as devoid of passion himself enjoys freedom from passion. The yogi who meditates upon Siva as full of passion will certainly himself enjoy passion.'[31] Other texts have advanced the somewhat tortuous argument that the erect phallus is a symbol of chastity since the semen has not yet been shed and the linga thus symbolizes concentrated sexual vitality, which, in the Hindu tradition, it is incumbent upon yogis to transform into mental power. Psychologically, the linga does not have an erotic connotation, if by eroticism one means the direction of sexuality towards the world of 'objects', the desire for others. In other words, the linga is not a symbol of object libido but of narcissistic libido, of sexual investment in the self. Thus, although sexuality is the essence of the symbol, the linga is both 'chaste' and 'erotic' at the same time.

Given the dominant psycho-social themes of Indian infancy and childhood, we can see why the symbol of the linga is charged with such emotional power in the psychology of its devotees. The linga stands for the promise of potent manhood at the same time that it incorporates the defensive fantasies of the grandiose self and self-sufficient bisexuality in the service of narcissism. It condenses the manifold and the contradictory into a single visual image, an evocation of all that is impossible or difficult to put in so many words.

The Revolutionary Yogi: Childhood of
Swami Vivekananda

To identify and understand those specific constellations in the Indian inner world that help or hinder an individual's efforts to adapt to rapidly changing historical circumstances, I intend to go back in history to the nineteenth century and consider the life and work of

Swami Vivekananda, a man who was both a passionate proponent of the traditional Hindu world-image and a prophet of change in the modern western sense. Introspective yogi and activist monk, sensitive poet and fiery orator, a religious philosopher who reinterpreted ancient Hindu thought to make it more accessible to modern consciousness and who, at the same time, was the dynamic organizer of the Ramakrishna Order of monks, Vivekananda is one of the most fascinating figures in the history of modern India. On the one hand, as a practising yogi and religious teacher in the ancient Indian tradition of the sage-guru, he exhorted his countrymen to make the traditional ideals of enhancement of the inner world and fusion of 'I' and the 'Other' a living actuality in everyday life. Yet, on the other hand, he was also a firm believer in the value of activity directed towards necessary social change, a dedicated advocate of furthering scientific and technical education among Indians and the founder of an order of monks who not only took the traditional vows of personal striving for *moksha* but gave a new, unprecedented pledge of service to the Indian masses, a pledge that was carried out in mundane activities such as the running of schools, orphanages, dispensaries and relief campaigns during famines and epidemics.

In the political sphere, Vivekananda synthesized apparent cultural contradictions in a new nationalism that combined both religious and political ideals; redemption from alien subjection became both a patriotic and religious duty, the means to immediate independence and ultimate salvation too. A western disciple, Sister Nivedita, described Vivekananda thus:

In his consciousness, the ancient light of the mood in which man comes face to face with God might shine, but it shone on all those questions and all those puzzles which are present to the thinkers and workers of the modern world. . . . I see in him the heir to the spiritual discoveries and religious struggles of innumerable teachers and saints in the past of India and the world, and at the same time the pioneer and prophet of a new and future order of development.[32]

From all accounts, those of disciples, contemporaries and biographers, the man himself must have had a tremendous—there is no other word for it—*presence*. As in descriptions of all charismatic leaders credited with this quality of magnetic presence, Vivekananda's counterplayers emphasize that particular aspect of his personality that is most meaningful in the context of their own lives, while aware that the essence of the man's charisma is indefinable. Thus some stress Vivekananda's vigour and vitality, others his tenderness and serenity; some talk of the luminous profundity of his eyes, others of a Savonarola-like fearless outspokenness; some marvel at his power and lucid intellectuality while others admire his spirituality.

In historical retrospect, Vivekananda stands out as a leader of prodigious faith and scepticism, a catalyst of India's national consciousness. In psychological terms, Vivekananda created, as he represented, an early version of modern Indian identity. In the last part of the nineteenth century, as Indian society began to recover from its first intoxication with the West and to resist the political domination of Britian, Vivekananda's speeches and writings provided a rudder of self-respect and intellectual *explication* for the emerging militant nationalist movement. Because of its roots deep within the Indian tradition and because of its implications for the future shape of Indian polity, the ideology of nineteenth-century nationalism is more significant, in a psycho-historical sense, than the disintegration of its political organization soon after Vivekananda's death. The development of the ideology of militant nationalism, the religious basis of patriotism, the concept of the nation as an organic spirit, the importance of popular identification with the nation and mass participation in its self-assertion, psychological and cultural self-confidence as a necessary prelude to political action and finally, the qualified legitimacy of revolutionary violence: this is Vivekananda's legacy.[33]

In Vivekananda's view, the development of a modern Indian identity had only one legitimate basis: the traditional Hindu world-image. The past, he believed, had to be retrieved, in fact essentially rediscovered, before a modern Indian national identity could emerge and take shape and become powerful in the world of nations. In a speech at Madras, on his triumphant return from the United States in 1897, he stated this conviction with passion:

Each nation, like each individual, has one theme in this life which is its centre, the principal note around which every other note comes to form the harmony. If any one nation attempts to throw off its national vitality, the direction which has become its own through the transmission of centuries, that nation dies ... In one nation political power is its vitality, as in England. Artistic life, in another, and so on. In India religious life forms the centre, the key-note of the whole music of the national life. And therefore, if you succeed in the attempt to throw off your religion and take up either politics or society, the result will be that you will become extinct. Social reform and politics have to be preached through the vitality of your religion

... Every man has to make his own choice; so has every nation. We made our choice ages ago.³⁴

Vivekananda was passionately convinced that the regeneration of religious vitality required a massive effort in raising cultural consciousness so that the Hindu world-image would come to pervade every form of individual and social endeavour, which in turn called for elementary measures of economic and sheer physical emancipation. Religion cannot be preached to empty bellies, he asserted. Or, as Bertolt Brecht would later put it, *'Erst kommt das Fressen und dann das Moral'* ('Eating comes first, morality later'). The Indian masses had to become strong, had first to gain pride and faith in themselves; the energy that had for so long gone into the mortification of the body needed now, to meet modern tests, to be directed towards the development of physical strength:

No more is this the time for us to become soft. This softness has been with us till we have become like masses of cotton. What our country now wants is muscles of iron and nerves of steel, gigantic will, which nothing can resist, which can accomplish their purpose in any fashion, even if it means going down to the bottom of the ocean and meeting death face to face. That is what we want, and that can only be created, established, and strengthened by understanding and realizing the ideal of Advaita, that ideal of the oneness of all. Faith, faith, faith in ourselves! . . . Not the English; it is we who are responsible for all our degradation. Our aristocratic ancestors went on treading the common masses of our country underfoot till they became helpless, till under this torment the poor, poor people nearly forgot that they were human beings. They have been compelled to be merely hewers of wood and drawers of water for centuries, so that they are made to believe that they are born as slaves, born as hewers of wood and drawers of water.³⁵

Vivekananda's answer to Indian dependence was activism:

We want that energy, that love of independence, that spirit of self-reliance, that immovable fortitude, that dexterity in action, that bond of unity of purpose, that thirst for improvement checking a little the constant looking back to the past, we want that extensive vision infinitely projected forward; and we want that intense spirit of activity (*Rajas*) which will flow through every vein, from head to foot.³⁶

In periods of emotional strain—and intense, 'altered' mental states were a recurring feature of his life—Vivekananda's assertive imagery of struggle directed outward would give way to that of acceptance, passivity and turning inward. In the aftermath of these periods of emotional crisis, he was wont to maintain that the ideas of activity and progress were delusions. Things never got better; they remained as they were. Only individuals grew better through the changes they made in themselves: 'The musk deer, after vain search for the cause of the scent of the musk, at last will have to find it in himself.'[37] After an especially severe crisis at the age of thirty-five, four years before his death in Calcutta, Vivekananda gravely informed his disciples that he had been all wrong and that his patriotism and zeal as a nationalist reformer had completely vanished. Two years later, in a letter to a friend, he could write: 'And work? What is work? Whose work? Whom to work for? I am free. I am Mother's* child. She works, She plays. Why should I plan? What shall I plan? Things came and went, just as She liked, without my planning, in spite of planning. We are Her automata. She is the wire-puller.'[38]

A great man's contradictions are an integral part of his greatness; they may indeed fuel his historic initiatives. As Erikson in his biography of Luther, another *homo religiosus*, emphasizes, the state of inner repose, a simple enjoyment of life, an ordinary decency and conflict-free sense of purpose and direction are not the lot of intensely creative men with a sense of their own historical destiny.[39] Although I reject the pathographic approach which would diagnose Vivekananda as a 'classic' manic-depressive, the hagiographic adulation of his direct and indirect disciples, Nivedita and Nikhilananda, and admirers like Romain Rolland, who explain Vivekananda's heightened propensity for emotional conflict, his mystical visions and intense mental experiences as an expression of the Divine, the manifestation of a spiritual 'supra-consciousness', doesn't tell us much either. Rather, I intend to bring the insights of psycho-analytic psychology to bear on some aspects of Vivekananda's life and to try to weave a pattern of meaning (not causality) from the tangled threads of conflict and contradiction. My purpose is threefold: first, to identify the principal motivational themes of Vivekananda's life and thus to show that the divergent facts of his personality do indeed have a core of psychological consistency; second, to trace in a concrete life history some of the themes I have suggested are characteristic of a modal Indian personality; and third, to illustrate the psychological dilemma of modernization in the life of a charismatic Indian leader.

*The Great Goddess.

Narendranath*—or Naren, as he was affectionately called as a boy —was born in Calcutta in January, 1863 in a Bengali upper-middle-class family belonging to the Kayastha community. The Kayasthas, one of the higher castes of Hindu society, are mentioned in early Sanskrit texts as hereditary government officials, although the community probably crystallized as a separate *jati* around the thirteenth century. Staffing the bureaucracies of the princely states through the many upheavals of Indian history, the Kayasthas proved to be an adaptable people, capable and willing to adopt the mores and even the language of the rulers they successively (and successfully) served—whether they were Muslim or British. Thus, whereas in the period of Muslim rule, they had diligently learned Persian, when the British conquered Bengal the Kayasthas quickly became proficient in English. Given the nature of their occupation and their access to those who ruled, the Kayasthas were always in the front lines of the cultural confrontation that attends imperial conquest. In the eighteenth and nineteenth centuries, the Kayasthas were one of the first Hindu communities to be exposed to the new social and ethical philosophies emanating from the West. Together with the other communities of Bengal's traditional intelligentsia, the Brahmins and the Vaidyas, the Kayasthas reacted strongly to the British cultural penetration of a conservative society, as ever larger numbers experienced the inner conflicts aroused by cultural and social dislocation. The first response of many was a revolt against the restraining norms of Hindu tradition and an indiscriminate acceptance of all things British. Caught in the cultural cross-current and uniquely sensitive to it, this traditional intelligentsia initiated the early movements to reform the conservative Hindu social order. In fact, as early as the 1850s, one of Naren's uncles was writing pamphlets on such subjects as the education of Indian women and the unequal distribution of land and wealth—causes which Vivekananda later adopted and 'radicalized'.

During Naren's childhood in the latter part of the nineteenth century, the conflict between the old, Brahmin-dominated Hindu orthodoxy and the new, British-inspired liberalism championed by many members of his community was at its peak. As his brother writes, 'He was born when Hindu society was again on the road to regain its dynamism. In his own Kayastha community the blow fell terribly. Parents and sons, husbands and wives used to be separated

*Vivekananda's real name.

because the son either has changed his religion or has become a reformer or has gone to England for study.'⁴⁰ Many of the more progressive members of the community who had not identified with the British in India, nevertheless saw in the western scientific and rationalist world-view a means of purging Indian social institutions of the dead weight of tradition. But once the seeds of self-criticism had been sown among these sensitive Bengali intellectuals, it was not long before their uncritical emulation of the British developed into hypercritical ambivalence, then rejection, and finally into a revival of hyperbolic reverence for the Hindu tradition. Thus, to understand Naren's intellectual and psychological development fully, we must bear in mind the ideological instability (perhaps chronic to Bengal) of his time which manifested itself acutely—paradigmatically— among the members of his community.

Naren's father, Vishwanath Datta, was a lawyer practising at the Calcutta High Court. He was westernized and 'modern', a man well-versed in Persian and English literature, agnostic in religious outlook, and a *bon vivant* who is said to have thoroughly enjoyed the good things of this world. I have an impression of him as the proto-type of the modern Indian who moves in the professional and business circles of large Indian cities, although one hundred years ago this new class of westernized Indians was confined to small oases in Calcutta, Bombay and Madras. Viswanath Datta was a member of India's new professional class, which was beginning to provide civil servants, military and police officials, engineers, doctors, teachers and other professionals, the vanguard of modernization.

Naren's mother, Bhuvaneshwari Devi, was a traditional Hindu woman. Deeply religious, steeped in Puranic mythology and lore she took her cosmology and values from the ideals of the *Ramayana* and *Mahabharata*, the repository of Hindu culture. Indeed, she could recite large portions of the beloved epics from memory. Bhuvaneshwari Devi, with her religious piety, steadfast devotion to tradition and calm efficiency in running the household, typified in the eyes of her sons the ideal of Indian womanhood. This combination of a westernized father and a traditional Hindu mother is not uncommon in the higher castes and upper-middle classes of India even today; it is a striking fact that many of India's leaders during the nationalist movement and since independence are the offspring of this parental combination.

Naren was born into an extended family in which his father's uncle was the *pater familias*. In addition to Vishwanath, his wife and children, the family included the large families of the uncle's two sons (Vishwanath's cousins). Naren's mother's place in this family was that of the outsider with manifold obligations to other family members and very few rights or enjoyments. She was necessarily a dutiful and compliant daughter-in-law and her husband was not a son but a nephew of the family. Her status in the family hierarchy was minimal, and she suffered a great deal under the strict regimen of her husband's aunt, the female head of the family.[41] Before Naren's birth, his mother had borne one son and four daughters, but the son and two daughters had died in infancy. Given these circumstances, it is not difficult to imagine her longing for a son during this, her sixth, confinement. We are told that while Naren was still in the womb, Bhuvaneshwari Devi, as other pious Hindu mothers then and since, took religious vows, prayed and fasted that she might be blessed with a son. Especially she prayed to Shiva; and it is reported that 'one night she dreamt that this supreme Deity aroused himself from his meditation and agreed to be born as her son. When she awoke she was filled with joy.'[42] We cannot know of course whether the dream is a fact, or one of those adventitious legends that grow up around the 'birth of a hero'. Apocryphal or not, it reveals the mother's devotional attitude and emotional investment in the infant Naren. She named him Vireshwara at first, after Shiva, a name the family later changed to Narendranath. To Bhuvaneshwari Devi, her eldest living son was a special object of maternal affection and ministration. In later life, Vivekananda too rarely talked about his father but often of his mother's 'unselfish love and purity', maintaining that his mother was the one being in the world, if any, whom he loved.

Naren's unique position among Bhuvaneshwari Devi's many children comes through clearly in a biography of Vivekananda written by his younger brother, Bhupendranath. Although the purpose of this book is to highlight Vivekananda's contributions to modern India, its reminiscences reveal something of the younger brother's rivalry and envy towards the mother's favourite. Thus, after a stint in jail for his revolutionary activity against the British, which had been given wide press coverage, Bhupendranath 'jokingly' remarks to his mother, 'You never got any recognition for being Vivekananda's mother, but you got public reception for being my mother.'[43] On another occasion, when Vivekananda's American disciples ask to meet his mother, Bhupendranath prohibits such a meeting, exclaiming to her angrily, 'As half of your body falls in my share, I will cut you into two with a see-saw [*sic*] if your eldest son insists about it.'[44]

'A man who has been the indisputable favourite of his mother,' Freud once remarked, 'keeps for life the feeling of a conqueror, that confidence of success that often induces real success.'[45] Even as a child, Naren had this conquistador feeling; he assumed as a matter of course that in the game of 'king and the court' he would be the monarch who assigns the roles of ministers and courtiers to the other playmates who would accept his right to do so without question and submit meekly to his dictates. Later, this same charismatic authority informed his leadership of the Ramakrishna order, and even when he deviated from traditional ideals of monkhood in the United States, his brother-monks accepted as a matter of course his plans, proposals, and even his whims as the natural prerogatives of the 'chosen one'.

This sense of being chosen as the bearer of a superior destiny never left Vivekananda, even in his 'dark nights of the soul'. As he once wrote in a piece of perceptive self-analysis:

There are two sorts of persons in the world—the one strong-nerved, quiet, yielding to nature, not given to much imagination, yet good, kind, sweet, etc. For such is this world—they alone are born to be happy. There are others, again, with high-strung nerves, tremendously imaginative, with intense feelings—always going high, and coming down the next moment. For them there is no happiness. The first class will have almost an even tenor of happiness. The second will have to run between ecstasy and misery. But of these alone geniuses are made. There is some truth in a recent theory that genius is a sort of madness.

Now persons of this class, if they want to be great, must fight to be so—clear the decks for battle. No encumbrance—no marriage—no children, no undue attachment to anything except the one idea, and live and die for that. I am a person of this sort.[46]

Although it clearly originated in his earliest relationship with his devoted mother, Naren's indelible sense of superior mission was reinforced by his family. His paternal grandfather, after the birth of Naren's father Vishwanath, had renounced the world and put aside his responsibilities as a *grihastha* to lead a monk's life. Many thought that Naren's striking resemblance to this grandfather 'proved' that he had been reborn in the child, or, in other words, that the child Naren was his father's father. If we add to this Naren's dominance over his playmates, his leadership in school, his intellectual and rhetorical gifts that in college won him universal praise and admiration from his teachers, his being chosen at the age of eighteen by Ramakrishna as his foremost disciple and spiritual heir, it is not difficult to argue that Naren's environment conspired—he was an unconsciously willing co-conspirator—to maintain and enhance the intra-psychic construction of archaic grandiosity ('I am great'). Whereas the 'reality testing' of most children gradually reveals their limitations and sooner or later they lose their original sense of primacy, of 'specialness', Naren's encounters with the real world simply confirmed his sense of special destiny.

The sense of being the bearer of a superior destiny can generate in a child an inner drivenness to become 'great' and thereby fulfil his parents' expectations as well as the imperatives of his own self-image. Yet this unconscious conviction of superiority *vis-à-vis* parents and the other adults around him can also be a source of great conflict and psychological tension for a young child. For one thing, his fantasied grandiosity is not matched by the realities of his physical stature and stage of ego development; the precocity of the small boy's unconscious wishes and ideals contrasts starkly with the anxious self-doubt and confusion that all too easily can overwhelm the still tentative identity. The conflict between the fantasies of greatness and the reality of dependence upon parents and other adults in the family makes its appearance in Vivekananda's earliest memory, a 'cover memory' in the psycho-analytic sense, for it condenses a continuing and pervasive childhood conflict in a single dramatic scene:

When I was only two years old, I used to play with my *syce* (coachman) at being *vairagi* (monk, renunciant,) clothed in ashes and *kaupina*. And if a *sadhu* came to beg, they would lock me in, upstairs, to prevent my giving too much away. I felt that I *was* this [a holy *vairagi*), and that for some mischief I had to be sent away from Shiva. No doubt my family increased this feeling, for when I was naughty they would say, 'Dear, Dear! So many austerities, yet Shiva sent us this demon after all, instead of a good soul.' Or when I was very rebellious they would empty a can of water over me, saying 'Shiva! Shiva!' Even now, when I feel mischievous, that word keeps me straight. 'No!' I say to myself, 'not this time!'[47]

Such a scene not only reflects the 'chosen' child's deep sense of hurt and humiliation at being treated so unceremoniously *by his mother*[48] but also the guilty fear that his budding initiative and curiosity might lead to some kind of exile from his mother and home as he was once sent away from Shiva. The remembered scene also suggests the contrapuntal role assumed by Naren's mother in their relationship, namely, she idealizes her son and yet rejects his somewhat cocky display of independence and initiative, or what she calls his 'rebelliousness'. The inner tension created by a mother who mistrusts or mocks her son's actual behaviour even as she elicits his ambitions and stretches his expectations is at the heart of a child's (and for that matter, vestigially, of an adult's) unstable self-concept and fluctuations in self-esteem.

The struggle to free himself from his mother and the advocacy of a thoroughly masculine courage and initiative (both in personal relations and on the collective plane of nationalist politics) were lifelong themes in Vivekananda's inner world, and in adulthood the maternal counterplayer would be Kali, the Divine Mother. Vivekananda was aware of this inner struggle; indeed, he believed it enhanced and befitted a man: 'Yes, let the world come, the hells come, the gods come, let Mother come. I fight and do not give in. Ravana got his release in three births by fighting the Lord himself! It is glorious to fight Mother.'[49] The struggle manifested itself in his historic mission to infuse Indian nationalism with a militant revival of tradition, to bring resolute 'manly' activity and radical social transformation to 'that awful mass of conservative jelly-fish',[50] that 'nation of women',[51] as he characterized the India of his time. And the same inner struggle would immobilize him during those frequent 'spells' in which he repudiated this ideal and denied his mission.

When a boy's early years have been characterized by intense emotional attachment and identification with his mother, the struggle for individuality and potence is an unremitting one. The unconscious dynamics of the struggle are these: the attempt to separate himself arouses guilt that not only dims the benevolent mother imago, but threatens the sense of one's own uniqueness of which she was the original guarantor. The 'bad mother' may then become magnified and stifle the pretension to greatness. The internal psychological 'work' of restitution thus becomes necessary; the threatening 'bad mother' must be propitiated by the child's renouncing any claim to independence and by claiming once again protection from Putana and Agasur, the maternal monsters who, in the deepest recesses of the inner world, are as alive as the 'good' Bhuvaneshwari Devi. This swinging back and forth between an 'agentic' adult manliness and the dependency of childhood was a recurrent feature of Vivekananda's life. In fact, the years of his greatest success and achievement,

years when his name became a household word all over India,
coincided with severe personal crises.

I want to quote at length here from a disciple's eye-witness
account of the 'culminating' crisis in Vivekananda's life (in 1897),not
only because it illuminates his personal conflict but also because it
reflects a fundamental constellation in the Hindu inner world:

In some imperceptible way, at all events, the Swami's attention appeared to shift, during the month of August, from Shiva to the
Mother. He was always singing the songs of Ram Prasad,* as if he
would saturate his own mind with the conception of himself as a
child. He told some of us once, that wherever he turned he was conscious of the presence of the Mother, as if she were a person in the
room. It was always his habit to speak simply and naturally of
Mother, and some of the older members of the party caught this, so
that such phrases as 'Well, well! Mother knows best!' were a constant
mode of thought and speech amongst us: when, for instance, some
cherished intention had to be abandoned.

Gradually, however, his absorption became more intense. He complained bitterly of the malady of thought, which would consume a
man, leaving him no time for sleep or rest, and would often become
as insistent as a human voice. He had constantly striven to make
clear to us the ideal of rising beyond the pair of opposites, beyond
pain and pleasure, good and evil alike—that conception which forms
the Hindu solution of the problem of sin—but now he seemed to
fasten his whole attention on the dark, the painful, and the inscrut-
able . . . 'The worship of the Terrible' now became his whole cry.
Illness or pain would always draw forth the reminder that 'She is the
organ. She is the pain. And she is the Giver of pain, Kali! Kali! Kali!!'
His brain was teeming with thoughts, he said one day, and his
fingers would not rest till they were written down. It was the same
evening that we came back to our houseboat from some expedition,
and found waiting for us, where he had called and left them, his
manuscript lines on 'Kali the Mother'. Writing in a fever of inspiration, he had fallen on the floor, when he had finished—as we learnt
afterwards—exhausted with his own intensity.

KALI THE MOTHER

The stars are blotted out
The clouds are covering clouds
It is darkness vibrant, sonant.
In the roaring, whirling wind,
Are the souls of a million lunatics,
Just loosed from the prison house,

*Eighteenth century singer and poet whose songs of longing for the Mother
are very popular in Bengal.

Wrenching trees by the roots
Sweeping all from the path.
The sea has joined the fray
And swirls up mountain waves,
To reach the pitchy sky.
The flash of lurid light
Reveals on every side
A thousand, thousand shades
Of death, begrimed and black.
Scattering plagues and sorrows,
Dancing mad with joy,
Come, Mother, Come!
For terror is Thy name.
Death is Thy breath.
And every shaking step
Destroys a world for e'er.
Thou 'Time' the All-Destroyer!
Come, O Mother, come!
Who dares misery love,
Dance in destruction's dance,
And hug the form of death,—
To him the Mother comes.

About this time, he had taken the boat away from our vicinity, and only a young Brahmo doctor, who was also living in Kashmir that summer—and whose kindness and devotion to him were beyond all praise—was allowed to know where he was, and to inquire about his daily needs. The next evening the doctor went as usual, but finding him lost in thought, retired without speaking, and the following day, September the thirteenth, he had gone, leaving word that he was not to be followed, to Kshir Bhowani, the coloured springs.* He was away, from that day till October the sixth.

In the afternoon of that day we saw him coming back to us, up the river. He stood in front of the *dunga*, grasping with one hand the bamboo roofpole, and with the other holding yellow flowers. He entered our houseboat—a transfigured presence, and silently passed from one to another blessing us, and putting marigolds on our heads. 'I offered them to Mother', he said at last, as he ended bv handing the garland to one of us. Then he sat down. 'No more "Hari Om!" It is all "Mother" now!' he said, with a smile. We all sat silent. Had we tried to speak, we should have failed, so tense was the spot, with something that stilled thought. He opened his lips again. 'All my patriotism is gone. Everything is gone. Now it's only "Mother, Mother!" '

'I have been very wrong', he said simply, after another pause. 'Mother said to me, "What, even if unbelievers should enter My

*There is a well-known ruined temple of Kali at this spot.

temples, and defile My images! What is that to you? Do you protect Me? Or do I protect you?" So there is no more patriotism. I am only a little child!'[52]

Symbolically, Vivekananda had the hair on his head shaved off. With uncanny insight, he connected his physical symptoms (among them, severe asthmatic attacks) with his mental conflict; while the mood seemed to deepen and grow upon him that he was a child, 'seated in the Mother's lap and being caressed by her . . . the thought came to us, unspoken, that these Her kisses might make themselves known to mind and nerves as anguish, yet be welcomed with rapture of recognition.'[53]

To do full justice to Vivekananda's 'encounter' with Kali, we must view his crisis against the backdrop of Indian culture in which mother-religions and the worship of Kali in her many manifestations, especially in Bengal, form the deepest layer of Hindu religiosity. Without going into detail, I would only stress that the rapture of recognizing (and being recognized by) the mother's affirming presence together with the ambivalent anguish in response to her individuality-destroying embrace are the complementary affects evoked and condensed in the worship of Kali. In her gracious (*sundarmurti*) manifestations of world-mother (*jagadamba*) and world-nurse (*jagaddhatri*), Kali awakens an intense nostalgia for the abundance and benevolence of maternal nurturing, approval and reassurance. At the same time, in her hideous (*ghorarupa*) form, as the bone-wreathed lady of the graveyards, quaffing a skull full of seething blood, Kali symbolizes the ominous dimension in every Hindu's maternal imagery. Through the sanctioned rituals of her religion and the collective sharing of a symbol hallowed by generations of worship, Kali provides her devotees with a powerful symbolic and ritual integration of the two faces of Hindu motherhood, the trust and the dread, the rapturous sense of being cared for and the formidable fear of annihilation in that care.

At the time of the Hindu son's second birth, which coincides with the oedipal period of psycho-sexual development, the grandiose infantile self usually becomes somewhat dented as the child comes up against the world of men. In Naren's case, this developmental transition was complicated by his fantasy (somewhat corroborated by other family members) of being his father's father, if not the father-of-them-all, Shiva. In a boy's unconscious fantasy, to feel or imagine himself superior to his father means to replace that father, to have the power to annihilate him, a psychic process laden with enormous guilt. Most boys succeed in reducing this guilt through idealization and gradual identification with their father; the oedipal conflict is typically resolved within the everyday realities of the family and family relationships. For an uncommon child such as Naren, adored by his mother and intensely attached to her, determined almost involuntarily to maintain his original superiority and sense of greatness intact, convinced early on that he was 'chosen' to fulfil a special destiny, the way of idealization and identification with the father seems to have been difficult, especially since his father, according to the testimony of Naren's younger brother, was a 'weak' man.[54] That is, Vishwanath had low status among the Dattas; he was completely subservient to the wishes of his uncle, the head of the extended family. In spite of the cruel treatment meted out to his wife, Bhuvaneshwari Devi, who for a long time had only one sari to clothe her, Vishwanath had neither the temerity to protest nor the wherewithal to break away from the joint family to whose economic maintenance he contributed the lion's share. More or less passively accepting the decisions affecting the welfare of his wife and children, Vishwanath sought refuge from family tensions and quarrels in a wide circle of friends whom he was in the habit of entertaining lavishly. That he was a sensitive and gifted man who loved his eldest son dearly is beyond question; it is reported that when young Naren wanted to go to England to study law, he was not permitted to do so because Vishwanath could not bear to be separated from his son. Yet Vishwanath can scarcely be called a rock of strength, a father to be unconditionally idealized and identified with, a means of safe passage out of the mother's ambivalently consequential embrace. I do not mean that Naren did not identify with his father at all but I am suggesting that this identification must have been a tenuous one that required inward vigilance and constant struggle to maintain. For in spite of the availability of other adult males in his extended family, manliness and the clear sanction for it that are normally absorbed by a boy in his unconscious identification with his father remained emotionally charged issues in Vivekananda's life: individuation as a man, separate from the maternal presence, remained the central, unresolved life task.

Again and again, as a grown man and nationalist leader, Vivekananda comes back to India's (and his own?) need for manliness as the all-encompassing cure for the country's ills, the means of political development and independence. 'Who cares for your *bhakti* and *mukti*?' he would retort angrily to brother monks who chided him on his western activist ideas so different from those of their guru Rama-krishna. 'Who cares what your scriptures say? I will go into a thousand hells cheerfully if I can rouse my countrymen, immersed in *tamas* (darkness), to stand on their own feet and be *men* inspired with the spirit of Karma yoga.'[55] Or: '. . . the older I grow, the more every-thing seems to me to lie in manliness. This is my new gospel. Do even evil like a man! Be wicked, if you must, on a grand scale,'[56] Or: 'No more weeping, but stand on your feet and be men. It is a man-making religion that we want. It is man-making theories that we want:'[57] 'I want the strength, manhood, *kshatravirya* or the virility of a warrior . . .'[58] And: 'O Thou Mother of the Universe, vouchsafe manliness unto me! O thou Mother of Strength, take away my weak-ness, take away my unmanliness, and—*Make me a Man!*'[59]

This obsession with manliness carried over into an admiration for India's conquerors, the Muslims and the British. Vivekananda often proclaimed that he wanted to build an India with a Muslim body and a Vedantist brain, and maintained that no race understood as the British did 'what should be the glory of a man'.[60] For the young men of India who were Vivekananda's primary constituency, this was (and still is) a powerful call for freedom from the conflicting embrace of the Great Mother—the appeal of this kind of masculinist campaign touching a deep current of potential militance and aggressive activity in Indian society.

As a child, Naren's solution to the early version of the conflict over 'manly' individuation was to withdraw from the world around him, to become (and remain) wholly self-absorbed. Symbolically, this withdrawal from reality to fantasy is condensed in a striking incident. Following his mother's example, Naren had obtained for himself images of Rama and Sita, bedecked them with flowers and ritually, regularly worshipped these deities, who are the idealized parental couple of Hindu India. At the age of four or five, he dis-carded the couple and installed in their place an image of Shiva, the self-sufficient god of renunciation. Apparently, Naren, oblivious of the world around him, would sit for hours 'meditating' before Shiva's image, sometimes opening his eyes to see whether his own hair, like that of fabled holy men who meditate for years at a stretch, had grown long and entered the earth.

Yet internal pressures cannot be held at bay indefinitely, no matter how intricate and 'successful' the fantasies, no matter how grand the self-image. In moments of stress, and whenever the watchfulness of the ego is relaxed, the elation of 'I am All' can give way to the despair of 'I am Nothing': deeply buried knowledge of the 'rebellious' boy who might be banished from his mother's presence, or of the presumptuous son who might provoke dire punishment should he outdo his father in any way (even in fantasy) presses insistently from within. I believe Vivekananda's long-time presentiment that he would meet his death in a Shiva temple, the ultimate vengeance of the father-god for the son's oedipal hubris, and his fainting before the ice phallus of Shiva in the cave at Amarnath when he was thirty-four, reveals the anxiety accompanying the claims of the grandiose self. In Vivekananda's adult life, states of depression invariably followed when he was unable to repress the ever restless, unresolved childhood anxieties, 'If I become an independent man my mother will abandon me' and 'If I am greater than my father I will be punished.' He struggled against depression by escaping into transient mental states in which grandiose fantasy took over completely. 'Black and thick are the folds of sinister fate,' Vivekananda would write in one period, 'but I am the master. I raise my hand, and lo, they vanish! All this is nonsense and fear. I am the Fear of fear, Terror of terror. I am the fearless, secondless One! I am the Ruler of destiny, the Wiper-out of fact.'[61] Or, in another letter:

'He whose joy is only himself, whose desires are only in himself, he has learnt his lessons. This is the great lesson we have to learn, through myriads of births and heavens and hells: There is nothing to be sought for, asked for, desired beyond one's self. I am free, therefore I require none else for my happiness. Alone through eternity because I was free, am free and shall remain free for ever . . . Yes, I am. I am free—Alone. I am the One without a second . . . if the universe tumbles round my ears, what is that to me? I am Peace that passeth understanding. Understanding only gives us good or evil. I am beyond—I am Peace.'[62]

At other times, in response to the same inner pressure, the fantasy of complete isolation, of being 'One without a second', would be replaced by its opposite, the 'regressive' imagery of the fervent wish for fusion with the mother. Here, the lonely splendour of Shiva would become transformed into the infant Krishna's longing for unconditional acceptance and peace that beloved sons find in the 'good mother's' embrace. In these periods of vulnerability, Vivekananda inadvertently made use of standard contemporary psycho-analytic techniques of retracing early psychological experience in order to recover the past creatively. His letters at these times have the flavour of free associations in psychotherapy:

I am drifting again, with the bright warm sun ahead and masses of vegetation around, and in the heat everything is so still, so calm, and I am drifting, languidly, in the warm heat of the river. I dare not make a splash with my hands or my feet for fear of breaking the wonderful stillness, stillness that makes you feel it is an illusion! Behind my work was ambition, behind my love was personality, behind my purity was fear, behind my guidance was a thirst for power. Now they are vanishing and I drift. I come, Mother, I come, in Thy warm bosom, floating wheresoever Thou takest me, in the voiceless, in the strange, in the wonderland, I come, a spectator, no more an actor.

Oh, it is so calm; my thoughts seem to come from a great, great distance in the interior of my own heart. They seem like faint distant whispers, and peace is upon everything, sweet, sweet peace . . .[63]

This alternation of vivid fantasies of isolation and fusion by means of which Vivekananda dealt with conflict reflects one of the dominant cultural concerns of India. In his relatively conflict-free periods of initiative and political leadership, this underlying polarity provided the energy and the direction for his historic achievements. For whereas most people are likely to be incapacitated by the relentless (and illusory) claims of a poorly integrated grandiose self, the ego of a gifted person may be pushed to its utmost capacity by such pressure and embark on objectively outstanding achievements.[64] In a charismatic leader such as Vivekananda, the importance of this turn towards the self in childhood and the drive (beset with anxiety and guilt, to be sure) to realize his superior destiny, cannot be underestimated. The turn towards the self gave him a central focus inside, an internal audience in the psyche, which might severely disapprove or enthusiastically applaud, but which gave Vivekananda the ability to act according to an inner light, independent of the judgements of others as to the 'realism' of a particular course of action. By carrying within him a sense of his own psychological inviolacy, coupled with a stubborn will that held to the self-chosen course in the face of all outer obstacles, Vivekananda could, when the time came, project his vision with a passionate conviction capable of striking such a responsive chord in his audience that action on a large scale and resistance to the status quo (political and cultural) became possible. Yet this activist potential was never fully realized, and Vivekananda's vision of India's rejuvenation never became a mass movement. For one thing, the 'contents' of his vision were ultimately dissonant with the prevailing direction of political organization and anti-British resistance; but more important, the very nature of his conflict led him intermittently to withdraw from (if not reject outright) the responsibilities of ideological and organizational leadership against a foreign 'enemy' to a deeply private region where his psychic energies were fully deployed in combating or appeasing the demons within.

In 1870, at the age of seven, Naren entered school where his exceptional intelligence was quickly recognized by both teachers and classmates. In contrast with the brooding moodiness of his early childhood at home, the *leitmotif* of the so-called latency stage, which extended in Naren's case well into adolescence, was boundless activity and inexhaustible energy, especially of the locomotor kind. He organized a gymnasium and an amateur theatrical company, took lessons in the 'manly' sports of fencing, rowing and wrestling, and was the leader of a gang of mischievous youngsters who climbed the neighbourhood trees to pluck fruit and flowers, to the indignant (and apparently futile) remonstrances of tree-owners. Shiva and Kali, Rama and Sita, the *vairagis* and the meditating holy men whose hair took root in the earth, were apparently 'forgotten', and the dreamy maternal cosmos of his early years appears to have been temporarily superseded by the fascinations of the 'world of men', as the boy constructed models of the gas works and aerated-water factory lately introduced to Calcutta—much as an American boy today might make space-ship models in preconscious homage to the dominant technological image of our time.

With the advent of adolescence, however, 'forgotten' childhood themes were reactivated and Narendra's ego controls, the psychosocial gains of middle childhood, were buffeted by the renewed instinctual pressures of this stage. Once more, he found he could not always cope with the claims of archaic grandiosity and the anxiety and guilt associated with its breakthrough. Increasingly, he experienced periods of hypomanic excitement; once, on a journey with his parents to a small town in Madhya Pradesh when he was fifteen, they passed through a narrow pass surrounded on both sides by lofty peaks, and it is reported that Narendra 'spied a large bee-hive in the cleft of a giant cliff and suddenly his mind was filled with awe and reverence for the Divine Providence. He lost outer consciousness and lay thus in the cart for a long time.'[65] There were repeated *déjà vu* experiences as childhood repressions were momentarily lifted; on occasions he would, trance-like, break into song extolling divine glories, much to the astonishment of his college friends. It was as if the youth Narendra, whom Vivekananda would later look back upon as something of a fanatic, lived simultaneously in several *personas*. He was the activist patriot, convinced that his country's future depended upon the acquisition of a modern identity and that his own supreme task lay in promoting and hastening this process. At other times, he was the young man with 'burning eyes', prone to ecstasies, in search of a guru. He apparently went from one eminent religious teacher to another, asking each (much to their embarrassment) whether he had ever really seen God face to face. And there were others in what we might call his 'identity repertoire': the ascetic young man with a 'passion for purity' who had repudiated the demands of his sexual nature; the son who refused to marry and settle on a professional career in law as his parents desired. And from childhood, the unconscious selves of the 'great one', the *vairagi* and the father's father, made their own insistent demands. To put it briefly, more than most other youths, Narendra's identity was a fragmented one; he was looking for someone to provide him with a single integrated image of himself and the world, of himself *in* the world, someone to whom he could offer his complete devotion and who, in return, would make him whole.

This 'someone' was of course the remarkable Ramakrishna Paramahansa, whom millions of Hindus believe to have been an *avatar*,* the ultimate tribute paid in India to a liberated man. Ramakrishna's struggle to persuade his chosen spiritual heir to accept the Great Mother in whom lies the perfect synthesis of 'good' and 'bad' mother imagery as the fundamental reality of his inner cosmos; and the intimate, quasi-therapeutic relationship that developed between the patient, loving and motherly teacher and his imperious, stubborn disciple who openly mocked his guru's childlike *bhakti*-religiosity—these are subjects that would take us beyond the boundaries of our present study. Perhaps it is enough to note here that during the last two years of his six-year apprenticeship to Ramakrishna, and after the death of his father when he was twenty-one years old, Narendra was under intense mental strain, highly vulnerable and suggestible. Ramakrishna

*Incarnation of the godhead.

stepped into the void his pupil's inner world had become—indeed, he was already at home there—and serving as a mighty mentor, he helped to set the inner stage for the emergence of Vivekananda, the revolutionary monk and one of the greatest men India has produced in the last one hundred years.

For much of his adult life, Vivekananda managed successfully to integrate his divergent strivings for individuation as a man with the yearning for fusion with some ultimate divine matrix in the propagation of a specifically Indian form of nationalism that captured the imagination of his countrymen. By combining elements of an activist, self-assertive manhood with those of emotional and religious mysticism, Vivekananda equated patriotism with an identification with Mother-India; his powerful oratory stirred the masses with its appeal to *their* pride and *their* tradition, and used symbols meaningful to *them*. The theme of phallic grandiosity was as much a part of his appeal as the bliss inherent in the imagery of a strong, bounteous and fertile Motherland—his reassurance that the skull-garlanded Kali 'of blackest gloom' could be transformed into the resplendent Durga if only her sons would come back to her and to their ancient *dharma*. Vivekananda ultimately failed politically in that he was unable to sustain or substantiate the religious-emotional identity he purveyed with a tight, efficient political organization. As Pamela Daniels puts it, 'Religious and political ideals briefly and powerfully combined under the banner of militant nationalism, but the alliance was not sustained. The politicians went their way, and the mystics theirs.'[66] The task of fashioning the tools of power with which to effect nationalist aspirations was left for Vivekananda's more pragmatic successors, for men such as Gandhi, Nehru and Patel. I have suggested above that Vivekananda's 'failure' was rooted in the same psychic constellation that gave his message its powerful appeal, in the vestiges of the archaic narcissism of Hindu childhood. For to the extent that an individual or a movement succeeded in consolidating a vigorous sense of existential or political independence and in exalting the good mother, that very success brought in its wake the *alter imago* of the bad mother—the dark Kali who allows neither individuation nor a blissful union but only permits an anxious abject surrender. A profound ambivalence towards manhood and its representations such as Shiva and the British *raj*, towards the 'good mother' and her symbols—Durga and the motherly Ramakrishna —cast a long shadow on the Indian independence movement.

Let us step back to consider the validity of this sketch of Vivekananda's emotional development. How far is this rough chart of his inner territory 'true' and how much of it is mere conjecture? This is a recurring question in the psycho-biographical study of historical figures in that the modification, extension or revision of preliminary hypotheses on the basis of the subject's responses, corrections and questions is not possible. Nevertheless, this rough map strikes me as probable in that it connects and integrates a series of (sometimes contradictory) episodes in Vivekananda's life history, it is consistent with psycho-analytic theory and, especially in the biographer's own empathic reactions towards his subject—his 'countertransference'—persists in having a ring of truth.

CHAPTER VI

Conclusion: Childhood and Social Change

This book has explored the developmental significance of Hindu infancy and childhood, and their consequence in Indian identity formation. Drawing upon anthropological evidence, life-historical and clinical data, mythology and folklore, the exploration has taken us into the shadowy realms of collective fantasy as well as the daily worlds of Hindu social organization in search of the psycho-social foundations of our inner world. The emphasis has been on the mutual reinforcement of psyche and culture, in the sense that within a given cultural and social order, particular psychological themes become internalized in the individual psyche, later to be projected back onto the culture's institutions and social forms and thereby perpetuated from generation to generation. Thus far, we have skirted the wider implications of the inner world—the childhood layer of the mind—for the processes of modernization and social change. Yet it is critical that we understand and underscore the relevance of childhood, in India, as in any culture, to the ways in which a culture responds to the press of social change, to the tension between innovation and conservation in the generation of solutions to age-old and brand-new questions.

Vivekananda's vision of a modern Indian identity that would integrate a rational, scientific model of inquiry and the aims of technological modernization with the essentials of the traditional Hindu world image, remains an unrealized ideal. As we have seen, in his despairing moments he tended to see the 'rational' and the 'traditional' elements in this vision of 'modern Indian identity' as irreconcilably antithetical. In such moments, he fell back upon the widely and deeply held Hindu belief in the fundamental futility of all change and proclaimed that no alteration of the outer social and physical environment ever made life 'better' but that this goal depended wholly on the devoted and systematic cultivation of the inner world. In this respect, Vivekananda shared Freud's scepticism regarding the very idea of social change, a scepticism based on the belief that the central reality for any individual is the internal one and that social, political and economic institutions have no separate, independent existence but are collective responses to or defences against the turbulence of the inner world.

Freud viewed social institutions as a 'response', in the sense of sublimations and defences, to the anxiety and guilt created by human sexual and aggressive strivings. Changes in these institutions over the course of history, he claimed, were only 'apparent', merely the manifestation of new editions of the elementary repertoire of defences and sublimations summoned to cope with the increased anxiety that follows a break-through of the two 'unchanging' impulses. Thus, for example, Freud characterized the Marxist position as a fragile, untenable psychological illusion. 'In abolishing private property', he maintained, 'we deprive the human love of aggression of one of its instruments, certainly a strong one, though not the strongest; but we have in no way altered the differences in power and influence which are misused by aggressiveness nor have we altered anything in its nature. Aggressiveness was not created by property.'[1]

In the later development of psycho-analytic thought, this rigid reductionist formulation of the relationship between the individual psyche and society's institutions has been amended. As noted in the first chapter, Freud himself increasingly acknowledged the influence of the society at large on the development of the individual psyche, especially its two sub-structures, the ego and the superego. Without denying the existence and the mercurial voice of the id, the mainstream of psycho-analytic thinking today does not view social institutions as instances of collective wish-fulfilment but acknowledges their independent existence and function.

In the cycle of generations, changes in a society's values and institutions, transmitted through the family, inevitably amend or alter the psychic structure of individuals belonging to the society. This psychological change may appear to be a transformation of identity, noticeably in the superficial 'behavioural' layers of personality, more subtle and gradual in the deeper layers, while the deepest layer (the bedrock of the inner world) may remain relatively unaffected through many generations. We must not forget, however, that the ego, on both the individual and the collective plane, continuously responds to social change as it endeavours to synthesize its previous experience with

13

new demands and thus to maintain the continuity of the self and its integration with the outer world. In other words, there are no insurmountable psychological obstacles to the development of the modern Indian identity Vivekananda envisioned. The traditional Indian identity elaborated throughout this book can, in principle and in theory, evolve in such a way that both its historical continuity and its integration with a changing environment are maintained.

Unfortunately, this theoretical model of evolutionary and cultural identity development presupposes only so much historical and environmental uncertainty as is manageable, in the sense that the environment—social, political, economic and technological—may be unsettled, but not to the point of 'turbulence'. If change is sudden, or so revolutionary in content that its demands on the individual are sharply discontinuous with his previous experience—as in the aftermath of revolution, foreign invasion, famine—or both sudden and discontinuous at the same time, then severe disruption in the ways individuals have learned to experience themselves and the world are unavoidable. Cataclysmic dislocations do not have the psychological effect of transforming and consolidating identity around emerging socio-political issues; rather, they are experienced as a threat to the integrity of the self, to the psychological status quo. Such a threat brings in its wake a collapse of self-esteem which, in turn, demands restitutive and reparatory counter-measures. Some individuals may make determined, even violent efforts to restore an earlier 'idyllic' state, while others may regress further, reacting with depressive modes of apathy, resignation and withdrawal. In moments of profound uncertainty and revolutionary disaffection, the same defensive measures adopted and 'learned' by individuals in dealing with the prototype of narcissistic injury during childhood are called into play.

The process of social change in India during the last one hundred and twenty-five years has been a gradual one, though there are indications of its pace having recently accelerated. I do not imply that all sections of society remained unscathed by the upheavals of Indian history during the nineteenth and twentieth centuries. Consider, for instance, the Muslim feudal classes after the British conquest of India or the aristocracy of the princely states following their integration into the new Indian nation-state after 1947. The response to the nationalist movement and to the 'modern' tasks of an independent polity have ranged from (actual or fantasied) efforts at a violent restoration of an earlier state, to despair and resignation among those groups who were exposed to sudden narcissistic injuries that shatter the collective grandiose self.

For the large majority of India's people, social change has been gradual and bearable. Most Indians have remained true to the traditional Indian identity in which the maternal cosmos of infancy and early childhood *is* the inner world. As we have seen, in the living 'mythology' of this cosmos, the central unconscious concerns are a simultaneous longing for and a dread of fusion with the maternal matrix, the celebration of dyadic intimacy and the struggle for individuation, the development of sensory modes and emotional sensibilities, and a fascination with everything in mental life that is born and flourishes in an individual's earliest, 'primary', relationship. The economic ethos of social institutions, which corresponds to a later developmental stage of childhood, remains subordinate to the religious ethos, which is related to the first stage of the human life cycle and has its developmental counterpart in man's earliest relationship with the mother. In Vivekananda's theological language, most Indians continue to believe that 'When God is worshipped as Mother, the Hindus call such worship the "right-hand" way; and it leads to spirituality but never to material prosperity. When God is worshipped in His terrible aspect (as the father?), that is, in the "left-hand" way, it leads usually to great material prosperity but rarely to spirituality and eventually it leads to degeneration and the obliteration of the race that practises it.'[2]

As one of the 'last bastions of the Mother' in an increasingly instrumental, technocratic and rational age, India is coming under increasing political, economic and demographic pressure to abandon its cultural emphasis on the emotional, aesthetic and instinctual qualities of life, on the primacy of primary group relationships and on the communal sharing of responsibility for individual lives. To predict the social consequences of these pressures, which are impinging on the childhood layer of the mind in an uprecedented way, is to venture into the business of crystal-gazing and the following observations may be viewed as a concluding counterpart to the 'Personal Word' in the introduction to this study.

A sudden increase in the intensity and tempo of social conflict or environmental pressure would undoubtedly result in sharp discontinuities of experience for large sections of Indian society who have maintained the traditional identity more or less intact. These discontinuities, in so far as they incorporate mandates of rational individual deliberation and decision making, regard for objectivity and empirical fact, and loss of the warmth and connectedness provided (and symbolized) by the primary groups of family and *jati*, may be experienced as injuries to self-esteem and may indeed evoke a 'regressive' employment of the full repertoire of psychological defences acquired in a Hindu childhood. In the outer world of society and politics, this might trigger in some groups outbreaks of violent rioting on inconsequential pretexts, as individuals react with narcissistic rage to the attack on the idealized parental image incorporated and elaborated in traditional norms and cultural values.[3] Others might withdraw into alcoholism or drug addiction, while still others might take refuge in the mystical and occult cults that tend to flourish in periods of social dis-ease.

The regressive phase would in all probability be followed by (or concurrent with) attempts at recovery; in the political and social arena, there would be a frantic search for, and an uncritical submission to charismatic leaders without regard for the political contents of their cause or ideology. At the same time, we might expect both a strengthening of the old collective sub-identities based on caste, religion, regional and ethnic affiliations, as well as the emergence of new groups espousing 'modern', totalist ideologies. As when the extended family take over the maternal care-taking role during the period of narcissistic crisis in the Hindu boy's life, individuals may be impelled to seek those wider groupings which, above all, promise to take encompassing *care* of their members. In the beginning at least, conventional Indian tolerance of deviance and respect for non-violence are likely to diminish as both the new and the old groupings seek to develop absolute value systems to govern where once the idealized parental image did, and to espouse elitist or militant expansionist ideologies to reconstitute and replenish the impoverished grandiose self of individual members. Whether these group identities are parochial or in the larger interest of the society, selfish or altruistic, revolutionary or reactionary, criminal or humanist, would in all likelihood have little effect on their ability to attract and hold their constituents. This ability would be based more on the satisfaction of archaic needs that have once again become virulent. Whereas initially the appeal of these groups may be limited to sections of society who are most susceptible to the pressures of social change—for example, youth and urbanized classes—we can expect an ever-widening circle of participation as more and more people are sucked into the wake of modernization. Even today, the popularity of the cults of Sai Baba, Rajneesh and many others, can be viewed as a response to increasing disturbances in narcissistic economy. They do not reflect any great increase in the quest for 'self-realization' but are more a reaction to the threat of impending depression and the consequent efforts at the restoration of a lost sense of self-esteem and 'meaning'. And I would postulate the same underlying psychological dynamics in the case of many new political movements such as the Anand Marg or the Shiv Sena. In short, we can expect an increasing destruction of the nascent, western-style individualism as more and more individuals seek to merge into collectivities that promise a shelter for the hurt, the conflicted and the shipwrecked.

Another important psychological factor related to the problem of social change is the notion that there are two kinds of reality—absolute and relative, ultimate and worldly—which is firmly (and unconsciously) embedded in the Hindu psyche. As we have seen, the 'ultimate' reality of the maternal cosmos of infancy is held superior to the 'worldly' reality of post-maternal childhood. Glaring economic and social inequalities which are a part of the worldly reality, have the status of *facts* and can never feel as real as the *moksha* ideals which give *meaning* to the Hindu life cycle, and especially to old age. However much concern may be expressed for the problems of worldly reality, the Hindu commitment to this reality cannot be a total one. It is as if there is a core self which, with a fluctuating intensity depending on the individual's stage of life, is always facing the ultimate reality and the maternal cosmos.

I am tempted to conclude from this that a psychological revolutionary situation in India can only come about if large sections of Hindu society question the usefulness of 'ultimate' reality, bring up to awareness its origins in Hindu infancy and firmly reject many of its social and cultural manifestations as vestiges of an archaic personal and historical past. I am, however, also acutely aware of the loss that such a rigid adherence to the world of facts implies—namely, the despair of old age, devoid of meaning, the shadowy underside of all societies which have accepted the verifiable world of facts as the only *really real* image of the world. Yet without a more equitable balance between different kinds of reality and without an integration of the material and the instinctual with the 'spiritual', Hindu culture may soon find itself entrapped in a field of critical environmental stresses. Like many other cultures which have overdeveloped only a part of man's nature and stressed only a part of his life experience, Hindu culture too may be caught up in contradictions and dead ends. This would be a great loss since the many insights to be gleaned from the nature of traditional Hindu childhood and society are of vital importance for mankind's radical need for a holistic approach to man's nature.

The Child in Indian Tradition

The maternity room in the southwest corner of the house, facing east, is light and airy. Two days ago, amid much ceremony—the trumpeting of conchshells, the playing of music and the beating of drums—the expectant mother entered this room accompanied by four older women of the family, all of them mothers of long standing. Together with the rest of the family, the women had worshipped the family priest and his apprentices before they had left for the room ritually prepared for imminent childbirth.

The room, its walls whitewashed and its floor freshly swept, is uncluttered. Simple mats, woven of bamboo reeds, are spread on the floor to be used as beds. Beside the expectant mother's mat, there is a clay pot containing the sacred *turyanti* plant, a jar of water, a mace, a spear and a sword—all of which help to ward off the evil spirits that threaten newborn infants. In one corner of the room, the *sutika* (impure) birth-fire burns brightly in a brazier; the flames fed with rice chaff and mustard seeds.

The woman reclines on her mat. As the labour pains begin, her limbs are massaged and rubbed with a herbal paste and she is addressed with comforting words of reassurance and practical instructions delivered in the calm voice of authority and experience. Outside, the rest of the family perform rites to ensure a safe delivery, and an apprentice priest goes around the house opening all the windows and doors and unlocking all the locks—practising sympathetic magic to loosen the foetus from its moorings in the womb. As the baby is born, one of the ministering women strikes stones near its ears while another dashes cold and warm water against its face to stimulate breathing. A third woman removes the mucus from the baby's mouth and throat with a lint of sterile cotton. *Ghee* and *Saindhav* salt are then given to the infant so that it will cough up any amniotic fluid it may have swallowed. The father now comes in to look at the baby's face. The paternal act of looking at a first-born son, the sacred texts assure him, will absolve him of all his debts to the gods and to the ancestors. But for a sensible man, and the father prides himself on being a sensible man, even the birth of a girl would have been only slightly less meritorious; her gift in marriage brings the father spiritual merit, and appreciably increases the store of his good *karmas*. Having seen the infant's face, the father goes out and takes a ritual bath. Accompanied by the priests and family elders the father then re-enters the maternity room for the birth ceremonies. The room is getting quite crowded.

The first rite is designed to stimulate the newborn's mental development. While a priest holds aloft a cup of butter and honey, the father alternately dips a gold spoon and the fourth finger of his right hand into the mixture and touches it to the infant's mouth. While the father recites the sonorous Gayatri *mantra* with its prayer for the growth of talent and intellect, the infant screams away lustily, oblivious to the women's ineffectual efforts to hush it into a semblance of ceremonial seriousness. Ignoring the commotion, the father bends down and whispers the child's secret name (it will be known only to the parents) into the boy's ear. Prompted by the priest, he haltingly recites in verse examples of immortality—the immortality of the ocean, of nectar, of sacrificial fire, of ancient sages—so as to prolong the child's own life. His efforts are supplemented by the priests who stand around the child breathing forcefully and rhythmically—longdrawn out breaths intended to quicken and prolong the breath of life in the infant. The birth rites continue as the father kneels down on the floor and with folded hands says a prayer of thanks to the spot of earth where the birth took place. He turns toward the mother and, following the priest's lead, recites a verse thanking and praising her for having borne a strong son. The child is then washed and ceremoniously given to the mother.

The birth ritual is not yet over. Before the men leave the maternity room, the father places a jar of water near the pillow and says, 'O water, you watch with gods. As you watch with the gods, thus watch this our mother, who is confined, and her child.' The men now leave the room, the father taking away the birth-fire which he will place outside the room, ceremoniously fuelling it twice a day till the mother gets up from childbed and re-enters the family. Depending upon the mother's condition and the auspiciousness of the astrological constellations, this may happen on the tenth, twelfth, fifteenth or even the thirty-second postpartum day, and will be an occasion for yet another ritual. For the moment, at least, a relative quiet descends on the delivery room. The women busy themselves with various tasks while the mother sinks into an exhausted sleep with the baby snuggled against her breast. Outside, the sounds of the great feast in which family members, friends and community elders are taking part, slowly gather momentum and volume.[1]

Once the birth ritual has introduced the baby to the family and the community, we arrive at the starting point of this inquiry: what are the traditional conceptions of the nature of children and childhood in India that inform the behaviour of the newborn's caretakers and influence their interaction with this new human being in their midst? Can we systematically identify a *cultural awareness* of the child that will help us to clarify our own adult attitudes toward the child before us? To answer these questions, I have looked at views of children expressed and reflected in various parts of the Indian cultural tradition. There are passages dealing with children in the law books, especially *The Laws of Manu*, and on the care and upbringing of infants and children in the three primary texts of traditional Indian medicine, *Ayurveda*. There are references to children and childhood in the *Ramayana* and the *Mahabharata* although I have only focused on the latter. And of course there are descriptions of childhood in ancient and medieval literature, although in this essay I have limited myself to the devotional poetry of Surdas and Tulsidas, which depicts the childhood of Krishna and Rama. The chief *samskaras* of childhood also contribute to the formation of an Indian consciousness and conception of childhood. These *samskaras* set temporal and behavioural limits to childhood and delineate childhood stages. In addition, their symbolic content and that of the traditional folk songs that accompany them, provide some indication of the chief characteristics of a given stage of childhood.[2] Perhaps I also need to mention at the outset that large parts of the Indian tradition of childhood are solely concerned with boys and ignore, if not dispossess, girls of their childhood.

The Child in Law

In ancient Indian law, and here I specifically refer to the *Laws of Manu*, the child is located very near the bottom of a social pyramid at the apex of which stands the householder, an adult male belonging to one of the twice-born castes. At the bottom of the pyramid, the child finds himself in motley company: persons belonging to the lowest castes and those who have lost their caste by practising forbidden occupations, the mentally deficient and the mentally disturbed, slaves and hired servants, actors and vagrants, the old and the sick, newly-married women and those who are pregnant.[3] The lower social status of the child is also evident in Manu's mourning prescriptions: the younger the deceased, the shorter the mourning period, and the otherwise elaborate funeral rites are minimal in case of a child's death.[4]

A close examination of Manu's injunctions reveals a sharp line of cleavage through the social pyramid, a line that divides the lower orders into two clearly differentiated groups. Towards one of these groups, comprising the casteless and the lowest castes, the violators of Brahminical social ethics and the rejectors of a brahminical pietistic life style, Manu consistently takes an authoritarian and punitive stance. Children, however, belong to the second group—consisting of women, the aged, the sick and the infirm—who deserve society's protection and claim its indulgence. Thus, even before serving invited guests (and guests, as we know, are almost on a par with gods in the Hindu tradition) the householder is enjoined to feed pregnant women, the sick and the young.[5] Although a man may not quarrel with learned men, priests and teachers, he is also forbidden to speak harshly to the aged, the sick and children.[6] Whereas the king is within his rights to exact retribution on those who question his authority or inveigh against his person, he is required to forgive children (as also the old and the sick) who may be guilty of lese-majesty. Although punishments, including fines, are prescribed for anyone soiling the king's highways, children are specifically exempted; they are only to be reprimanded and required to clean up after themselves.[7]

The protective indulgence shown towards the child is manifested most clearly where it matters the most (at least to the child)—namely, in Manu's pronouncements on the chastisement of children. Children (and women) are only to be beaten with a rope or a bamboo stick split at the end. The split bamboo, as we may remember from circus clowns' mock fights, makes a loud noise without inflicting much pain. Moreover, even this punishment is to be carried out only on the back and never on a 'noble part'—that is, not on the head or the chest.[8] To those who hold progressive views of child discipline, the beating of children may hardly seem like 'protective indulgence'. However, the extent of this indulgence becomes strikingly clear when we compare Manu's *Laws* with legal texts of other ancient societies. For example, there is evidence in the law codes and digests of ancient Rome to suggest that brutal forms of child abuse were common mistreatment, which the more enlightened emperors attempted to mitigate;[9] it was only as late as A.D. 374 that infanticide was declared a capital offence in the Roman world.[10]

In short, though by modern standards Manu's *Laws* have been severely condemned as a repository of inequity, sanctioning the repression of the weak and the poor, their attitude toward children —one of protective nurturance—is unexceptionable, at least within the premises of the patriarchal society which gave the *Laws* their birth.

The Child in Medicine

The treatment of the child constitutes one of the eight branches of the traditional Ayurvedic system of Indian medicine. I hesitate to equate this branch of medicine (known as *Balanga* in *Ashtangahridya* and *Kumarbhrutya* in the *Caraka* and *Susruta Samhitas*) with modern pediatrics, primarily because child development in the Indian system is thought to begin not with birth but with conception. Observations and speculations on foetal development comprise a large portion of the Ayurvedic literature on the child. The pre-natal period is considered equally important (if not more so) as the period of childhood proper, for the physical and mental development of the individual. This concern with the psychological development of the foetus distinguishes the content of *Balanga* from that of modern embryology. Clearly, the Hindu worldview has played an important role in defining the scope and content of Indian medical specialization dealing with the child—as doubtless Western images of the origins of life and the nature of man have informed the training of the modern pediatrician.

Since life is presumed to begin with conception, birth in the Indian tradition is a relatively later event that marks the end of the first stage of the life cycle rather than its beginning. According to the metaphysical doctrine of rebirth and transmigration of the soul, a doctrine shared by ancient Indian medics, it is at the moment of fertilization that the soul, in its 'subtle body' (which includes the mind) from previous life, enters the conceptus. The qualities of the sperm, the ovum, the *rasa* ('organic sap' or 'nutrition') and the soul's 'subtle body'—that is, its psychic constellation from its previous incarnation—are the determinants of the embryo's structural and functional growth.[11]

The critical period for the psychological development of the individual is said to commence from the third month of pregnancy (the fourth, in *Susruta Samhita*), when the latent 'mind' of the foetus becomes 'activated' or 'conscious' (*chetan*). In this stage of *dauhridaya* (literally, 'bi-cardiac'—where one heart belongs to the foetus and the other to the mother), the unborn child and the mother function psychologically as a unit mutually influencing each other. The feelings and affects of the foetus—a legacy from its previous birth—are transmitted to the mother through the channels of nutrition (*dhamanis*). For the future psychic well-being of the individual it is imperative—the texts are unanimous on this point—that the wishes and

cravings of the pregnant woman be fully gratified and the unit of expectant mother and foetus be completely indulged. For these desires
of the mother, Ayurveda claims, are but the mental strivings of the
foetus, deflected and distorted through the prism of the mother's
body and psyche. Of course, care should be taken while fulfilling the
mother's desires that nothing is done or given to her which is harmful
either to her or to her unborn child. If the pregnant woman's longing
becomes overwhelming, it is better—the texts go so far in their indulgence—that she be given the desired object even if it is injurious
to her health—care being taken to neutralize the object's baneful influence through appropriate countermeasures.[12] Finally, in the Ayurvedic tradition, the desires of the pregnant woman in *dauhridaya* are
thought to contain clues to the unborn child's psychological predispositions and character.

For a student of human development, all this is quite fascinating,
especially since Ayurveda claims, with much justification, to be a
science of rational therapeutics based on the collected observations
of a host of ancient doctors. Unfortunately, this claim to empirical
validity cannot always be substantiated. Our credulity is strained,
and the empirical likelihood of certain observations on child development becomes doubtful, when we read the predicted behaviour of the
unborn child—predictions based on the longings of his mother during
a particular period of pregnancy. Thus, for instance, the mother's desire to see a king means that the son will become rich and famous;
her wish for the fine clothes and ornaments signifies that the child
will have an aesthetic nature; her desire to visit a hermitage suggests
that the child will be self-controlled; and so on. There is a long list
of traits presumed to correlate with the expectant mother's culinary
cravings—each craving presaging that the unborn individual will have
the traits ascribed to that particular animal or bird. For instance, the
expectant mother's wish to eat beef means that her child will grow
up into a strong and hardy adult, the craving to eat partridge foretells
a timid and fearful disposition, and so on. There are other lists too,
cataloguing certain maternal activities and their influence on the
foetus; many of the items on these lists have little or no possible
basis in observation.

The hypothesized relationship between the feelings and behaviour
of the expectant mother and those of her offspring seems closer to the
omens, auguries, prophecies and soothsaying of the magical realm of
thought. This mixture of genuine medical opinion based on observa-

tion and practice on the one hand, and speculations and attitudes deriving from the magico-religious realm on the other, are not only characteristic of the Ayurvedic literature on the child but are a feature of Ayurveda as a whole.[13] However, my purpose is not the evaluation of the scientific merit of Ayurvedic observations on child development. Rather, let me note two prominent Ayurvedic notions that contribute to the Indian *idea* of the child.

The first is that the child, as a subject of study or treatment, cannot be viewed in isolation but must be understood as part of a larger matrix in which the mother-child unit, epitomized in the *dauhridaya* stage of pregnancy, is fundamental. Measures to promote the child's growth or to alleviate its distress are thus to be directed towards this 'unit', whose centre shifts only gradually from the mother to the child. Thus, for example, even as late as the end of the first year after birth, while the child is still being breast fed, many of its diseases are apt to be diagnosed as due to the 'vitiation' of the mother's milk. Therapeutic measures, including the administration of drugs, are directed toward the mother to remove this 'vitiation'. Whatever the medical rationale for these practices, their symbolic and psychological thrust is unmistakable; they emphasize the symbiosis of the mother and child and express the conviction that during the foetal period and for a while after birth, the removal of the mother's tensions and diseases is the key to the child's well-being.[14]

The second central idea in 'Indian child development' is the belief that the basic contours of personality are laid down *in utero*. In contrast with the Western, post-Freudian emphasis on early childhood as the vital period for psychological development, this period is relatively underplayed in the Hindu tradition, in favour of the embryonic period, especially the *dauhridaya* stage. It is not correct, however, that the Indian medical tradition has little to say about childhood proper. In fact, the Ayurvedic texts contain detailed and copious instructions on the care of the young child. These wide-ranging instructions—on such diverse topics as the time when a child should be encouraged to sit up or the specification of toys with regard to colour, size, shape and texture—reveal great solicitude concerning the period of infancy and early childhood. The voices of ancient doctors, in spite of the archaic language through which they reach us, sound strangely modern and positively Spockian as they expound on the relationship between child-rearing practices and personality development. The practice of persuading the child to eat or to stop crying by conjuring up threatening visions of ghosts, goblins and ferocious animals, they tell us, is to be avoided since it has a very harmful effect.[15] The child should not be awakened from sleep suddenly, they go on to say, nor should he be snatched or thrown up in the air. He should not be irritated, and he should be kept happy at all costs, as this is crucial for his psychological development and future well-being.[16]

In summary, Ayurvedic theory of optimal child development is an intriguing blend of the superstitious and the rational, the arcane and the modern. In its consistently humane attitude towards the child, however, ancient Indian medicine is irreproachable. With compassion and tenderness for the young, Ayurveda strives to develop the adult caretaker's capacity to comprehend the needs and emotions of the child—needs that are apt to be overlooked since they are articulated in voices that are frail and words that are indistinct.

Children in the Mahabharata

Of the three hundred and fifty odd references to children in the *Mahabharata*, many are mere records of birth, with perhaps a score having a supplementary verse that eulogizes the infant's physical and mental qualities. Later on in the epic, from the *Drona Parva* onward, 'children' are increasingly mentioned in the context of parental mourning as their sons die in the great war. In these descriptions, however, the child *qua* child is incidental—memories of his play and playfulness serving only to enhance the parents' grief at the loss of an adult son. Arjuna and Subhadra's distraught lamentations at Abhimanyu's death, Yudhishtira's grief when Ghatotkacha is killed, Dhritarashtra's poignant memories of the childhood of his sons, and many other instances of mourning are more evocative of the Hindu concept of death, and designed to help the survivors bear the death of their children with equanimity, rather than with giving us insight into the childhood of those who were slain in the battle.

For the rest, in the *Mahabharata* if there is one predominant child-related theme it is the importance attached to, and the intense longing expressed for, the birth of a son. A number of myths and didactic passages repeatedly emphasize that begetting a son is one of man's highest duties and the only way he can discharge the debt he owes to his ancestors.[17] Consider the story of Jaratkuru.

The renowned ascetic Jaratkuru, full of merit and great spiritual power derived from his sustained asceticism, was wandering around the world when one day he came across a deep pit. In this pit, the spirits of his ancestors—the *pitris*—were hanging head down, their feet tied to a tree trunk by a single skein of rope that was gradually being nibbled away by a large rat. It was evident that the *pitris* would fall down into the deep darkness of the pit. Moved by their pitiable condition, Jaratkuru enquired whether he could somehow save them from this fate, expressing his readiness to do so even if he had to give up all the rewards to which his great asceticism entitled him. 'Venerable *brahmacharin*', the *pitris* answered, 'thou desirest to relieve us! . . . O child, whether it is asceticism, or sacrifice, or whatever else there be of very holy acts, everything is inferior. These cannot count equal to a son. O child, having seen all, speak unto that Jaratkuru of ascetic wealth . . . tell him all that would induce him to take a wife and beget children.'[18]

Similarly, the sage Agastya, having failed to procreate, beholds his *pitris* in a like predicament.[19] Another ascetic, Mandapala, is told in no uncertain terms that in spite of his most ascetic efforts, certain celestial regions will forever remain closed to him, for they can be reached only by those who have had children—'Beget children therefore!' Mandapala is instructed; 'Thou shalt then enjoy multifarious regions of felicity!'[20]

Sons in the *Mahabharata* are not only seen as instrumental in the fulfilment of a sacred *duty* which, however agreeable and meritorious, still carries the connotation of religious necessity and social imposition, they are also portrayed as a source of emotional and sensual gratification. Listen to Shakuntala asking Dushyanta to acknowledge his son: 'What happiness is greater than what the father feels when the son is running towards him, even though his body be covered with dust, and clasps his limbs? Even ants support their own eggs without destroying them, then why shouldst not thou, virtuous as thou art, support thy own child? The touch of soft sandal paste, of women, of (cool) water is not so agreeable as the touch of one's own infant son locked in one's embrace. As a Brahmana is the foremost of all bipeds, a cow, the foremost of all quadrupeds, a protector, the foremost of all superiors, so is the son the foremost of all objects, agreeable to the touch. Let, therefore, this handsome child touch thee in embrace. There is nothing in the world more agreeable to the touch than the embrace of one's son.'[21]

In contrast to the joyous celebration at the birth of sons, girls generally receive a muted if not a totally cold reception. The religious merit reaped at the birth of a daughter is minimal; her entry into the world is accompanied by forebodings on the part of the parents. Thus, Indra's charioteer Matali, father of the beauteous Gunakeshi, laments: 'Alas, the birth of a daughter in the families of those that are well-behaved and high-born and possess reputation and humility of character, is always attended with evil results. Daughters, when born in respectable families, always endanger the honour of these families, their maternal and paternal families and the family into which they are adopted by marriage.'[22] And though King Drupada, for very good reasons of his own, wishes for the birth of a son, he seems to go to ludicrous lengths to deny the sex of the daughter who is finally born, futilely begs Shiva to change her sex and (after her birth) conceals her real identity and performs the rites prescribed for a male child.[23]

We find that the random remarks on children scattered throughout the epic do not permit us to discern any single, consistent view of the child. In the rare passages where the ascetic mode prevails, the attitude towards the child, because of the child's strong association with the procreative act, is one of unrelieved disgust. 'In consequence of the keen desire that men entertain for women, offspring proceed from them, due to (the action of) the vital seed. As one casts off from one's body such vermin as take their birth there but as are not on that account any part of oneself, even so should one cast off those vermin of one's body that are called children, who, though regarded as one's own, are not one's own in reality. From the vital seed as from sweat (and other filth) creatures spring from the body, influenced by the acts of previous lives or in the course of nature. Therefore, one possessed of wisdom should feel no regard for them.'[24] As I have indicated above, however, such a life-negating and rejecting attitude towards children is a minor theme in the *Mahabharata*. Most references to children in the text are positive, full of acceptance and a joyous generativity that is actively solicitous and protectively caring of the next generation. Indeed in a few passages the child is thoroughly idealized as a creature 'without desires and aversions'—and thus nearer to God.[25] In other passages, where the Bhakti mode prevails, one of the attributes of God is that of his *being* a child: 'Salutations to thee that art of the form of the rising sun, and that art of the form of a child, that art the protector of attendants (Krishna's cowherds), all of whom are of the form of children.'[26]

On the familiar problem of whether heredity or environment exerts a greater influence on the child's personality, the *Mahabharata* comes down firmly in favour of heredity. Heredity, we must remember, in the *Mahabharata* as in the rest of Indian tradition, is not simply a matter of biology. Together with the father's 'seed', the *karmic* balance from the previous life gives the child certain predispositions that are all-determining in their impact on individual behaviour. The *Mahabharata* thus holds the contribution of 'nurture' during the impressionable childhood years to be negligible, when compared with the influence of 'nature' which it conceives of in terms of a metaphysical biology.

In contrast to the Ayurveda, which accords some recognition to the part played by the mother's 'ovum', the *Mahabharata* is patriarchically imperious in granting legitimacy only to the father's 'seed' in the formation of a son's personality. There are many passages in the text with an identical refrain: namely, that the father himself is born as the son, and with the placing of his seed in the womb he has placed his own self.[27] Child-rearing practices and the environment of the early years cannot alter the basic nature of the child, which has received this strong 'biological' stamp. This view comes through clearly in the story of Matanga, who was sired by a Shudra but adopted at birth by a Brahman. The Brahman brought Matanga up as his own son and with due performance of all the rites of infancy and childhood ordained for Brahmans. One day, Matanga was asked by his father to fetch some materials speedily for a sacrifice. Matanga set out on a cart drawn by a young ass, who, instead of obeying the carter, set out in the direction of its mother. Angry, Matanga began to strike the animal on its nose with a goad. On seeing these marks of violence on her offspring's nose, the she-ass said: 'Do not grieve, O child, for this treatment. A *chandala* it is that is driving thee . . . He is simply proving the order of his birth by conducting himself in this way. The nature which he hath derived from his sire forbids the rise of those sentiments of pity and kindness that are natural to the Brahmana.'[28]

We may then conclude that the *Mahabharata* elaborates and deepens our understanding of the two themes in the traditional Indian view of childhood encountered in ancient law and medicine. First, there is an intense parental longing for children, and their upbringing is characterized by affectionate indulgence. This 'child-centredness', however, as the *Mahabharata* makes clear, is limited to boys: the Indian tradition is indifferent, if not overtly hostile, to the developmental fate of girls. Secondly, the Indian tradition subscribes to an ideology that downgrades the role of the environment and nurture in the development of a child, and instead emphasizes a deterministic conception of mystical heredity. Whereas in Ayurveda this mystical heredity is still loose and composed of many factors, in the *Maha-bharata* it is reduced to the *karmas* of the previous life and the attributes of the father (especially his caste) transmitted through his 'seed'.

The Child in Literature

In classical Sanskrit literature, children rarely figure as individuals in their own right, with activities, reactions and feelings separate from those of their all-powerful parents. The child usually appears as a wish—that is, in the context of a couple's, or more often a father's, longing for offspring—or as the fulfilment of the wish—in descriptions of parental happiness when a child is born and in lyrical accounts of parental love, usually of a father for his son. Thus, to take two well-known examples, Bhavabhuti describes Rama's love for Lava and Kusha, while Banabhatta rhapsodizes over Prabhakar-vardhan's love for his son, Harsha.[29] The greatest of all Sanskrit poets, Kalidasa, both follows and deviates somewhat from this pattern. He too is lyrical about the father's feeling for his child, for instance, in his descriptions of Dushyanta's feelings for his son Sarvadamana and of Dilip's love for Raghu in *Raghuvamsha*. Here is Dilip's response to Raghu's birth:

He went in immediately [on hearing the news] and as the lotus becomes motionless when the breeze stops, he gazed at his son's face with the same still eyes. Just as tides come into the ocean when it sees the moon, similarly the King [Dilip] was so happy on seeing his son that he could not contain the happiness in his heart.[30]

However, in addition, Kalidasa sensitively portrays, with much empathy, the sage Kanva's love for his *daughter* Shakuntala.

Classical Sanskrit literature is not a living tradition in the same sense that classical law and traditional medicine are; rather, its influence is indirect and hard to pin down. For an account of children and childhood in the Indian literary tradition, we must turn to the classics of the regional languages. Here, however, I will tap only one literary stream, the medieval Hindi literature associated with the Bhakti movement, and look especially at the poems and songs of Surdas and Tulsidas. My reasons for choosing Bhakti-inspired literature (in addition to its accessibility) are not hard to comprehend. First, this is the most powerful surviving literary tradition in the

Hindi-speaking belt of northern and central India. Through the continuing popularity of its songs and poems, it has moulded folk consciousness in a way that is rare for *any* literature. Second, this literature in general, and the poems of Surdas in particular, are unique among the literary traditions of the world (as far as I know) in that children and childhood—Krishna's childhood in Surdas and Rama's childhood in Tulsidas—are placed close to the centre of poetic consciousness and creativity, rather than at its periphery. Surdas, in fact, composed five hundred verses on Krishna's childhood alone![31] Apart from their religious significance, these verses are a rich source for Hindu ideals of childhood and for delineating the topography of a culturally approved utopia of childhood.

A concept such as the 'utopia of childhood' suggests that I will treat the literary material on the child somewhat differently from similar material in legal and medical texts. Whereas with law and medicine the effort was to summarize and rearrange the scattered textual material on the child into unified and coherent constructs, here with the literature, I propose to add, and *consciously* emphasize, a point of view. This point of view is frankly psychological. It is based on the assumption that poetic descriptions of the infancy and childhood of Krishna and Rama also contain certain desires that both *relate* to, and *derive* from, the period of childhood. These desires, often not conscious, constitute the *fantasy* of childhood, which is not idiosyncratic to the poet-creators but instead, by virtue of being widely shared by audiences through the centuries, has acquired the status of an Indian child-utopia. Before we consider the main themes of this child-utopia, however, let us look at its genesis and position in the Bhakti literature more closely.

The religious poetry of the Bhakti—the devotional approach to the Divine—is chiefly of two types. In one, the poet (and through him, the devotee) places himself in relation to the Godhead as a child to his parent; he seeks forgiveness for transgressions and tries to evoke the parental response of nurturance. This is, of course, a common theme in the religious literatures of the world, although Indian Bhakti poetry differs from devotional literature in other societies by the fact that it conceives of the Divine in terms of a maternal rather than a paternal matrix. To give two brief illustrations: the first a short poem by Kabir (fifteenth century):

> Mother, I am your child
> Why not forgive my faults?

The child misbehaves on many days.
They are not the days the mother remembers.
He catches her hair and hits her.
She does not reduce her affection.
Kabir says, it is evident.
A child's unhappiness is the mother's pain.[32]

The second is by the Bengali religious poet Ramprasad (seventeenth century):

O Mother! my desires are unfulfilled;
My hopes are ungratified;
But my life is fast coming to an end.
Let me call Thee, Mother, for the last time;
Come and take me in Thy arms.
None loves in this world;
This world knows not how to love;
My heart yearns, O Mother, to go there,
Where Love reigns supreme.[33]

Both these songs mirror a widespread, and perhaps universal, pattern of spiritual longing for a transcendence of separation from the Godhead. The attributes of the child (devotee) emphasized in this poetry are his yearning for infinite and unconditional love, the wish for a forgiving acceptance of his imperfections, and his search for the caretaker's responsive face.

The uniqueness of Bhakti poetry, however, lies more in its second school, where we find a surprising reversal. Here the poet (devotee) is as a mother towards God, who is the child. The celebration of the Divine, as in Surdas's poems of Krishna, takes place through the metaphor of celebration of the child. The aspects that are admiringly emphasized as divine attributes, as Kinsley has pointed out, are the child's freedom and spontaneity, his simplicity, charm and delight in self.[34]

Krishna is singing in the courtyard.
He dances on his small feet, joyous within.
Lifting up his arms, he shouts for the black
and white cows.
Sometimes he calls Nandbaba, sometimes he
goes in and out of the house.
Seeing his reflection, he tries to feed it.
Hidden, Yashoda watches the play that makes
her so happy.
Surdas says, to see Krishna's play every day
is bliss.[35]

Tulsidas sings:

> Self-willed he [Rama] insists on having the moon.
> He sees his shadow and is frightened.
> Clapping his hands, he dances.
> Seeing his child-play
> All mother-hearts are brimming over with happiness.
> Becoming angry, he is obstinate.
> And remains stubborn till he gets what he wants.
> Tulsidas says, the sons of the King of Ayodhya live
> In the temple of his heart.[36]

In an adult-centred world that overvalues abstractions, prudence and reason, it is refreshing to find Bhakti poetry celebrating such childlike virtues as intensity and vivaciousness, capacity for sorrow and delight, mercurial anger and an equally quick readiness to forget and forgive injuries. In the Indian child-utopia these qualities are not seen as 'childish', to be socialized out of existence, but valuable attributes of human beings—of all ages—since they are but an expression of the Divine.

The second theme in the child-utopia of Bhakti poetry is the rapt play between mother and child. In poem after poem, we see Yashoda and Krishna, Kausalya and Rama, playfully, even blissfully, absorbed in each other. They are portrayed as oblivious to their surroundings, existing in a 'temporary world within the ordinary world, dedicated to the performance of an act apart'.[37] In this world, nothing exists for the mother but the child; the smallest expression of his being enhances the mother's erotic and affiliative leeway. Yashoda, for instance, is so full of joy at seeing Krishna's milk-teeth that, absorbed in her love for him, she loses consciousness of her own body. It is in these scenes of mother–child interplay that the Bhakti poets come into their own.

Surdas writes:

> O Nanda's small Krishna, leave the butter-churn.
> Again and again says Yashoda, Nanda's queen.
> Move to one side, my life, my wealth, I'll give
>   you the butter.
> My priceless treasure, do not be obstinate.
> He [Krishna] who is meditated upon by all beings
> Is kissed on the face by Yashoda and lifted upon
>   her shoulder.[38]

Similarly, Tulsidas:

> Queen Kausalya, with the beautiful Rama in her
>   lap, is gracing the bed.

Her eyes turned into *chakors*, they fly to Rama's
 face like the moon.
Sometimes she lies down and gives him her breast.
Sometimes she presses him to her heart.
Singing of his child-play, she is happily absorbed
 in drinking the nectar of love.
Behind the clouds, Brahma, Shiva, sages and the
 gods look on with happiness.
Tulsidas says, no one but Kausalya ever had such
 bliss.[39]

Analogous to the mother–child interplay, or rather as its extension, we find a third theme in Bhakti literature, in which the child is at the centre of an admiring circle of adults. If the mother is in the foreground, then the background consists of the adults in the community —the *gopis* of Gokul, the citizens of Ayodhya—milling around him. This particular theme reveals the child's primary need to be central to his world, rather than exist forlornly at its outskirts, to cause a glow in the eyes of adults rather than be looked at with indifference.

In medieval Bhakti literature, then, the child is truly an exalted being. To grow up at the centre of his human world, absorbed in interplay with the mother, admired for his spontaneity and self-delight, seem to be the poet's conception of a child's 'birthright'—the utopia of Indian childhood.

Stages of Childhood in the Indian Tradition

The conceptualization of the human life cycle unfolding in a series of stages, with each stage having its unique 'tasks' and the need for an orderly progression through the stages, is an established part of traditional Indian thought, best exemplified in the well-known scheme of *ashramadharma*.[40] *Ashramadharma*, however, focuses largely on the period of youth and adulthood, and neglects to assign any formal importance to the stages of childhood. For an understanding of how these stages have been envisioned in the Indian tradition, we must turn to Ayurveda and the ritual literature that describes the childhood *samskaras*—the expressive and symbolic performances, including rites and ceremonies that are so to speak held over the child and mark his transition from one stage to another. Parenthetically, I should perhaps add that the concept of a child developing through a series of stages requiring differential treatment by his caretakers, a notion that some historians of Western childhood consider 'modern', has always been a part of Indian folk-consciousness. It is expressed through such proverbs as 'Treat a son like a king for the first five years, like a slave for the next ten, and like a friend thereafter.'

The contribution of Ayurveda to the Indian image of childhood stages lies in its *formal* recognition of different periods of childhood and its assignment of 'appropriate' ages to each period. Consistent with the belief that life begins with conception rather than at birth, Ayurveda identifies five such childhood periods: (1) *Garbha*, or the foetal period; (2) *Ksheerda* (0–6 months), when the infant lives entirely on milk; (3) *Ksheerannada* (6 months–2 years), the period of early childhood in which weaning takes place; (4) *Bala* (2–5 years); and (5) *Kumara* (5–16) years.[41] As we shall see, this division of childhood is reflected and affirmed by ritual literature, in so far as the major rituals of childhood take place at ages that mark the transition from one period to another.

Looking at the timing and content of the various childhood *samskaras*, it appears that one of the major thrusts of these rituals is the gradual integration of the child into society, with the *samskaras*, as it were, beating time to a measured movement that takes the child away from the original mother–infant symbiosis into full-fledged membership in his community. Psychologically, through their periodic ritual reassurance of familiarity and mutuality, the *samskaras* seek to counteract the child's regressive longings and primal fears of abandonment and separation, which are invariably activated in the transition from one stage of life to another. By ceremoniously marking the transition points of a widening world of childhood and placing the child at the centre of rites that also command the intense participation of the whole family, the *samskaras* heighten a sense of both belonging and personal distinctiveness—that is, they strengthen the child's budding sense of identity.[42] Let us look at the major *samskaras* that mark the critical points of social development more closely.

A month after birth, in the naming rite of *namakarana*, the mother and infant emerge from the seclusion of the maternity room into the bustle of an expectant family, as the mother ceremoniously places the baby in the father's lap for the name-giving ceremony.[43] From the family, the mother and infant move into the wider world in the third or fourth month with the performance of *nishkramana*, the child's first outing or 'looking at the sun' and 'looking at the moon', as the texts poetically describe the infant's ritual introduction to the world and the cosmos. Between the sixth and ninth months, there is the important rite of *annaprasana*, the first time the child is given solid food, thus marking the onset of weaning and its psychological counterpart—the process of the child's individuation and separation from the mother.

If these rites are any guide, the process of individuation is deemed complete by the third year. At three, the child's 'psychological birth' is marked by the important rites of *chudakarana* or tonsure. The child is generally taken to the temple of a mother goddess (to the bank of a river in some regions) and his baby hair shaved and offered to the goddess. He is then dressed up in new clothes, which are a miniature replica of the clothes worn by adult members of his community. The symbolism of death and rebirth—in our terms, the death of the mother–infant symbiosis and the psychological birth of the child as a separate individual—is at the heart of the many rituals connected with *chudakarana*. Thus, for instance, in the Bhojpuri region of northern India, before the child's head is shaved and he is dressed in new clothes, the women of the family take the child to the Ganges and ceremoniously cross the river in a boat.[44] Moreover, the folk songs sung at the time of *mundan* (as the *samskara* is called in north India) are the *sohras*, the songs that are also sung at birth. In the popular tradition, it is only after the child's tonsure that he is considered ready for the process of discipline and the family's socialization efforts.

The rite of *vidyarambha* between the fifth and seventh years, when the child is supposed to be old enough to learn to read and write, is followed by the major *samskara* of *upanayana*. *Upanayana* marks the culmination, the grand end of childhood. Traditionally performed (depending upon the caste) anywhere between the eighth and twelfth year, *upanayana* initiates the child's 'social birth' into the wider community. As a text puts it, 'Till a boy is eight years old he is like one newly born, and only indicates the caste in which he is born. As long as his *upanayana* ceremony is not performed the boy incurs no blame as to what is allowed or forbidden.'[45] The initiation ceremony is elaborate, its preparatory rites designed to drive home the fact of the child's separation from his family and the final break with his mother. In its traditional version, the child is smeared with a yellowish paste and expected to spend the whole night in a pitch-dark room in absolute silence—a re-creation of the embryonic state—before he emerges the next morning for one of the most moving and poignant ceremonies of this *samskara*, the sharing of a meal with his mother, which is the last time the mother and son will ever eat together. Thus although as an initiation rite, *upanayana* contains many rituals symbolizing a hopeful beginning, it nevertheless also clearly marks the regretted end of a familial and familiar world—the world of childhood.

The question of the extent to which this traditional image of the stages of childhood remains part of modern consciousness is difficult to answer with any certainty. We do know that most of the childhood *samskaras*, especially those of birth, tonsure and initiation, are performed in the case of boys of the upper and intermediate castes in the same order and at approximately the same ages as outlined above.[46]

In fact, the omnibus reference to the 'child' in the discussion of the stages of childhood in the Indian tradition conceals two omissions: girls and children belonging to the lower castes have been largely excluded from this tradition—as indeed women and the lower castes have been excluded from most of the prescriptions and formulations of the Hindu tradition. To take just one example, the *sohras*—the joyous songs of celebration sung at the birth of a child in the Hindi-speaking belt—are almost never sung for newborn daughters. Indeed, many *sohras* express the mother's relief that this has not been the case and her worst fears have proven to be unfounded: 'As the *turiyan* leaf trembles with a gust of wind, my heart trembles at the thought that I may give birth to a daughter.'[47] With the proviso that 'child' primarily refers to a boy belonging to one of the upper castes and that the ages shown under each stage of childhood are only approximate or, more precisely, that they are the 'usual' ages,[48] the Hindu scheme of social development of the child can be schematically presented as in the chart below (see p. 208).

Traditions of Childhood: Indian and Western

Considering its fateful implications for the lives of children—and adults—the highlighting of a society's traditions of childhood, the historically derived pattern of deprivations and compensations offered to its children, becomes an important task. For this task to be properly fulfilled, one would also expect that the Indian tradition of childhood would be compared and contrasted with the childhood traditions of other societies. Such a comparative perspective, besides highlighting specific elements of one's own tradition, can also be socially therapeutic in so far as it shows us the range of human caretaking patterns that lie between the necessary minimum to keep the

Stages of Childhood: The Hindu Scheme of Social Development

Childhood period	Stage	Central mode of relationship	Rite marking transition into following stage
I. *Garbha*	1. Foetus	Symbiotic ('*dauhridya*')	*Jatakarma*
II. *Ksheerda*	2. Early infancy (0—1 month)	Dyadic intimacy	*Namakarana*
	3. Middle infancy (1—3/4 months)	Dyad in family	*Nishkramana*
	4. Late infancy (3/4—6/9 months)	Dyad in world	*Annaprasana*
III. *Ksheerannada*	5. Early childhood (6/9 months—2/3 years)	Dyadic dissolution (psychological birth)	*Chudakarana*
IV. *Bala*	6. Middle childhood (2/3—5/7 years)	Familial	*Vidyarambha*
V. *Kumara*	7. Late childhood (5/7—8/12 years)	Familial dissolution (social birth)	*Upanayana*

child physically and emotionally alive and the anxious maximum beyond which the child's development is apt to be stunted. Such a systematic comparison with other traditions cannot be attempted here, especially since for most societies (including the Indian) the histories of childhood still remain to be written. In conclusion, therefore, I shall content myself with noting a few impressions of the contrast between the Indian and Western traditions of childhood.

For an Indian, the most striking aspect of recent Western scholarship on childhood is its depiction of an enduring ideological conflict between the rejecting and accepting attitudes towards the child.[49] Some Western scholars of childhood have discerned a definite movement within this conflict, a steady evolution that has made the Western ideology of the child increasingly humane and nurturant.[50] In Western antiquity and till perhaps the thirteenth century, adult attitudes toward children were generally dominated by an ideology that had little empathy for the needs of children. This ideology looked upon the child as a nuisance and an unwanted burden, perfunctorily tolerating brutal treatment of children by their parents as well as such associated phenomena as infanticide, the sale of children and their casual abandonment.[51] It is, however, also demonstrable that there has been a gradual progression in the Western ideology of the child. From the earlier external suppression that permitted the grossest physical torture and when sexual abuse of children was commonplace, by the sixteenth and seventeenth centuries the ideological emphasis was decisively shifting towards an *internal* suppression in which child training and discipline were stressed. Here, for instance, is how an eminent scholar of the American family describes attitudes towards the child in colonial America: 'And what of the young in colonial America? There remain from the period various books and essays on the proper deportment of children, which convey some impression at least of what was expected. A central theme in these works—especially, but not exclusively, in the writings of the Puritans—is the need to impose strict discipline on the child virtually from the beginning of life. Here is the advice of Reverend John Robinson, a leading preacher among the Pilgrims just prior to their departure for America: "Surely there is in all children . . . a stubbornness and stoutness of mind arising from natural pride which must in the first place be broken and beaten down, so that the foundation of their education being laid in humility and tractableness, other virtues may in their time be built thereon." The key terms are "broken" and "beaten down". The child was regarded as coming into the world with an inherently corrupted and selfish nature, and this created *the* central problem for parents.'[52]

From parental efforts aimed at conquering the child's will, the Western ideology of caretaking progressed further towards according the child a greater freedom, as in the nineteenth and twentieth centuries awareness of the sensibilities and needs of children increased appreciably. This movement towards the fostering attitude continues unabated. The spate of recent books on the rights of children, the effect of working mothers on the development of children, 'The Year of the Child' announced by the United Nations and so on, are some of the expressions of this progress: current manifestations of an old movement towards evolving an ideology of childhood which makes the child and its needs central to the caretaking process.

The conflict between the rejecting and fostering attitudes towards the child, so marked in the Western tradition and which perhaps provides it with its evolutionary impetus, is simply not a feature of the Indian tradition. As we have seen in this essay, the evidence from textual sources is overwhelming that the child in Indian tradition is ideologically considered a valuable and welcome human being to whom the adults are expected to afford their fullest protection, affection and indulgence. Consider, for instance, the reflection of this ideology in linguistic usage where the notion of the child being autonomous and self-directing is much more pronounced than in English or German. In Hindi for example, what adults do to children is *palna posna*—protecting–nurturing; they are not 'reared', 'brought up'. With its implications of training the child, teaching him to conform to social norms and 'channelling his impulses', the model of *socialization* (which governs contemporary Western caretaking) is a logical next step in a historical evolution where the preceding model was that of disciplining and conquering the child's will. In its general orientation and focus, such a model is necessarily foreign to the Indian tradition that did not have to overcome an original burden of rejection of children. In fact, as we saw in our discussion of the child-utopia that is reflected in Bhakti songs and poems, there is a specific stream in the Indian tradition of childhood that values precisely those attributes of the child which have *not* been 'socialized'. In this tradition, it is the child who is considered nearest to a perfect, divine state and it is the adult who needs to learn the child's mode of experiencing the world. Here the proper form of interaction between adults and children is not conceived of in terms of socialization but *interplay*. Closer to that Indian tradition, interplay as a paradigm of growing up would emphasize the *adult-child unit*, concern itself with their *mutual* learning and mutual pleasure in each other. It would thus sharply differ from the socialization model that concentrates solely on the child and his movement towards adulthood.

Before losing ourselves in any self-congratulatory panegyrics, we must also note the gravest drawback of the Indian tradition—its relative rejection of girls. By rejection I do not mean to imply that the texts we have considered show any great hostility or contain instances of dramatic and overt violence towards female children. Even in the myths of abandonment of children in the *Mahabharata*, Menaka's abandonment of her new-born daughters Pramadvara and Shakuntala is counterbalanced by Kunti abandoning the infant Karna. It is more in its exaggerated emphasis on sons, in the joyous din at the birth of male children, that the silent rejection of female infants stands out so clearly and has had such grave consequences for Indian women and society.[53] Again, by 'grave consequences' I am not alluding to the failure of Indian tradition to erect an ideological bulwark against female infanticide among certain castes at certain periods of history. Infanticide by sheer violence has probably always been exceptional all over the world. Rejection, or at best, ambivalence towards girls has always worked (and continues to do so) in a more subtle and insidious manner. It is reflected in statistics that show a higher rate of female infant mortality and underlies the crushed spirit of countless women for which no statistics but only folk-songs are available. Without the removal of this ambivalence towards the female child, without an ideological change that will ensure society's protection and nurturance to *all* its children, the Indian tradition of childhood, with all its dazzling 'achievement', remains gravely flawed.

Notes and References

CHAPTER I: Introduction

1. Anna Freud, 'The Concept of Developmental Lines', *The Psychoanalytic Study of the Child*, vol. 18, New York: International Universities Press, 1963. pp. 245–65. See also Lawrence Kohlberg and R. B. Kramer, 'Continuities and Discontinuities in Childhood and Adult Moral Development', *Human Development*, 12, 1969, 93–120.
2. Erik H. Erikson, *Identity: Youth and Crisis*, New York: W. W. Norton, 1968.
3. See Heinz Kohut, 'Introspection, Empathy and Psychoanalysis', *Journal of American Psychoanalytic Association*, 7, 1959, 459–83.
4. For an authoritative statement of the psycho-analytic view on the relationship between man and his culture, see Heinz Hartmann, Ernst Kris and Rudolph M. Loewenstein, 'Some Psychoanalytic Comments on Culture and Personality', in G. B. Wilbur and W. Muensterberger (eds.), *Psychoanalysis and Culture*, New York: International Universities Press, 1951, pp. 3–31; see also Sidney Axelrad, 'Comments on Anthropology and the Study of Complex Cultures', in W. Muensterberger (ed.), *Man and his Culture*, London: Rapp and Whiting, 1969, pp. 273–93.
5. For earlier psycho-analytic discussions on the functions of a myth, see Sigmund Freud, *Totem and Taboo* (1913), The Standard Edition of the Complete Psychological Works of Sigmund Freud, ed. J. Strachey, vol. 13, London: Hogarth Press, 1958 (hereafter cited as Standard Edition), and Otto Rank, *Das Inzest-Motiv*, Leipzig and Vienna: Deuticke, 1912. An even earlier, non-psycho-analytic writer with essentially the same view of myths is Kierkegaard; see Soren Kierkegaard, *Der Begriff Angst*, Hamburg: Rowohlt Verlag, 1960, p. 44. For later, ego-psychological writings on the subject, see Jacob A. Arlow, 'Ego Psychology and the Study of Mythology', *Journal of American Psychoanalytic Association*, 9, 1961, 371–93; Max M. Stern, 'Ego Psychology, Myth and Rite', in W. Muensterberger et al. (eds.), *The Psychoanalytic Study of Society*, vol. 3, New York: International Universities Press, 1964, pp. 71–93, and Harry A. Slochower 'Psychoanalytical Distinction between Myth and Mythopoesis', *Journal of American Psychoanalytic Association*, 18, 1970, 150–64.
6. Wolfgang Loch, 'Determinaten des Ichs. Beitrüge David Rapaport's zur psychoanalytischen Ich-Theorie', *Psyche*, 25, 1971, 395. See also Paul Parin and W. Morgenthaler, 'Ego and Orality in the Analysis of West Africans', in W. Muensterberger et al., *The Psychoanalytic Study of Society*, vol. 3, p. 197, and P. Parin et al., *Die Weisse Denken Zuviel*, Zurich: Atlantis, 1963.
7. J. W. McCrindle, *Ancient India as Described by Megasthenes and Arrian* (2nd rev. edn.), Calcutta: Chukervertty, Chatterjee & Co., 1960, p. 100.
8. Quoted in Aubrey Lewis, 'Chairman's Opening Remarks', in A. V. S. De Rueck and R. Porter (eds.), *Transcultural Psychiatry*, London: J. and A. Churchill, 1965, p. 1.
9. This view is shared by David G. Mandelbaum who in a similar context remarks that 'No generalization can be proved, disproved or modified before it is formulated', see *Society in India*, vol. 1, Berkeley and Los Angeles: University of California Press, 1970, p. 8.
10. Alfred L. Kroeber and Clyde Kluckhohn identified 160 definitions in the English language! See *Papers Peabody Museum*, 47, 1952, 181.
11. For a concise discussion of the cultural background of personality, see Theodore Lidz, *The Person: His Development throughout the Life Cycle*, New York and London: Basic Books, 1968, pp. 10–16.

12. George Devereaux, 'Normal and Abnormal: The Key Concepts of Ethno-psychiatry', in W. Muensterberger (ed.), *Man and his Culture*, pp. 113–36.
13. In one of his letters to Fliess in 1897, Freud writes of civilization as a 'progressive renunciation'; Freud, Standard Edition, vol. 1, p. 257.
14. The notable exceptions are the writings of Herbert Marcuse, *Eros and Civilization*, Boston: Beacon Press, 1955, and Norman Brown, *Life against Death*, London: Routledge and Kegan Paul, 1959.
15. In Heinz Hartmann's well-known phrase, 'his average expectable environment'. See *Ego Psychology and the Problem of Adaptation*, New York: International Universities Press, 1958, p. 23.
16. E. H. Erikson, *Identity: Youth and Crisis*, p. 47.
17. Freud, *New introductory Lectures in Psychoanalysis* (1933), Standard Edition, vol. 22, p. 67.
18. For an excellent summary of the 'ego-psychological' views on the relationship between individual and society from earliest infancy, see David Rapaport, *Collected Papers of David Rapaport*, ed. Merton M. Gill, New York: Basic Books, 1967, pp. 596–624. See also Fred I. Weinstein and Gerald Platt, *Psychoanalytic Sociology*, Baltimore and London: John Hopkins University Press, 1973.
19. Pandurang V. Kane, *History of Dharmasastra*, Poona: Bhandarkar Oriental Research Institute, vol. 2 (part 1), 1933, p. 188.
20. Jawaharlal Nehru, *The Discovery of India*, Calcutta: The Signet Press, 1946, p. 30.
21. Ibid., pp. 38–9.

CHAPTER II: The Hindu World Image

1. By 'community unconscious' I do not mean Jung's collective unconscious but suggest the term in the Eriksonian sense of the community dimension of identity.
2. E. H. Erikson, *Gandhi's Truth*, New York: W. W. Norton, 1969, p. 34.
3. *Brihadaranyaka Upanishad*, 4. 3. 21. In this particular Upanishad the number of states is given as three, and the nature of liberation (*moksha*) is said to be revealed in the third and last state. The doctrine of four states, the commonly accepted number in Samkhya psychology, is set forth in the *Mandukya* and other Upanishads.
4. *The Portable Blake*, ed. A. Kazin, New York: Viking Press, 1946, p. 486.
5. S. Freud, *Civilization and its Discontents* (1930), Standard Edition, vol. 21, p. 64.
6. Roland Fischer, 'The Cartography of Ecstatic and Meditative States', *Science*, 174, 1971, 897–904.
7. Arthur Osborne, *Ramana Maharishi and the Path of Self-knowledge*, London: Rider, 1970, p. 45.
8. Ibid., p. 46.
9. H. Hartmann, *Essays in Ego Psychology*, New York: International Universities Press, 1964, p. 127.
10. E. H. Erikson, *Identity: Youth and Crisis*, pp. 220–4.
11. Swami Vivekananda, *The Yogas and Other Works*, ed. S. Nikhilananda, New York: Ramakrishna–Vivekananda Center, 1953, p. 593.
12. S. Freud, *New Introductory Lectures* (1933), Standard Edition, vol. 22, p. 73.
13. Vivekananda, op. cit., pp. 608–9.
14. Bernard Apfelbaum, 'On Ego Psychology: A Critique of the Structural Approach to Psychoanalytic Theory', *International Journal of Psychoanalysis*, 47, 1966, 451–75.
15. S. Freud, *An Outline of Psychoanalysis* (1940), Standard Edition, vol. 23, p. 148.
16. S. Freud, *Civilization and its Discontents*, p. 140.
17. See Lewis Thomas, *The Lives of a Cell*, New York: Viking Press, 1974, especially p. 24.

18. Siva Purana, 10. 187, quoted in Wendy D. O'Flaherty, *Asceticism and Eroticism in the Mythology of Siva*, London: Oxford University Press, 1973, p. 173.
19. *Anandabhairava* of Prema-Dasa, quoted in O'Flaherty, op. cit., p. 113.
20. Swami Narayanananda, *The Mysteries of Man, Mind and Mind-Functions* (2nd rev. edn.), Rishikesh: Narayanananda Universal Yoga Trust, 1967, p. 664.
21. Vivekananda, op. cit., p. 629. Perhaps I should emphasize that the unconscious has always occupied the central place in Hindu psychological theory. It's a curious fact that in spite of a growing amount of literature on the subject now available in Western languages, the insights and discoveries of Indian depth psychology have neither been yet recognized nor evaluated in the West. Parochial treatments of the subject, for example, H. F. Ellenberger, *The Discovery of the Unconscious: The History and Evolution of Dynamic Psychiatry*, New York: Basic Books, 1970, are a rule rather than an exception.
22. Ibid., p. 609. See also Swami Sivananda, *Mind: Its Mysteries and Control*, Sivanandanagar, U.P.: Divine Life Society, 1974, pp. 242–3.
23. *Amitayur-dhyana-sutra*, trans. F. Takakusu,, in M. Müller (ed.), *Sacred Books of the East*, vol. 49, Oxford: Clarendon Press, 1910, p. 161 ff. Although this quotation is from a Mahayana Buddhist text, the instructions for the *samayama* phase of yoga are exactly the same; in fact, Vivekananda (op. cit., p. 620) uses almost the same metaphors.
24. Margaret S. Mahler, *On Human Symbiosis and the Vicissitudes of Individuation*, New York: International Universities Press, 1969.
25. Medard Boss, *A Psychiatrist Discovers India*, Calcutta: Rupa and Co., 1966, pp. 165–6.
26. Sarvepalli Radhakrishnan, 'Foreword', in Osborne, op. cit., pp. xi–xii.
27. Vivekananda, op. cit., p. 210.
28. For a detailed discussion of the psycho-analytic vision of reality, see Roy Schaeffer, 'The Psychoanalytic Vision of Reality', *International Journal of Psychoanalysis*, **51**, 1970, 279–97.
29. See Richard Lannoy, *The Speaking Tree*, London: Oxford University Press, 1971, pp. 47–56.
30. Ibid., pp. 76–7.
31. Erna M. Hoch, 'A Pattern of Neurosis in India', *American Journal of Psychoanalysis*, **20**, 1966, 17. The classical Hindu view is expressed by Swami Sivananda: 'The body with its organs is no other than the mind. The physical body is the outward manifestation of the mind . . . Whatever you hold in your mind will be produced in the physical body. Any ill-feeling or bitterness towards another person will at once affect the body and produce some kind of disease in the body. Intense passion, hatred, longstanding bitter jealousy, corroding anxiety, fits of hot temper actually destroy cells of the body and induce diseases of heart, liver, kidneys, spleen and stomach . . . When the mind is agitated, then this body also is agitated. When both the body and mind are agitated, the Prana flows in a wrong direction. Instead of pervading the whole body steadily and equally, it will vibrate at an unequal rate (unrhythmically). Then the food is not digested properly. Diseases orginate. If the primary cause is removed, then all diseases will disappear.' See Sivananda, op. cit., pp. 31 and 34.
32. See D. W. Winnicott, *Playing and Reality*, London: Tavistock Publications, 1971, p. 19.
33. Ramana Maharishi describes this experience as follows: 'I was sitting alone in a room on the first floor of my uncle's house . . . a sudden violent fear of death overtook me . . . The shock of the fear of death drove my mind inwards and I said to myself mentally, without actually framing the words: "Now death has come; what does it mean? What is it that is dying? This body dies." I lay with my limbs stretched out stiff as though *rigor mortis* had set in.' See Osborne, op. cit., p. 18. Ramakrishna's description is even stronger: 'One day I was torn by a terrible anguish. I felt that my heart was being wrung out like a wet cloth. Suffering was destroying me. Suddenly I saw the

great sword that was hanging in the shrine. I decided to make an end of it. I threw myself forward like a demented man to seize it, and suddenly at last the Blessed Mother showed herself. The buildings in their various sections, the temple and all the rest vanished before my eyes and left no trace. In their place I saw an ocean of consciousness without limits, infinite and splendid. As far as my eyes could see, I perceived brilliant waves that rose from all sides and broke over me with a terrifying roar, ready to drown me. I could no longer breathe. Caught in the whirlpool of the waves, I fell lifeless.' See *The Gospel of Sri Ramakrishna*, trans. S. Nikhilananda, New York: Rama-krishna–Vivekananda Center, 1942, p. 14.

34. Quoted in Kane, op. cit., vol. 1 (Part 3), p. 3.
35. *Bhagavada Gita*, III. 35.
36. Quoted in Pandarinath N. Prabhu, *Hindu Social Organisation*, Bombay: Popular Book Depot, 1954, p. 73.
37. Nivedita, *The Master as I Saw Him*, Calcutta: Udbodhan Office, 1910, p. 118.
38. In this context, see Gerald Platt and Fred I. Weinstein, *The Wish to be Free*, Berkeley and Los Angeles: University of California Press, 1970.
39. See Sudhir Kakar, 'The Human Life Cycle: The Traditional Hindu View and the Psychology of Erik Erikson', *Philosophy East and West*, **28**, 1968, 127–36.
40. Oscar Lewis, *Village Life in Northern India*, New York: Vintage Books, 1968, p. 25.
41. Oswald Spengler, *The Decline of the West*, London: George Allen and Unwin, 1959, p. 131.
42. *Dhammapada*, I. 1.
43. *Vaisesikasutra*, I. 38.
44. Spengler, op. cit., p. 117.

CHAPTER III: Mothers and Infants

1. I am adopting Simmel's term 'dyad' for the mother–infant relationship since no other word conveys so well the feeling of complementarity and interdependence of two independent entities.
2. Sigmund Freud, *An Outline of Psychoanalysis* (1940), Standard Edition, vol. 23, p. 188. For a comprehensive historical account of Freud's writings on the mother–infant relationship, see John Bowlby, 'The Nature of the Child's Tie to His Mother', *International Journal of Psychoanalysis*, **39**, 1958, 350–73.
3. The literature on the earliest human relationship has grown rapidly during the last few years; a complete bibliography of sources would cover many pages. The most important psycho-analytic writings upon which this summary is based are René A. Spitz, *The First Year of Life*, New York: International Universities Press, 1965; D. W. Winnicott, *The Family and Individual Development*, London: Tavistock Publications, 1952; Erik H. Erikson, *Childhood and Society*, New York: W. W. Norton, 1950; Edith Jacobson, *The Self and the Object World*, New York: International Universities Press, 1964, especially Part 1; Margaret S. Mahler, *On Human Symbiosis and the Vicissitudes of Individuation*, New York: International Universities Press, 1969; L. B. Murphy, 'Some Aspects of the First Relationship', *International Journal of Psychoanalysis*, **45**, 1964, 31–43; and J. Bowlby, *Attachment*, New York: Basic Books, 1969. And of course no psycho-analytic study of motherhood (however liable to cultural specialization) can be complete without reference to Helene Deutsch, *The Psychology of Women*, vol. 2 (*Motherhood*), New York: Grune and Stratton, 1945.
4. Spitz, op. cit., p. 96.
5. For an elaboration of this view, see Bowlby, *Attachment*, pp. 265–96.
6. Spitz, op. cit., p. 95.
7. See Chapter II, 'Life Task and Life Cycle'.

8. For a psycho-analytic consideration of some of these issues, see, for example, Grete L. Bibring *et al.*, 'A Study of the Psychological Processes in Pregnancy and of the Earliest Mother–Child Relationship', *The Psychoanalytic Study of the Child*, vol. 16, New York: International Universities Press, 1961, 9–72, and H. A. Moss, 'Sex, Age and State as Determinants of Mother–Infant Interaction', *Merrill-Palmer Quarterly*, 13, 1967, 19–36.

9. Although the patrilineal and patrilocal family type is dominant all over India, there are some castes and communities, especially in Southern India which are matrilineal and in which women enjoy relatively greater freedom. For the similarities and contrasts in kinship organization of different regions in India, see Irawati Karve, *Kinship Organization in India*, 3rd edn., Bombay: Asia Publishing House, 1968.

   My remarks are intended to apply only to the dominant patriarchal culture where by unconscious necessity it is the *mater* who is of primary symbolic significance, or, as the Jungians would put it, the mother is the primary constituent of a man's *anima*. The problem of feminine figures in the myths of a patriarchal society is compounded by the fact that these *animas* are not solely male projections but also represent some aspects of feminine psychology in these cultures. The reason for this intertwining of *anima* images and feminine psychology is that very early in childhood, girls learn to accurately perceive and conform to the patriarchal images of femininity entertained by the men around them in the household. In this connection see Marie-Louise von Franz, *The Feminine in Fairy Tales*, Zurich: Spring Publications, 1972.

10. The anthropological accounts which have a bearing on this section are T. N. Madan, *Family and Kinship: A Study of the Pandits of Rural Kashmir*, Bombay: Asia Publishing House, 1965; Leigh Minturn and John T. Hitchcock, 'The Rajputs of Khalapur, India' in *Six Cultures: Studies of Child-rearing*, ed. B. B. Whiting, New York: John Wiley and Sons, 1963, pp. 301–61; L. Minturn and W. W. Lambert, *Mothers of Six Cultures*, New York: John Wiley, 1964; Oscar Lewis, *Village Life in Northern India*, New York: Vintage Books, 1958; S. C. Dube, *Indian Village*, New York: Harper and Row, 1967; M. N. Srinivas *Marriage and Family in Mysore*, Bombay: New Book Co., 1942; Edward B. Harper, 'Spirit Possession and Social Structure', in *Anthropology on the March*, ed. B. Ratnam, Madras: The Book Centre, pp. 165–97; and Aileen D. Ross, *The Hindu Family in its Urban Setting*, Toronto: University of Toronto Press, 1961. Two other useful studies, essentially descriptive, based on intensive interviewing with women who represent the progressive, well-educated parts of Indian society are Margaret Cormack, *The Hindu Woman*, Bombay: Asia Publishing House, 1961, and Promilla Kapur, *Love, Marriage and Sex*, Delhi: Vikas Publishing House, 1973. For older, impressionistic yet sensitive studies of Indian women, see Mary F. Billington, *Woman in India* (18—?), New Delhi: Amarko Book Agency, 1973, and Frieda M. Das, *Purdah, the Status of Indian Women*, New York: The Vanguard Press, 1932.

11. The infant mortality rate in 1969 for females was 148.1 as compared to 132.3 for males; the life expectancy between 1961–71 was 45.6 for females, 47.1 for males, while the number of girls enrolled in the educational system in 1970–1 was 18.4 per cent as compared to 39.3 per cent for boys. See the relevant statistical tables in Indian Council of Social Science Research, *Status of Women in India: A Synopsis of the Report of the National Committee on the Status of Women* (1971–4), New Delhi: Allied Publishers, 1975, pp. 140–75.

12. *Atharvaveda*, VI. 2. 3, quoted in R. M. Das, *Women in Manu and His Seven Commentators*, Varanasi: Kanchana Publications, 1962, p. 43. See also *Atharvaveda*. VIII. 6. 25, VI. 9. 10, III. 23. 3, for prayers in a similar vein.

13. A. A. MacDonell, *Vedic Religion*, p. 165, quoted in R. M. Das, op. cit., p. 43.

14. See, for example, Minturn and Hitchcock, op. cit., pp. 307–8; Madan,

op. cit., p. 77; Dube, op. cit., pp. 148–9; Cormack, op. cit., p. 11. See also, William J. Goode, *World Revolution and Family Patterns*, New York: The Free Press, 1963, pp. 235–6; and D. G. Mandelbaum, *Society in India*, vol. 1, Berkeley: University of California Press, 1970, p. 120. Cases of *post-partum* depression, for example, are much more commonly reported among mothers who give birth to a daughter than among those who have a son. See M. R. Gaitonde, 'Cross-Cultural Study of the Psychiatric Syndromes in Out-Patient Clinics in Bombay, India, and Topeka, Kansas', *International Journal of Social Psychiatry*, **4**, 1958, 103.

15. Lewis, op. cit., p. 195.
16. Karve, op. cit., p. 206.
17. See Das, op. cit., p. 44. A contemporary Bengali proverb expressess this thought more bluntly, 'Even the piss of a son brings money; let the daughter go to hell.'
18. Sudhir Kakar, 'Aggression in Indian Society: An Analysis of Folk Tales', *Indian Journal of Psychology*, **49 (2)**, 1974, 124.
19. Ibid., pp. 125–6.
20. Cormack, op. cit., pp. 75–8.
21. Karve, op. cit., p. 210.
22. See Ross, op. cit., pp. 150–1; Dube, op. cit., pp. 148–9; Srinivas, op. cit., p. 173; Whiting, op. cit., p. 303; Harper, op. cit., pp. 171–2; Madan, op. cit., p. 77; and Cormack, op. cit., p. 9. Folk songs from all over India also bear witness to this close mother–daughter tie. See, for example, songs no. 4, 5, 6, 7, 8, and 9 in Karve, op. cit., p. 205.
23. Karve, op. cit., p. 205.
24. As Helene Deutsch expresses it, 'In her relation to her own child, woman repeats her own mother–child history.' See *The Psychology of Women*, vol. 1, op. cit., p. 205. See also Nancy Chodorow, 'Family Structure and Feminine Personality', in *Woman, Culture and Society*, ed. M. Rosaldo and L. Lamphere, Stanford: Stanford University Press, 1975, pp. 52–3.
25. Thus in many ballads whereas the women are depicted as tolerant, self-sacrificing and faithful, the men are weak, timid and faithless. See Sankar Sen Gupta, *A Study of Women of Bengal*, Calcutta: Indian Publications, 1970, p. 107.
26. Srinivas, op. cit., p. 195.
27. For example, in the *Dasa Puttal Brata* of Bengali girls it is wished that 'I shall have a husband like Rama, I shall be *sati* like Sita, I shall have a *devara* (younger brother-in-law) like Lakshman. I shall have a father-in-law like Dasharatha; I shall have a mother-in-law like Kousalya; I shall have sons as Kunti had, I shall be a cook like Draupadi, I shall acquire power like Durga; I shall bear the burden like earth; I shall be like Sasthi whose offspring know no death.' See Akshay Kumar Kayal, 'Women in Folk-Sayings of West Bengal', in Sen Gupta, op. cit., p. xxii.
28. Das, op. cit., p. 49.
29. Ibid., p. 72.
30. Jerome S. Bruner, 'Myths and Identity', *Daedalus*, Spring 1959, p. 357. In a study carried out in the north Indian province of Uttar Pradesh 500 boys and 360 girls between the ages of 9 and 22 years were asked to select the ideal woman from a list of 24 names of gods, goddesses and heroes and heroines of history. Sita was seen as the ideal woman by an overwhelming number of respondents: there were no age or sex differences. See P. Pratap, 'The Development of Ego Ideal in Indian Children', unpublished Ph.D. Thesis, Banaras Hindu University, 1960.
31. *Ramayana of Valmiki*, trans. H. P. Shastri, vol. 1 (Ayodhyakanda), London: Shantisadan, 1962, p. 233.
32. Philip Slater, *The Glory of Hera*, Boston: Beacon Press, 1966, p. xi.
33. In this connection see also J. A. Arlow, 'Ego Psychology and the Study of Mythology', *Journal of American Psychoanalytic Association*, **9**, 1961, p. 375.
34. *Mahabharata*, trans. P. C. Roy, Calcutta: Oriental Publishing Co., n.d., vol. 3 (Vanaparva), p. 634.

35. Ibid., p. 633. The Savitri myth is also a striking demonstration of Ernest Jones's thesis that the conscious fantasy of dying together possesses the unconscious significance of the wish to have children. See E. Jones, 'On "Dying Together" with Special Reference to Heinrich von Kleist's Suicide' and 'An Unusual Case of Dying Together', *Essays on Applied Psychoanalysis*, London: Hogarth Press, 1951, pp. 9–21.
36. Ibid., p. 488.
37. Ibid., pp. 506–7.
38. *Siva Purana*, 2. 2. 5. 1–68, 6. 1–62. The translation is from W. O'Flaherty, *Asceticism and Eroticism in the Mythology of Siva*, London: Oxford University Press, 1973, p. 64–5. A perusal of Hindu law texts reveals that our ancient law-givers—Manu, Kautilya, Kullika, Medhatithi—were obsessed with the chastity of young, unmarried girls. The punishments for all conceivable kinds of chastity-violation, depending on the castes of the actors, their sex (whether the violator is a man or a woman), the degree of consent and so on, are elaborately detailed. Thus, for example, if a man forcibly 'pollutes' a maiden with his fingers, the fingers shall be amputated and he shall pay a fine of 500 *panas*. If the man is of equal caste, the fine is reduced. If the fingers have been inserted with the consent of the maiden, the fingers are not amputated and the fine is reduced to 200 *panas*. If the initiative is taken by the girl, the punishment is lighter or non-existent; instead her guardians are to be punished in so much as they presumably did not keep a proper watch on her. There are similar fines in the case of an older woman seducing a young girl, depending on their castes and the 'violation'. See Das, op. cit., pp. 63–70.
39. Rangila Bhasur go tumi keno deyor haila na.
Tumi jodi haita re deyor khaita batar pan
(aar) ranga rasa kaitam katha juraito paran.
Sen Gupta, op. cit., p. 94.
40. The mean age according to the 1961 census was 15.8 years. For a discussion of the subject, see K. P. Singh, 'Women's Age at Marriage', *Sociological Bulletin*, 23 (2), 1974, 236–44. See also William J. Goode, op. cit., pp. 232–6.
41. See Ross, op. cit., p. 151.
42. Lewis, op. cit., p. 161; see also Karve, op. cit., p. 137 for evidence on the widespread existence of this custom.
43. Here is an example from Bengal (freely translated):
O, Kaffu [a bird], you are from my mother's side.
Speak, O speak in the courtyard of my parents.
My mother will hear you;
She will send my brother to fetch me.
O what sorrowful days have come!
I wish to get out of this,
I wish to reach my father's house.
Sen Gupta, op. cit., p. 149.
44. Folk-lore especially singles out the *sas* (mother-in-law) and the *nanad* (sister-in-law) as the natural enemies of the young bride. See Karve, op. cit., p. 130. Here are lines from some of the songs in Bengal depicting the bride's plight (and her anger) in these two relationships. 'My husband's sister is nothing but a poisonous thorn, her poisonous stings give me much pain'; 'My mother-in-law expired in the morning, if I find time in the afternoon after eating lunch, I will weep for her.' In north India the bride sings:

O my friend! My in-laws' house is a wretched place.
My mother-in-law is a very hard woman
She always struts about full of anger,

and so forth. There are also many songs which complain of the husband's indifference. For example, see songs no. 39, 40, 41, in Karve, op. cit., pp. 209–10. The presence of hidden hostility towards the new husband can also be inferred from the results of a Thematic Apperception Test administered to forty school girls in the South who were shown a picture of a death scene, with a covered unidentifiable body in the centre of the room and a doctor nearby consoling a young woman. In the stories written by the girls, by far the largest number (45 per cent) 'saw' the covered figure as the body of a dead husband. See D. Narain, 'Growing up in India', *Family Process*, 3, 1964, pp. 132–3.

45. *The Laws of Manu*, trans. G. Buhler, in M. Müller (ed.), *Sacred Books of the East*, vol. 25, Oxford: Clarendon Press, 1886, p. 196.
46. Ibid., p. 197.
47. Madhav S. Gore, 'The Husband–Wife and Mother–Son Relationship', *Sociological Bulletin*, **11**, 1961, 91–102. See also Ross, op. cit., p. 147, for evidence of a similar relationship existing in urbanized families.
48. *The Laws of Manu*, op. cit., p. 85. Similar sentiments are expressed in the *Mahabharata*.
49. See, for example, Mandelbaum, op. cit., p. 88, and Lewis, op. cit., p. 195.
50. Geeta Majumdar, *Folk Tales of Bengal*, New Delhi: Sterling Publishers, 1911, p. 17.
51. *The Laws of Manu*, op. cit., p. 344.
52. Ibid., p. 56.
53. *Mahabharata*, trans. P. C. Roy, vol. 1 (Adi-parva), pp. 177–8.
54. *Brahmavaivarta*, 3.2. 19–24, in O'Flaherty, op. cit., p. 225.
55. *The Laws of Manu*, op. cit., p. 354. Although it is primarily the son who is responsible for the performance of these rites, in case a couple has no son the rites may be performed by the daughter's son.
56. The Hindu attitude is similar to Malinowski's characterization of the Melanesians: 'The woman shows invariably a passionate craving for her child and the surrounding society seconds her feelings, fosters her inclinations, and idealizes them by custom and usage.' See B. Malinowski, *Sex and Repression in Savage Society*, New York: Harcourt, 1927, p. 21.
57. Helene Deutsch, *The Psychology of Women*, vol. 2, Chapter II.
58. Unless specifically mentioned, the following sections deal with the male infant only, the pattern being somewhat different in the case of daughters.
59. For anthropological accounts which confirm the widespread existence of this pattern of attachment all over India, see G. M. Carstairs, *The Twice Born*, London: Hogarth Press, 1957, pp. 63–4; S. C. Dube, *Indian Village*, pp. 148–9; Dhirendra N. Narain, 'Growing up in India', *Family Process*, 3, 1964, 134–7; John W. Elder, 'Industrialization in Hindu Society; A Case Study in Social Change', unpublished Ph.D. Thesis, Harvard University, 1959, p. 242.
60. Gardner Murphy, *In the Minds of Men*, New York: Basic Books, 1953, p. 56.
61. See Adrian C. Mayer, *Caste and Kinship in Central India*, London: Routledge and Kegan Paul, 1970; Ross, op. cit.; Gore, op. cit.; and D. Narain, 'Interpersonal Relationships in the Hindu Family', in R. Hill and R. Konig (eds.), *Families in East and West*, Paris: Mouton, pp. 454–80.
62. Jawaharlal Nehru, *Toward Freedom*, Boston: Beacon Press, 1961, p. 22.
63. Paramhansa Yogananda, *Autobiography of a Yogi*, Los Angeles: Self Realization Fellowship, 1972, p. 4.
64. Sigmund Freud, *Introductory Lectures on Psychoanalysis* (1916), Standard Edition, vol. 16, p. 407.
65. W. J. Wilkins, *Hindu Mythology* (1882), Delhi: Delhi Book Store, 1972, pp. 107–12 and 238–47.
66. E. H. Erikson, 'Ontogeny of Ritualization', in R. M. Loewenstein *et al.* (eds.), *Psychoanalysis—A General Psychology: Essays in Honor of Heinz Hartmann*, New York: International Universities Press, 1966, p. 604.
67. *Vaivarta Purana*, quoted in Wilkins, op. cit., p. 244.
68. J. Bowlby, *Separation: Anxiety and Anger*, London: Hogarth Press, 1973.
69. Ibid., p. 314.
70. *Satpatha Brahmana*, quoted in Wilkins, op. cit., p. 286.
71. J. Hitchcock, 'Pregnancy and Childbirth', quoted in D. Narain, 'Growing up in India', op. cit., p. 139.

72. William S. Taylor, 'Basic Personality in Orthodox Hindu Culture Patterns', *Journal of Abnormal Psychology*, **43**, 1948, 11. See also P. Spratt, *Hindu Culture and Personality*, Bombay: Manaktalas, 1966, pp. 181–6.
73. See Bowlby, *Separation*, p. 359, and D. W. Winnicott, 'The Capacity to be Alone', *International Journal of Psychoanalysis*, **39**, 1958, 416–20. A similar position has also been adopted by the intellectual spokesmen of what has come to be known as the 'counter-culture' in the United States. Thus Philip Slater suggests that the present American social order deeply frustrates three fundamental human needs: 'The desire for *community*—the wish to live in trust and fraternal cooperation with one's fellows. The desire for *engagement*—the wish to come directly to grips with social and interpersonal problems. The desire for *dependence*—the wish to share the responsibility for the control of one's impulses and the direction of one's life.' See *The Pursuit of Loneliness: American Culture at the Breaking Point*, Boston: Beacon Press, 1970, p. 5.
74. Sigmund Freud, *Introductory Lectures on Psychoanalysis* (1916), Standard Edition, vol. 16, p. 408, and *Inhibitions, Symptoms, and Anxiety* (1926), Standard Edition, vol. 20, p. 167.
75. See Bowlby, *Attachment*.
76. Erich Neumann, *The Great Mother: An Analysis of the Archetype* (2nd edn.), Princeton: Princeton University Press, 1963, pp. 147–203.
77. Slater, *The Glory of Hera*, p. 68. Slater's brilliant discussion of the mother-son constellation in ancient Greece shows some parallels, though not a complete identity, with the corresponding situation in modern India and has been a rich source of comparative material.
78. *Kalika Purana*, 47. 114–119, paraphrased from O'Flaherty, op. cit., p. 190.
79. *Matsya Purana*, 155. 1–34.
80. William N. Stephens, in a cross-cultural study of the family, has demonstrated these taboos to be positively correlated with indicators of sexual arousal. See *The Family in Cross-Cultural Perspective*, New York: Holt, 1963, pp. 80 ff.
81. *The Laws of Manu*, op. cit., p. 135.
82. *Aitareya Brahmana*, 1. 6. 1–6; see O'Flaherty, op. cit., p. 275.
83. Dube, op. cit., pp. 190–7.
84. Karen Horney, 'The Dread of Woman', *International Journal of Psychoanalysis*, **13**, 1932, 349–53.
85. *Brahma Purana*, 81. 1–5; paraphrased from O'Flaherty, op. cit., p. 204.
86. *Thirty Minor Upanishads*, trans. K. N. Aiyar, quoted in Spratt, op. cit., p. 118.
87. *Mahabharata*, vol. 2 (Vanaparva), pp. 102–5.
88. *Padma Purana*, 5. 26. 91–125; O'Flaherty, op. cit., p. 280.
89. *Ramayana of Valmiki*, vol. 1 (Aranyakanda), 18: 15–16. In psycho-analytic literature, it was Wilhelm Stekel who pointed to the relationship between the nose and feminine genitalia, basing some of his conclusions on the earlier work of Wilhelm Fliess, *Die Beziehungen zwischen Nase und weiblichen Geschlechtsorganen in ihrer biologisches Bedeutungen* (Vienna, 1897); see Stekel, *Conditions of Nervous Anxiety and their Treatment*, London: Paul, Trench and Trubner, 1923, p. 49.
90. Spratt, op. cit., p. 254.
91. Ibid., pp. 252–7.
92. I suspect this will be corroborated convincingly by clinical evidence, once this evidence becomes available in sufficient quantity and depth. Meanwhile, we cannot dismiss the common game of 'playing the wife' among boys of a certain age. The case history of a young boy who used to tie a piece of string around his prepuce and draw his penis so tightly into the scrotum that it was covered by the folds of the scrotum, thereby giving the genitalia a remarkable female resemblance is one aberrant manifestation of this identification. See G. Bose, 'The Genesis and Adjustment of the Oedipal Wish', *Samiksa*, **3**, 1949, p. 231. This behaviour is reminiscent of the commonly accepted (and admired) ability of Hatha-Yogis to draw the penis and

the testes back into the pubic arch so that the whole body takes on the appearance of a woman.

93. The second version of the Ganesha myth, in which Sani first avoids and then looks at the infant Ganesha (thus depriving him of his head) is reminiscent of cases of scotophilic women whose compulsive avoidance of, and looking at, men's genitals is a distorted expression of their castration wish.
94. *Mahabharata*, vol. 10 (Anusasnaparva), pp. 35–8.
95. Spratt, op. cit., p. 193, and p. 237.
96. Warner Muensterberger, 'Psyche and Environment', *Psychoanalytic Quarterly*, **38**, 1969, 204.
97. For Freud's distinction between the primary and the secondary processes, see *Formulations on the Two Principles of Mental Functioning* (1911), Standard Edition, vol. 12.
98. This is of course an impressionistic generalization based on personal and professional experience in Indian and Western societies. Empirical studies comparing Indian and Western children are rare. For an older study lending support to the impression that primary thought processes persist well beyond infancy in Indian childhood, see J. C. Hoyland, *An Investigation Regarding the Psychology of Indian Adolescence*, Jubbulpore: Christian Mission Press, 1921. In a study based on student responses to Rorschach cards, Asthana concludes that fantasy and imagination characterize the entire sample with some subjects given to intense and vivid imagery. See Hari S. Asthana, 'Some Aspects of Personality Structuring in Indian (Hindu) Social Organization', *Journal of Social Psychology*, **44**, 1956, 155–63.
99. Pinchas Noy, 'A Revision of the Psychoanalytic Theory of the Primary Process', *International Journal of Psychoanalysis*, **50**, 1969, 155–78.
100. Ibid., pp. 176–7.
101. See E. H. Erikson, *Identity: Youth and Crisis*, p. 174, for a discussion of the concept of negative identity.
102. Henry Whitehead, *The Village Gods of South India*, Calcutta: Association Press, 1921. p. 18.
103. *Mahabharata*, vol. 4 (Virataparva), p.12.
104. Milton Singer, 'The Radha-Krishna Bhajans of Madras City', in M. Singer (ed.), *Krishna: Myths, Rites, and Attitudes*, Honolulu: East-West Center Press, 1966, p. 130.
105. Swami Saradananda, *Sri Ramakrishna, The Great Master*, Madras: Ramakrishna Math, n.d., p. 238.

CHAPTER IV: Families and Children

1. For the sociological discussion of the Indian family, I have drawn on William J. Goode, *World Revolution and Family Patterns*, New York: The Free Press, 1963; Aileen D. Ross, *The Hindu Family in its Urban Setting*, Toronto: University of Toronto Press, 1962; and especially on David G. Mandelbaum's scholarly and sensitive work, *Society in India*, Berkeley: University of California Press, 1970, vol. 1, part 2.
2. For the Calcutta study, see Jyotirmoee Sarma, 'The Nuclearization of Joint Family Households in West Bengal', *Man in India*, **44**, 1964, 193–206; for the Gujarat studies, I. P. Desai, *Some Aspects of Family in Mahuva*, New York: Asia Publishing House, 1964, p. 69, and K. M. Kapadia, 'Rural Family Patterns', in *Sociological Bulletin*, **5**, 1956, 111–26; for the Madhya Pradesh study, Edwin D. Driver, *Differential Fertility in Central India*, Princeton: Princeton University Press, 1963; and for Bombay, Murray A. Straus and Dorothea Winkelmann, 'Social Class, Fertility and Authority in Nuclear and Joint Households in Bombay', in *Journal of Asian and African Studies*, **9**, 1969, 61–74.
3. See Chapter III, pp. 71–3.
4. This is an elaboration on William Goode's conclusion that 'Most people live

for part of their lives in a joint household, but at any given time most households are not joint.' Op. cit., p. 244.

5. Morris M. Lewis, *Language, Thought and Personality in Infancy and Childhood*, New York: Basic Books, 1964, p. 33.
6. Louis Dumont, *Homo Hierarchicus: Essai sur le Système des Castes*, Paris: Gallimard, 1966.
7. Henry Orenstein, *Gaon: Conflict and Cohesion in an Indian Village*, quoted in Mandelbaum, op. cit., p. 40.
8. *The Laws of Manu*, trans. G. Buhler, Oxford: The Clarendon Press, 1886, p. 145.
9. Sudhir Kakar, 'The Theme of Authority in Social Relations in India', *Journal of Social Psychology*, 84, 1971, 93–101.
10. Ibid., p. 100.
11. Erik H. Erikson, *Identity: Youth and Crisis*, New York: W. W. Norton, 1968, p. 23.
12. See, for example, Brij B. Sethi, V. R. Thakore and S. C. Gupta, 'Changing Patterns of Culture and Psychiatry in India'. *American Journal of Psychotherapy*, 19, 1965, 445–54.
13. The terms 'caste' and 'caste system' have often been used indiscriminately to characterize different things. Sometimes caste has meant *varna* which is more or less caste-as-archetype, the widescreen which provides the traditional lore for caste identity and caste status. At other times caste has not only meant *jati* but has also been a descriptive term for kinship groupings and *jati*-clusters. It is only recently that we are able to differentiate between the various subgroups of the Indian social order, thanks to painstaking anthropological and sociological studies carried out by Indian and foreign scholars alike. See, for example, M. N. Srinivas, *Caste in Modern India*, Bombay: Asia Publishing House, 1962; André Béteille, *Castes: Old and New*, Bombay: Asia Publishing House, 1969; and Dumont, op. cit.
14. Mandelbaum, op. cit., p. 14.
15. Nehru, *Toward Freedom*, Boston: Beacon Press, 1958, p. 353.
16. Personal communication from a relative reminiscing about his childhood and youth.
17. Shashi K. Pande, 'The Mystique of "Western" Psychotherapy: An Eastern Interpretation', *Journal of Nervous and Mental Disease*, 46, 1968, 425–32.
18. Lois Murphy *et al.*, *The Widening World of Childhood*, New York: Basic Books, 1967.
19. S. C. Dube, *Indian Village*, New York: Harper and Row, 1967, p. 149. For a related discussion of the effect of the 'second birth' on personality development in India, see K. V. Rajan, 'A Psychological Evaluation of Certain Trends in Indian Culture', *Indian Journal of Psychology*, 32, 1957, p. 127. Anthropological evidence gathered in different parts of India confirms the *fact* of this separation of son from mother and the boy's banishment into the male quarters; see L. Minturn and J. T. Hitchcock, 'The Rajputs of Khalapur', in B. B. Whiting (ed.), *Six Cultures: Studies of Child-rearing*, New York: John Wiley, 1963, pp. 347–50; C. V. Wiser and W. H. Wiser, *Behind Mud Walls*, London: Allen and Unwin, 1932, p. 10. See also H. S. Asthana, 'Some Aspects of Personality Structuring in Indian (Hindu) Social Organization', *Journal of Social Psychology*, 44, 1956, p. 104.
20. Heinz Kohut, *The Analysis of the Self*, New York: International Universities Press, 1971. The fact that the terms 'narcissistic' and 'narcissism' have been used in many different contexts in psycho-analytic literature has created a good deal of confusion. Clinically, narcissism has denoted a sexual perversion; genetically, a developmental stage; from the standpoint of object-relations, a specific kind for object choice and a specific mode of relating to the environment; and in psycho-analytic ego psychology, aspects of the sense of self-esteem. In agreement with much of the modern literature on the subject, I have used narcissism here to mean the concentration of mental interest on the self and the correlative conflicts stemming from problems of regulating self-esteem. For psychological discussions of narcissism, see W. G. Joffe and

14

Joseph Sandler, 'Some Conceptual Problems Involved in the Consideration of Disorders of Narcissism', *Journal of Child Psychotherapy*, **2**, 1967, 56–66; and Sydney E. Pulver, 'Narcissism: Concept and Metapsychological Conception', *Journal of American Psychoanalytic Association*, **18**, 1970, 319–41.

21. Kohut, op. cit., p. 25.
22. See E. H. Erikson, *Young Man Luther*, New York: W. W. Norton, 1958, pp. 123–4, and Erich Fromm, *The Crisis of Psychoanalysis*, London: Jonathan Cape, 1971, pp. 106–34.
23. Thus Mandelbaum, op. cit., p. 60, observes, 'Between father and son relations are supposed to be formal and restrained and are often so in reality', while Mayer, op. cit., p. 218, writes, 'The ideal pattern is sufficiently closely followed in most households without being enforced by corporal discipline. This ideal pattern is based on restraint between a father and his son.' See also Ross, op. cit., p. 100.
24. Paramhansa Yogananda, *Autobiography of a Yogi*, Los Angeles: Self-Realization Fellowship, 1972, p. 268. For an essentially similar account of a young man's relationship with his father in modern India, see Sudhir Kakar and Kamla Chowdhry, *Conflict and Choice: Indian Youth in a Changing Society*, Bombay: Somayia, 1971, pp. 27–8.
25. Mohandas K. Gandhi, *The Story of My Experiments with Truth*, Boston: Beacon Press, 1957, pp. 27–8.
26. Cited in D. Narain, 'Growing up in India', *Family Process*, **3**, 1964, pp. 149–50.
27. See Sudhir Kakar, 'Neuroses in India: An Overview and Some Observations', *Indian Journal of Psychology*, **50 (2)**, 1975, 172–9.
28. In an analysis of one hundred and sixty-six folk tales from seven Indian provinces, it was found that the father–son conflict in India was of a low intensity as compared to similar figures from forty-two other, so-called preliterate societies. The highest frequencies of this conflict were found among the Rajputs of Gujarat and Rajasthan. See Sudhir Kakar, 'Aggression in Indian Society: An Analysis of Folk Tales', op. cit., pp. 124–5.
29. Otto Fenichel, *The Psychoanalytic Theory of Neurosis*, London; Routledge and Kegan Paul, 1971, p. 89
30. See Harold Lincke, 'Das Überich—eine gefährliche Krankheit?', *Psyche*, **24**, 1970, 375–402.
31. O'Flaherty, op. cit., pp. 96–9.
32. Yogananda, op. cit., p. 107.
33. Ibid., p. 123.

CHAPTER V: Tracings: The Inner World in Culture and History

1. For a description of the essence of Krishna, see David R. Kinsley, *The Sword and the Flute: Kali and Krishna*, Berkeley: University of California Press, 1975, Chapters I and II. For an account of the early and medieval forms of the Krishna cult, see S. C. Mukherji, *A Study of Vaisnavism in Ancient and Medieval Bengal*, Calcutta: Punthi Pustak, 1966. See also Nicol Macnicol, *Indian Theism*, 2nd edn., Delhi: Munshiram Manoharlal, 1968.
2. *Bhagavata Purana* (my translation), XI. 14. 23–24. It is an interesting parallel that the 'gift of tears' was also a special mark of saintliness in medieval Catholicism.
3. McKim Marriot, 'The Feast of Love', in M. Singer (ed.), *Krishna: Myths, Rites, and Attitudes*, Honolulu: East-West Center Press, 1966, p. 202.
4. Ibid., pp. 203–4.
5. Ibid., pp. 210–11.
6. Ibid., p. 204.
7. The Govinda-lilamrita is explicit on this point: Krishna was dancing. He paused and admired the girls. He kissed some of them on cheeks and lips, looked at others with desire, and fondled the breasts of others, marking them with his nails. In that game of *rasa* he had sexual intercourse with Radha and

others, and thus had intercourse with himself. Cited in Kinsley, op. cit., p. 53.

8. *Bhagavata Purana*, XI. 14. 20.
9. Ibid., VII. 9. 10.
10. Thomas J. Hopkins, 'The Social Teachings of the *Bhagavata Purana*', in M. Singer (ed.), *Krishna: Myths, Rites, and Attitudes*, p. 22.
11. J. A. Arlow, 'Ego Psychology and the Study of Mythology', *Journal of American Psychoanalytic Association*, 9, 1961, 379.
12. Otto Rank, *The Myth of the Birth of the Hero*, New York: Brunner, 1952.
13. I am indebted to Philip Slater's analysis of the Heracles myths for an elucidation of certain parallels in Krishna legends. See Slater, *The Glory of Hera*, Boston: Beacon Press, 1966, Chapter XII.
14. In this context, see Melanie Klein, 'Bemerkungen uber einige schizoide Mechanismen', *Das Seelenleben des Kleinkindes*, Hamburg: Rowohlt Verlag, 1972, pp. 101–25.
15. The standard works on the double-bind theory of schizophrenia are Gregory Bateson *et al.*, 'Towards a Theory of Schizophrenia', *Behavioral Science*, 1, 1956, 251–64; and T. Lidz *et al.*, *Schizophrenia and the Family*, New York: International Universities Press, 1966. For a detailed discussion of the oral-narcissistic conflict mentioned here, see J. N. Rosen, *Direct Analysis*, New York: Grune and Stratton, 1953.
16. Henry, A. Bunker, 'Mother-Murder in Myth and Legend', *Psychoanalytic Quarterly*, 13, 1944, 198–207.
17. Kanhaiyalal M. Munshi, *Krishnavatara*, vol. 1, Bombay: Bharatiya Vidya Bhavan, 1967, pp. 65–7.
18. 'Homeric Hymn to Apollo', quoted in Slater, op. cit., p. 139. Serpent myths are ubiquitous in the mythologies of most societies. The symbolic range of these myths and the many different levels at which these symbols can be interpreted exemplify both the possibilities and the limitations of psychological analysis of myths. For discussions of the symbolism in serpent myths see Joseph Campbell, *The Hero With a Thousand Faces*, New York: Meridian Books, 1956; Joseph Fonterose, *Python: A Study of Delphic Myth and its Origins*, Berkeley: University of California Press, 1959; and R. F. Fortune, 'The Symbolism of the Serpent', *International Journal of Psychoanalysis*, 7, 1926, 237–43.
19. *Bhagavata Purana*, X. 8. 26–31.
20. Cited in Kinsley, op. cit., p. 47.
21. Ibid., p. 50.
22. For a detailed description of the ritual life of Shiva devotees see W. McCormack, 'On Lingayat Culture', in A. K. Ramanujan, *Speaking of Siva*, London: Penguin Books, 1973, 175–87. For a history of the development of Shaivism and the doctrines of its various sects see B. Bhattacharya, *Saivism and the Phallic World*, 2 vols., New Delhi: Oxford and IBH Publishing Co., 1975; see also Macnicol, op. cit., pp. 160–79.
23. Thorkil Vanggaard, *Phallos*, London: Jonathan Cape, 1972, p. 56.
24. See Annie Reich, 'Pathological Forms of Self-Esteem Regulation', *The Psychoanalytic Study of the Child*, 15, 1960, 215–32.
25. Sandor Ferenczi, *Thallassa: A Theory of Genitality*, New York: Psychoanalytic Quarterly, 1938, p. 16.
26. *Mahabharata*, vol. 11 (Anusasanaparva), trans. P. C. Roy, Calcutta, Oriental Publishing Co., n.d., p. 386.
27. *Siva Purana*, 49, 35–36, in W. O'Flaherty, *Asceticism and Eroticism in the Mythology of Siva*, London: Oxford University Press, 1973, pp. 130–1.
28. See P. Spratt, *Hindu Culture and Personality*, Bombay: Manaktalas, 1966, p. 338. Spratt (pp. 337–8) also recounts a legend, depicted in the sculpture of a Madurai temple, in which a couple faced the alternative of having a son of bad character who would outlive them or a virtuous son who would die before them and thus be unable to perform the all-important filial funeral rites. The couple chose a virtuous son. When the god of death came to fetch him, he clung so firmly to his father's penis that Yama was powerless and the boy had to be allowed to live.

29. See N. N. Chatterji, 'Notes on Disturbances of Ego in Schizophrenia', *Samiksa* 7, 1953, 49. In another paper, 'Oedipus Conflict and Defence of the Ego', *Samiksa*, 8, 1954, 125–32, Chatterji reports the case of a patient who, under the fantasied threat of anal penetration by the father and subsequent transformation into a woman, imagines that he eats both parents, thereby becoming *ardhnarishwara* and achieving sexual-sufficiency.

30. T. C. Sinha, 'Some Psychoanalytical Observations on the Siva Linga', *Samiksa*, 3, 1949, 39–41.

31. *Yogasastra*, cited in O'Flaherty, op. cit., p. 8.

32. Sister Nivedita, *The Master as I Saw Him*, Calcutta: Udbodhan Office, 1910, pp. 125–6.

33. See in this connection Pamela Daniels, 'Militant Nationalism in Bengal: A Study in the Shaping of Nations', unpublished Master's Thesis, Harvard University, 1963.

34. Swami Vivekananda, *The Yogas and Other Works*, ed. S. Nikhilananda, New York: Ramakrishna–Vivekananda Center, 1953, p. 118.

35. Ibid., p. 119.

36. Swami Vivekananda, *The Complete Works of Swami Vivekananda*, vol. 4, Almora: Advaita Ashrama, 1923, p. 337.

37. Letter to Mary Hale in Vivekananda, *The Yogas and other Works*, p. 92.

38. Ibid., pp. 157–8.

39. Erik H. Erikson, *Young Man Luther*, New York: W. W. Norton, 1958, p. 34.

40. Bhupendra Nath Datta, *Swami Vivekananda: Patriot-Prophet* Calcutta: Nababharat Publishers, 1954, p. 147. For details of Vivekananda's childhood and youth, I have checked the facts against two authoritative accounts: Sailendra Nath Dhar, *A Comprehensive Biography of Swami Vivekananda*, vol.1, Madras: Vivekananda Prakashan Kendra, 1975; and the official biography, *The Life of Vivekananda*, 8th ed., by His Eastern and Western Disciples, Almora: Advaita Ashrama, 1974.

41. Ibid. See also Dhar, op. cit.

42. Vivekananda, *The Yogas and other Works*, p. 1.

43. Datta, op. cit., p. 114.

44. Ibid., p. 115.

45. Ernest Jones, *The Life and Work of Sigmund Freud*, vol. 1, New York: Basic Books, 1953, p. 5.

46. Letter to Mary Hale, in Vivekananda, *The Yogas and other Works*, p. 165.

47. Nivedita, op. cit., p. 249.

48. Vivekananda, *The Yogas and other Works*, p. 2. In addition, since Indian mothers take care of infants much longer than the age given by Vivekananda for his childhood memory (even if portions of later childhood are incorporated in this memory), it is developmentally probable and reasonable in the Indian context to assume that by 'family' Vivekananda indeed means his mother.

49. Letter to Mrs Ole Bull, in Vivekananda, *The Yogas and other Works*, p. 945. See also Nivedita, op. cit., pp. 206–7.

50. Letter to Mary Hale in Vivekananda, *The Yogas and other Works*, p. 916.

51. Swami Vivekananda, *Lectures from Colombo to Almora*, Almora: Advaita Ashrama, 1933, p. 223.

52. Nivedita, op. cit., pp. 162–8.

53. Ibid., p. 170.

54. Datta, op. cit., pp. 97, 102 and 105.

55. Vivekananda, *The Yogas and other Works*, p. 128 (ital. in original).

56. Ibid., p. 151.

57. Ibid., p. 102.

58. Vivekananda, *Complete Works*, vol. 3, p. 224.

59. Ibid., vol. 4, p. 143.

60. Nivedita, op. cit., p. 297.

61. Letter to Nivedita, in Vivekananda, *The Yogas and other Works*, p. 951.

62. Letter to Mary Hale, in Vivekananda, *The Yogas and other Works*, p. 950.

63. Letter to Miss Macleod, in Vivekananda, *The Yogas and other Works*, p. 951.

64. See H. Kohut, *The Analysis of the Self*, New York: International Universities Press, 1971, pp. 108–9.
65. Vivekananda, *The Yogas and other Works*, p. 5.
66. Daniels, op. cit., p. 27.

CHAPTER VI: Conclusion: Childhood and Social Change

1. S. Freud, *Civilization and its Discontents*, Standard Edition, vol. 21, p. 113; see also Freud's critique of Marxism in the *New Introductory Lectures*, Standard Edition, vol. 22, pp. 176–81.
2. Vivekananda, *The Yogas and Other Works*, ed. S. Nikhilananda, New York: Ramakrishna–Vivekananda Center, 1953, p. 525.
3. For a discussion of the concept of narcissistic rage see H. Kohut, 'Narzissmus und narzisstische Wut', *Psyche*, 27, 1973, 513–54.

APPENDIX: The Child in Indian Tradition

1. I shall be greatly surprised if *jatakarma*, the Hindu birth ritual, has ever taken place exactly in the same way as I have described it above. I have constructed the birth and the ritual from the texts of Ayurvedic medicine and the elaborately detailed instructions given in the *Grihyasutras*, the ancient texts which contain directions for the various *samskaras*—the mandatory nexus of ceremonies, sacraments and rites which accompany a Hindu from the moment of his conception in the womb till the hour of death, and even further through the funeral ceremonies beyond death. In actual practice, of course, depending upon the region, the caste and the historical period, many of the prescribed *samskaras*, including the one at birth, have been shortened and condensed, blended with others or omitted altogether.
2. Excepting the folk songs, this material essentially belongs to the literate traditions of the upper castes. Yet, as Kosambi has pointed out in another context, such traditions are basically much the same in many lower groups; their continuous and continuing survival in large sections of society being one of the most distinctive features of Indian culture. See D. D. Kosambi, *The Culture and Civilization of Ancient India in Historical Outline*, New Delhi: Vikas, 1970, p. 16.
3. See George Bühler (tr.), *The Laws of Manu in Sacred Books of the East* (F. Max Mueller, ed.), Vol. XXV, Oxford: Clarendon Press, 1886; III, 114; VIII, 66–71; IX, 283.
4. Ibid., V, 67–71.
5. Ibid., III, 114.
6. Ibid., IV, 179.
7. Ibid., IV, 282–3.
8. Ibid., VIII, 299–300; IX, 230.
9. See Jerome Carcopino, *Daily Life in Ancient Rome*, New Haven: Yale University Press, 1940, Chapter IV on 'Marriage, Woman and the Family'.
10. Richard B. Lyman, Jr., 'Barbarism and Religion: Late Roman and Early Medieval Childhood', in L. De Mause (ed.), *The History of Childhood*, New York: Harper Torchbooks, 1975, p. 84.
11. *Caraka Samhita*, with Hindi translation by Jaideva Vidyalankar, Delhi: Motilal Banarsidass, 1975, Sarira 2: 33–6.
12. *Caraka*, Sarira 4: 15–9.
13. See Debiprasad Chattopadhya, *Science and Society in Ancient India*, Calcutta: R. I. Publishers, 1977, who has emphasized this fact.
14. The Ayurvedic view is identical to that of modern psychoanalysis which holds that in early life the infant must be thought of, 'not as an individual but only as a part of a nurturing unit, from which he gradually differentiates, as an individual, with the mothering partner serving as a catalyst and a living buffer': Margaret Mahler, *On Human Symbiosis and the Vicissitudes of*

228   *The Inner World*

Individuation, New York: International Universities Press, 1968, p. 229.
15. *Caraka*, Sarira 8: 96.
16. *Susruta*, Sarira 10: 38.
17. See, for instance, *Mahabharata* (M. N. Dutta, tr.), 12 vols., Calcutta: Oriental Publishing Co., n.d., vol. 1, pp. 107–80; vol. 2, p. 217; vol. 11, pp. 4, 55, 87.
18. Ibid., vol. 1 (*Adi Parva*), pp. 107–8.
19. Ibid., vol. 2 (*Sabha Parva*), p. 217.
20. Ibid., vol. 1 (*Adi Parva*), p. 510.
21. Ibid., pp. 177–8.
22. Ibid., vol. IV (*Udyog Parva*), p. 210.
23. Ibid., pp. 374–5.
24. Ibid., vol. IX (*Santi Parva*), p. 105.
25. Ibid., p. 136.
26. Ibid., p. 349.
27. See, for instance, vol. 1 (*Adi Parva*), p. 177; vol. IX (*Santi Parva*), pp. 267, 269.
28. Ibid., vol. X (*Anusasana Parva*), p. 155.
29. Bhavabhuti, *Uttara Rama-Charita*, 6: 13 and 6:22; Banabhattā, *Harshacarita*, 5: 99.
30. Kalidasa, *Raghuvamsha*: 3: 45–6.
31. Srinivas Sharma, *Adhunik Hindi Kavya Vatsalya Rasa*, quoted in Chandrabhan Rawat, *Sur Sahitya*, Mathura: Jawahar Pustakalaya, 1967, p. 230.
32. Rawat, *Sur Sahitya*, p. 229 (my translation).
33. Jadunath Sinha (ed.), *Ramaprosad's Devotional Songs*, Calcutta: Sinha, 1966, p. 7.
34. David R. Kinsley, *The Sword and the Flute: Kali and Krishna, Dark Visions of the Terrible and the Sublime in Hindu Mythology*, Berkeley: University of California Press, 1975, pp. 12–19.
35. Surdas, *Sursagarsar* (D. Verma, ed.), Allahabad: Sahitya Bhawan, 1972, p. 59 (my translation).
36. Goswami Tulsidas, *Kavitavali* (R. P. Tripathi, ed.), Allahabad: Bharati Niketan, n.d., p. 3 (my translation).
37. This is Huizinga's phrase to describe human play; quoted in Erik H. Erikson, *Toys and Reasons*, New York: W. W. Norton, 1977, p. 43.
38. Surdas, p. 57.
39. Tulsidas, *Gitavali* (translated in Hindi by V. N. Prasad), Gorakhpur: Gita Press, n.d., pp. 30–40 (my translation).
40. For a comparison of *ashramadharma* with a modern scheme of psychosocial development see my 'The Human Life Cycle. Traditional Hindu View and the Psychology of Erik Erikson', *Philosophy East and West*, 18 (3), 1968.
41. V. B. Athavale, *Balaveda*, Bombay: Pediatric Clinics of India, 1977, p. 1.
42. For a discussion of the psychology of rituals and ritualization see Erik H. Erikson, 'Ontogeny of Ritualization in Man' in *Psychoanalysis—A General Psychology* (R. M. Loewenstein *et al.*, eds.), New York: International Universities Press, 1966, pp. 601–6.
43. The contents of the *samskaras* have been extensively described in Raj B. Pandey, *Hindu Samskaras*, Delhi: Motilal Banarsidass, 1969.
44. See R. Sankrantyan and D. K. Upadhyaya (eds.), *Hindi Sahitya ka Vrihat Itihas*, Kashi: Nagaripracharni Sabha, vol. 16 (part 3), 19, p. 111.
45. P. V. Kane, *History of Dharmasastra*, Poona: Bhandarkar Oriental Research Institute, vol. 2 (part 1), 1933, p. 180.
46. In a study of growing up in 700 families in the urban complex of Poona, Champa Aphale tells us that *namakarana* was generally celebrated except in some families in the case of girls; *nishkramana* was confined to the children of upper and intermediate castes, *annaprasana* was omitted in the case of lower castes and *chudakarana* (*caula munda* in the local language) was universally performed except for girls of the upper castes. Girls were also excluded from the rite of *upanayana* which is not performed for boys belonging to the lower castes either. See Champa Aphale, *Growing Up in an Urban Complex*, New Delhi: National, 1976, pp. 53–6.

47. *Hindi Sahitya ka Vrihat Itihas*, p. 16.
48. In the literature on the *samskaras*, the age at which a particular *samskara* should be performed is not laid down with great rigidity but is flexible within certain, albeit wide, limits. Chronological flexibility, however, is characteristic of all schemes of 'stages of development'—Freud's stages of psychosexual development, Erikson's stages of psychosocial development, Piaget's stages of cognitive development and so on. As with these schemes, the Hindu ritual literature too gives us the earliest possible age for a given transition, the latest possible one and, sometimes, the optimal one.
49. In this connection, see the various contributions in *The History of Childhood*, and especially de Mause's review essay, 'The Evolution of Childhood', pp. 1–73.
50. de Mause identifies the following childrearing models: 1. Infanticidal (Antiquity to 4th century A.D.); 2. Abandonment (4th–13th centuries); 3. Ambivalent (13th–17th century); 4. Intrusive (18th century); 5. Socialization (19th–mid-20th century); 6. Helping (Begins mid-20th century): See de Mause, 'The Evolution of Childhood', pp. 51–4.
51. For example, as William Langer has shown, infanticide (contrary to the popular assumption that it was solely an Eastern practice) of both legitimate and illegitimate children was a regular practice in Western antiquity: See William L. Langer, 'Infanticide: A Historical Survey', *History of Childhood Quarterly*, 1 (3), pp. 353–65. In fact, it has been established that the killing of legitimate children in Europe was only slowly reduced during the Middle Ages and that illegitimate children continued to be regularly killed right into the 19th century: See de Mause, 'Evolution of Childhood', p. 25.
52. John Demos, 'The American Family in Past Time', *American Scholar*, 43 (3), 1974, p. 427.
53. I have discussed some of these psychological consequences in Chapter III.

Bibliography

Amitayur-dhyana-sutra, trans. F. Takakusu, in M. Müller (ed.), *Sacred Books of the East*, vol. 49, Oxford: Clarendon Press, 1910.

ANANT, S. S., 'Child Training and Caste Personality', *Race Quarterly*, **8**, 1967, 385–94.

APFELBAUM, B., 'On Ego Psychology: A Critique of the Structural Approach to Psychoanalytic Theory', *International Journal of Psychoanalysis*, **47**, 1966, 451–75.

ARLOW, J. A., 'Ego Psychology and the Study of Mythology', *Journal of American Psychoanalytic Association*, **9**, 1961, 371–93.

ASTHANA, H. S., 'Some Aspects of Personality Structuring in Indian (Hindu) Social Organization', *Journal of Social Psychology*, **44**, 1956, 155–63.

AXELRAD, S., 'Comments on Anthropology and the Study of Complex Cultures', in W. Muensterberger (ed.), *Man and his Culture*, London: Rapp and Whiting, 1969, 273–93.

Bahadur, K. P., *Folk Tales of Uttar Pradesh*, New Delhi: Sterling Publishers, 1972.

BATESON, G. *et al.*, 'Towards a Theory of Schizophrenia', *Behavioral Science*, **1**, 1965, 251–64.

BÉTEILLE, A., *Castes: Old and New*, Bombay: Asia Publishing House, 1969.

Bhagavad Gita.

Bhagavata Purana.

BHANDARI, L. C., 'Some Aspects of Psychoanalytic Therapy in India', in J. Masserman and J. Moreno (eds.), *Progress in Psychotherapy*, New York: Grune and Stratton, 1960, 218–20.

BHASIN, V., 'Aspects of Dependence–Independence Training in Joint Family', unpublished Ph.D. Thesis, University of Lucknow, 1959.

BHATTACHARYA, B., *Saivism and the Phallic World*, 2 vols., New Delhi: Oxford and IBH Publishing Co., 1975.

BIBRING, G. L. *et al*, 'A Study of the Psychological Processes in Pregnancy and of the Earliest Mother–Child Relationship', *The Psychoanalytic Study of the Child*, **16**, 1961, 9–72.

BILLINGTON, M. F., *Women in India*, New Delhi: Amarko Book Agency, 1973.

BLAKE, W., *The Portable Blake*, ed. A. Kazin, New York: Viking Press, 1946.

BOSE, G., 'The Genesis and Adjustment of the Oedipus Wish', *Samiksa*, **3**, 1949, 222–40.

BOSE, M., *A Psychiatrist Discovers India*, Calcutta: Rupa and Co., 1966.

BOSSAND, J. and BOLL, E., 'The Large Family Structure in Indian (Hindu) Social Organization', *Journal of Social Psychology*, **44**, 1956.

BOWLBY, J., 'The Nature of the Child's Tie to his Mother', *International Journal of Psychoanalysis*, **39**, 1958, 350–73.

——, *Attachment*, New York: Basic Books, 1969.

——, *Separation: Anxiety and Anger*, London: Hogarth Press, 1973.

Brahmavaivarta Purana.

Brihadaranyaka Upanishad.

BROWN, N., *Life Against Death*, London: Routledge and Kegan Paul, 1959.

BRUNER, J. S., 'Myths and Identity', *Daedalus*, Spring 1959.

BUNKER, H. A., 'Mother-Murder in Myth and Legend', *Psychoanalytic Quarterly*, **13**, 1944, 198–207.

CAMPBELL, J., *The Hero with a Thousand Faces*, New York: Meridian Books, 1956.

CARSTAIRS, G. M., *The Twice-Born*, London: Hogarth Press, 1957.

CHATTERJI, N. N., 'Nature of Disturbances of Ego in Schizophrenia', *Samiksa*, **7**, 1953, 39–52.

——, 'Oedipus Conflict and Defence of the Ego', *Samiksa*, **8**, 1954, 125–32.
CHAUDHRY, B. R., *Folk Tales of Rajasthan*, New Delhi: Sterling Publishers, 1972.
COHN, B. S., *India: The Social Anthropology of a Civilization*, Englewood Cliffs: Prentice-Hall, 1971.
CORMACK, M., *The Hindu Woman*, Bombay: Asia Publishing House, 1961.
CREMERIUS, J., 'Das Es und das Ich Freuds—und eine Schöpfungs-myth der alten Inder', *Zeitschrift fur psychosomatische Medizin*, **4**, 1957–8, 211–13.
DALY, C. D., 'Hindu-Mythologie und Kastrations-Komplex', *Imago*, **13**, 1927, 145–98.
——, 'The Mother Complex in Literature', *Samiksa*, **1**, 1947. 157–70.
DANIELS, P., 'Militant Nationalism in Bengal: A Study in the Shaping of Nations', unpublished Master's Thesis, Harvard University, 1963.
DAS, F. M., *Purdah, the Status of Indian Women*, New York: The Vanguard Press, 1932.
DAS, R. M., *Women in Manu and His Seven Commentators*, Varanasi: Kanchana Publications, 1962.
DESAI, I. P., *Some Aspects of Family in Mahuva*, New York: Asia Publishing House, 1964.
DEUTSCH, H., *The Psychology of Women*, 2 vols, New York: Grune and Stratton, 1945.
DEVEREAUX, G., 'Normal and Abnormal: The Key Concepts of Ethnopsychiatry', in W. Muensterberger (ed.), *Man and his Culture*, London: Rapp and Whiting, 113–36.
Dhammapada.
DRIVER, E. D., *Differential Fertility in Central India*, Princeton: Princeton University Press, 1963.
DUBE, S. C., *Indian Village*, New York: Harper and Row, 1967.
DUMONT, L., *Homo Hierarchicus: Essai sur le système des castes*, Paris: Gallimard, 1966.
ERIKSON, E. H., *Childhood and Society*, New York: W. W. Norton, 1950.
——, *Young Man Luther*, New York: W. W. Norton, 1958.
——, 'Ontogeny of Ritualization', in R. M. Loewenstein *et al.* (eds.), *Psychoanalysis—A General Psychology*, New York: International Universities Press, 1966.
——, *Identity: Youth and Crisis*, New York: W. W. Norton, 1968.
——, *Gandhi's Truth*, New York: W. W. Norton, 1969.
FENICHEL, O., *The Psychoanalytic Theory of Neurosis*, London: Routledge and Kegan Paul, 1971.
FERENCZI, S., *Thallassa: A Theory of Genitality*, New York: Psychoanalytic Quarterly, 1938.
FISCHER, R., 'The Cartography of Ecstatic and Meditative States', *Science*, **174**, 1971, 897–904.
FONTEROSE, J., *Python: A Study of Delphic Myth and its Origins*, Berkeley: University of California Press, 1969.
FORTUNE, R. F., 'The Symbolism of the Serpent', *International Journal of Psychoanalysis*, **7**, 1926, 237–43.
FREUD, A., 'The Concept of Developmental Lines', *The Psychoanalytic Study of the Child*, **18**, 1963, 245–65.
——, 'Comments on Aggression', *International Journal of Psychoanalysis*, **53**, 1972, 163–71.
FREUD, S., *Formulations on Two Principles of Mental Functioning* (1911), The Standard Edition of *The Complete Works of Sigmund Freud*, ed. J. Strachey, vol. 12, London: Hogarth Press, 1958.
——, *Totem and Taboo* (1913), Standard Edition, vol. 13.
——, *Introductory Lectures on Psychoanalysis* (1916), Standard Edition, vol. 16.
——, *Inhibitions, Symptoms and Anxiety* (1926), Standard Edition, vol. 20.
——, *Civilization and its Discontents* (1930), Standard Edition, vol. 21.
——, *New Introductory Lectures on Psychoanalysis* (1933), Standard Edition, vol. 22.
——, *An Outline of Psychoanalysis* (1940), Standard Edition, vol. 23.

FROMM, E., *The Crisis of Psychoanalysis*, London: Jonathan Cape, 1971.
GAITONDE, M. R., 'Cross-Cultural Study of the Psychiatric Syndromes in Out-Patient Clinics in Bombay, India, and Topeka, Kansas', *International Journal of Social Psychiatry*, 4, 1958, 98–104.
GANDHI, M. K., *My Experiments with Truth*, Boston: Beacon Press, 1957.
GOODE, W. J., *World Revolution and Family Patterns*, New York: The Free Press, 1963.
GORE, M. S., 'The Husband–Wife and Mother–Son Relationship', *Sociological Bulletin*, 11, 1961, 91–102.
——, *Urbanization and Family Change*, Bombay: Popular Prakashan, 1942.
Gospel of Sri Ramakrishna, trans. S. Nikhilananda, New York: Ramakrishna–Vivekananda Center, 1942.
GUPTA, N. N., 'Influence of Hindu Culture and Social Customs on Psychosomatic Disease in India', *Psychosomatic Medicine*, 18, 1956, 506–10.
HAMMETT, R. S., 'The Conceptual Psychology of the Ancient Hindu', *Psychoanalytic Review*, 16, 1929, 291–311.
HARTMANN, H., *Ego Psychology and the Problem of Adaptation*, New York: International Universities Press, 1958.
HARTMANN, H., *Essays in Ego Psychology*, New York: International Universities Press, 1964.
HARTMANN, H. *et al.*, 'Some Psychoanalytic Comments on Culture and Personality', in G. B. Wilbur and W. Muensterberger (eds.), *Psychoanalysis and Culture*, New York: International Universities Press, 1951, pp. 3–31.
HOCH, E. M., 'A Pattern of Neurosis in India', *American Journal of Psychoanalysis*, 20, 1966, 8–25.
HORNEY, K., 'The Dread of Women', *International Journal of Psychoanalysis*, 13, 1932, 349–53.
HOYLAND, J. C., *An Investigation Regarding the Psychology of Indian Adolescents*, Jubbulpore: Christian Mission Press, 1921.
HSU, F. (ed.), *Psychological Anthropology*, Homewood, Ill.: Irwin Dorsey, 1961.
INDIAN COUNCIL OF SOCIAL SCIENCE RESEARCH, *Status of Women in India: A Synopsis of the Report of the National Committee on the Status of Women in India (1971–4)*, New Delhi: Allied Publishers, 1975.
ISHWARAN, K., *Shivpur: A South Indian Village*, London: Routledge and Kegan Paul, 1968.
JACOBSON, E., *The Self and the Object World*, New York: International Universities Press, 1964.
JACKSON, S. W., 'Aspects of Culture in Psychoanalytic Theory and Practice', *Journal of the American Psychoanalytic Association*, 16, 1968, 661–70.
JAMES, W., *The Varieties of Religious Experience* (1902), New York: Collier Books, 1961.
JOFFE, W. G. and SANDLER, J., 'Some Conceptual Problems involved in the Consideration of Disorders of Narcissism', *Journal of Child Psychotherapy*, 2, 1967, 56–66.
JONES, E., *Essays on Applied Psychoanalysis*, London: Hogarth Press, 1951.
——, *The Life and Work of Sigmund Freud*, 3 vols, New York: Basic Books, 1953.
KAKAR, S., 'The Human Life Cycle: The Traditional Hindu View and the Psychology of Erik Erikson', *Philosophy East and West*, 28, 1968, 127–36.
——, 'The Theme of Authority in Social Relations in India', *Journal of Social Psychology*, 84, 1971, 93–101.
——, 'Aggression in Indian Society: An Analysis of Folk Tales', *Indian Journal of Psychology*, 49 (2), 1974, 119–26.
——, 'Neuroses in India: An Overview and Some Observations', *Indian Journal of Psychology*, 50 (2), 1975, 172–9.
——and CHOWDHRY, K., *Conflict and Choice: Indian Youth in a Changing Society*, Bombay: Somayia, 1971.
Kalika Purana
KANE, P. V., *History of Dharmasastra*, 5 vols, Poona: Bhandarkar Oriental Research Institute, 1933–58.
KAPADIA, K. M., 'Rural Family Patterns', *Sociological Bulletin*, 5, 1956, 111–26.

KARVE, I., *Kinship Organization in India*, 3rd edn., Bombay: Asia Publishing House, 1968.

KENNEDY, B. C., 'Rural–Urban Contrasts in Parent–Child Relations in India', *Indian Journal of Social Work*, 15, 1954, 162–74.

KELMAN, H., 'Psychoanalytic Thought and Eastern Wisdom', in J. H. Masserman (ed.), *Psychoanalysis and Human Values*, vol. 3, New York: Grune and Stratton, 1960, 124–32.

KHAN, I. A., 'A Comparative Study of the Attitudes of Adolescent Students and their Elders towards Authority and Discipline', Ph.D. Thesis, Aligarh Muslim University, 1961.

KIERKEGAARD, S., *Der Begriff Angst*, Hamburg: Rowohlt Verlag, 1960.

KINSLEY, D. R., *The Sword and the Flute*, Berkeley: University of California Press, 1975.

KOHLBERG, L. and KRAMER, R. B., 'Continuities and Discontinuities in Childhood and Adult Moral Development', *Human Development*, 12, 1969, 93–120.

KOHUT, H., 'Introspection, Empathy and Psychoanalysis', *Journal of American Psychoanalytic Association*, 7, 1959, 459–85.

——, *The Analysis of the Self*, New York: International Universities Press, 1971.

——, 'Narzissmus und Narzisstische Wut', *Psyche*, 27, 1973, 513–54.

KOLENDA, P. M., 'Regional Differences in Indian Family Structure', in R. I. Crane (ed.), *Regions and Regionalism in South Asian Studies*, Duke University Program in Comparative Studies in Southern Asia, Monograph no. 5, 1967, pp. 147–226.

KLEIN, M., *Das Seelenleben dos Kleinkindes*, Hamburg: Rowohlt Verlag, 1972.

LANNOY, R., *The Speaking Tree*, London: Oxford University Press, 1971.

The Laws of Manu, trans. G. Buhler, in M. Müller (ed.), *Sacred Books of the East*, vol. 25, Oxford: Clarendon Press, 1886.

LEWIS, M. M., *Language, Thought and Personality in Infancy and Childhood*, New York: Basic Books, 1964.

LEWIS, O., *Village Life in Northern India*, New York: Vintage Books, 1958.

LIDZ, T., *The Person: His Development Throughout the Life Cycle*, New York: Basic Books, 1968.

—— et al., *Schizophrenia and the Family*, New York: International Universities Press, 1966.

LINCKE, H., 'Das Überich—eine gefährliche Krankheit?', *Psyche*, 24, 1970, 375–402.

LOCH, W., 'Determinanten des Ichs. Beiträge David Rapaports zur psychoanalytichen Ich—Theorie', *Psyche*, 25, 1971.

MACNICOL, N., *Indian Theism*, 2nd edn., Delhi: Munshiram Manoharlal, 1968.

MADAN, T. N., *Family and Kinship*, Bombay: Asia Publishing House, 1965.

Mahabharata, trans. P. C. Roy, 12 vols., Calcutta: Oriental Publishing Co., n.d.

MAHLER, M. S., *On Human Symbiosis and the Vicissitudes of Individuation*, New York: International Universities Press, 1969.

MAJUMDAR, G., *Folk Tales of Bengal*, New Delhi: Sterling Publishers, 1971.

MALINOWSKI, B., *Sex and Repression in Savage Society*, New York: Harcourt, 1927.

MANDELBAUM, D. G., *Society in India*, 2 vols., Berkeley: University of California Press, 1970.

Mandukya Upanishad.

MARCUSE, H., *Eros and Civilization*, Boston: Beacon Press, 1955.

MARRIOT, M. (ed.), *Village India*, Bombay: Asia Publishing House, 1955.

MAYER, A. C., *Caste and Kinship in Central India*, London: Routledge and Kegan Paul, 1970.

Matsya Purana.

McCORMACK, W., 'On Lingayat Culture', in A. K. Ramanujan, *Speaking of Siva*, London: Penguin Books, 1973, 175–87.

McCRINDLE, J. W., *Ancient India as Described by Megasthenes and Arrian*, Calcutta: Chuckervertty, Chatterjee and Co., 1960.

MINTURN, L. and HITCHCOCK J. T., 'The Rajputs of Khalapur, India', in B. B.

WHITING (ed.), *Six Cultures: Studies of Child-rearing*, New York: John Wiley, 1963.

MINTURN, L. and LAMBERT, W. W., *Mothers of Six Cultures*, New York: John Wiley, 1964.

MITCHELL, J. D., 'The Sanskrit Drama Shakuntala', *American Imago*, 14, 1957, 389–405.

MOHANTY, S. *Folk Tales of Orissa*, New Delhi: Sterling Publishers, 1970.

MOSS, H. A., 'Sex, Age and State as Determinants of Mother–Infant Interaction', *Merrill-Palmer Quarterly*, 13, 1967, 19–36.

MUENSTERBERGER, W., 'Psyche and Environment', *Psychoanalytic Quarterly*, 38, 1969, 191–216.

MUKHERJEE, S. C., *A Study of Vaisnavism in Ancient and Medieval Bengal*, Calcutta: Punthi Pustak, 1966.

MURPHY, G., *In the Minds of Men*, New York: Basic Books, 1953.

MURPHY, L. B., 'Some Aspects of the First Relationship', *International Journal of Psychoanalysis*, 45, 1964, 31–43.

—— *et al., The Widening World of Childhood*, New York: Basic Books, 1967.

MUNSHI, K. M., *Krishnavatara*, vol. 1, Bombay: Bharatiya Vidya Bhavan, 1967.

NARAIN, D., 'Interpersonal Relationships in the Hindu Family', in R. Hill and R. Konig (eds.), *Families in East and West*, Paris: Mouton, 1964, 454–80.

——, 'Growing up in India', *Family Process*, 3, 1964, 127–54.

NARAYANANANDA, S., *The Mysteries of Man, Mind and Mind-Functions*, Rishikesh: Narayanananda Universal Yoga Trust, 1965.

NEHRU, JAWAHARLAL, *The Discovery of India*, Calcutta: The Signet Press, 1946.

——, *Toward Freedom*, Boston: Beacon Press, 1961.

NEUMANN, E., *The Great Mother: An Analysis of the Archetype*, Princeton: Princeton University Press, 1963.

NIVEDITA, *The Master as I saw Him*, Calcutta: Udbodhan Office, 1910.

NOY, P., 'A Revision of the Psychoanalytic Theory of the Primary Process', *International Journal of Psychoanalysis*, 50, 1969, 155–78.

O'FLAHERTY, W., *Asceticism and Eroticism in the Mythology of Siva*, London: Oxford University Press, 1973.

ORENSTEIN, H., *Gaon: Conflict and Cohesion in an Indian Village*, Princeton: Princeton University Press, 1965.

OSBORNE, A., *Ramana Maharishi and the Path of Self-knowledge*, London: Rider, 1970.

Padma Purana.

PANDE, S. K., 'The Mystique of "Western" Psychotherapy: an Eastern Interpretation', *Journal of Nervous and Mental Diseases*, 46, 1968, 425–32.

PARIN, P. and MORGENTHALER, W., 'Ego and Orality in the Analysis of West Africans', *The Psychoanalytic Study of Society*, vol. 3, New York: International Universities Press, 1964.

PARIN, P. *et al., Die Weisse Denken Zuviel*, Zurich: Atlantis, 1972.

PLATT, G. AND WEINSTEIN, F. I., *The Wish to be Free*, Berkeley: University of California Press, 1970.

YOGANANDA, *Autobiography of a Yogi*, Los Angeles: Self-Realization Fellowship, 1972.

PATEL, R., 'Understanding the Culture through Mythological Stories', *American Journal of Psychoanalysis*, 20, 1960, 83–5.

PRABHU, P. N., *Hindu Social Organization*, Bombay: Popular Book Depot, 1954.

PRATAP, P., 'The Development of Ego Ideal in Indian Children', Ph.D. Thesis, Benares Hindu University, 1960.

PULVER, S. E., 'Narcissism: Concept and Metapsychological Conception', *Journal of American Psychoanalytic Association*, 18, 1970, 319–41.

RAJAN, K. V., 'A Psychological Evaluation of Certain Trends in Indian Culture', *Indian Journal of Psychology*, 32, 1957.

Ramayana of Valmiki, H. P. Shastri, London: Shantisadan, 1962.

RANK, O., *Das Inzest Motiv.*, Leipzig and Vienna: Deuticke, 1912.

——, *The Myth of the Birth of the Hero*, New York: Brunner, 1952.

RAPAPORT, D., *Collected Papers of David Rapaport*, ed. M. M. Gill, New York: Basic Books, 1967.

REICH, A., 'Pathological Forms of Self-Esteem Regulation', *The Psychoanalytic Study of the Child*, **15**, 1960, 215–32.

ROLLAND, R., *Prophets of the New India*, London: Cassell, 1930.

ROSEN, J. N., *Direct Analysis*, New York: Grune and Stratton, 1953.

ROSS, A. D., *The Hindu Family in its Urban Setting*, Toronto: University of Toronto Press, 1962.

RUECK, A. V. S. and PORTER, R. (eds.), *Transcultural Psychiatry*, London: J. and A. Churchill, 1965.

SALIN, C. N., 'Identity, Culture and Psychosexual Development', *American Imago*, **24**, 1967, 181–247.

Satapatha Brahmana.

SARADANANDA, *Sri Ramakrishna, The Great Master*, Madras: Ramakrishna Math, n.d.

SARMA, J., 'The Nuclearization of Joint Family Households in West Bengal', *Man in India*, **44**, 1964, 193–206.

SASTRY, N. S. N., 'Symbolism in Hindu Gods', *Indian Journal of Psychology*, **19**, 1949, 190–193.

SCHAEFFER, R., 'The Psychoanalytic Vision of Reality', *International Journal of Psychoanalysis*, **51**, 1970, 279–97.

SEN GUPTA, S., *A Study of Women of Bengal*, Calcutta: Indian Publications, 1970.

SEETHALAKSHMI, K. A., *Folk Tales of Tamil Nadu*, New Delhi: Sterling Publishers, 1969.

SHEOREY, I., *Folk Tales of Maharashtra*, New Delhi: Sterling Publishers, 1973.

SETHI, B. B. and NATHAWAT, S. S., 'Neurotic and Depressive Patterns in India', *Transcultural Psychiatric Research Review*, **9**, 1972, 133–5.

SETHI, B. B., THAKORE, V. R. and GUPTA, S. C., 'Changing Patterns of Culture and Psychiatry in India', *American Journal of Psychotherapy*, **19**, 1965, 46–54.

SINGER, M. (ed.), *Krishna: Myths, Rites, and Attitudes*, Honolulu: East-West Center Press, 1966.

SINGH, K. P., 'Women's Age at Marriage', *Sociological Bulletin*, **23 (2)**, 1974, 236–44.

SINHA, T. C., 'Some Psychoanalytical Observations on the Siva Linga', *Samiksa*, **3**, 1949, 37–42.

Siva Purana.

SIVANANDA, S., *Mind: Its Mysteries and Control*, Shivanandanagar, U.P.: Divine Life Society, 1974.

SLATER, P., *The Glory of Hera*, Boston: Beacon Press, 1966.

——, *The Pursuit of Loneliness: American Culture at the Breaking Point*, Boston: Beacon Press, 1970.

SLOCHOWER, H. A., 'Psychoanalytical Distinction between Myth and Mythopoesis', *Journal of American Psychoanalytic Association*, **18**, 1970, 150–64.

SPENGLER, O., *The Decline of the West*, London: George Allen and Unwin, 1959.

SPITZ, R., *The First Year of Life*, New York: International Universities Press, 1965.

SPRATT, P., *Hindu Culture and Personality*, Bombay: Manaktalas, 1966.

SRINIVAS, M. N., *Marriage and Family in Mysore*, Bombay: New Book Co., 1942.

——, *Caste in Modern India*, Bombay: Asia Publishing House, 1962.

STEKEL, W., *Conditions of Nervous Anxiety and their Treatment*, London: Paul, Trench and Trubner, 1923.

STEPHENS, W., *The Oedipus Complex*, Glencoe, Ill.: The Free Press, 1962.

——, *The Family in Cross-Cultural Perspective*, New York: Holt, 1963.

STERN, M., 'Ego Psychology, Myth and Rite', *The Psychoanalytic Study of Society*, **3**, 1964, 71–93.

STRAUSS, M. A. and WINKELMANN, D., 'Social Class, Fertility and Authority in Nuclear and Joint Family Households, in Bombay', *Journal of Asian and African Studies*, **9**, 1969, 61–74.

TAYLOR, W. S., 'Basic Personality in Orthodox Hindu Culture Patterns', *Journal of Abnormal Psychology*, **43**, 1948, 3–12.

——, 'Behavioural Disorders and the Breakdown of the Orthodox Hindu Family System', *Indian Journal of Social Work*, **4**, 1943, 163–70.
THOMAS, L., *The Lives of a Cell*, New York: Viking Press, 1974.
VANGGAARD, T., *Phallos*, London: Jonathan Cape, 1972.
Vaisesikasutra.
VIVEKANANDA, *The Yogas and other Works*, ed. S. Nikhilananda, New York: Ramakrishna–Vivekananda Center, 1953.
——, *Collected Works of Swami Vivekananda*, 8 vols., Calcutta: Advaita Ashrama, 1970.
VON FRANZ, M. L., *The Feminine in Fairy Tales*, Zurich: Spring Publications, 1964.
WEINSTEIN, F. I. and PLATT, G., *Psychoanalytic Sociology*, Baltimore: John Hopkins University Press, 1973.
WHITEHEAD, H., *The Village Gods of South India*, Calcutta: Association Press, 1921.
WILKINS, W. J., *Hindu Mythology*, Delhi: Delhi Book Store, 1972.
WINNICOTT, D. W., 'The Capacity to be Alone', *International Journal of Psychoanalysis*, **39**, 1958, 416–20.
——, *The Family and Individual Development*, London: Tavistock Publications, 1952.
——, *Playing and Reality*, London: Tavistock Publications, 1971.
WISER, C. V. and WISER, W. H., *Behind Mud Walls*, London: George Allen and Unwin, 1932.

Index

Index of Appendix